DREAMS COME DUE

Government and Economics As If Freedom Mattered

A Libertarian Agenda

JOHN GALT

SIMON AND SCHUSTER   New York

We have made every effort to trace the ownership of all copyrighted material and to secure permission from copyright holders. In the event of any question arising as to the use of any material, we will be pleased to make the necessary corrections in future printings. Thanks are due to the following authors, publishers, publications, and agents for permission to use the material indicated.

Addison-Wesley Publishing Company: From Charles Peters, *How Washington Really Works*, © 1983, Addison-Wesley, Reading, Massachusetts. Excerpted material, reprinted by permission.

Arno Press Books: From *Liberty and the Great Libertarians* by Charles T. Sprading; *The God of the Machine* by Isabel Paterson; and *Our Enemy, The State* by Albert J. Nock.

Dow Jones and Company: From *The Wall Street Journal*, chart by Stephen Wermiel from "High Court Faces Workload Crisis but Disagrees on Causes, Solutions," © 1982 by Dow Jones & Company. All rights reserved. Reprinted by permission.

Facts on File®: From *The Quotable Woman* by Elaine Partnow, © 1983, by Elaine Partnow. Reprinted by permission of Facts on File, Inc., New York.

Freedom House: Map of Freedom—January 1986. With permission of Freedom House.

Harper & Row, Publishers: Specified extract from *Managing in Turbulent Times* by Peter F. Drucker. Copyright © 1980 by Peter F. Drucker. Specified extracts from *The True Believer* by Eric Hoffer. Copyright 1951 by Eric Hoffer. By permission of Harper & Row, Publishers, Inc.

Houghton Mifflin Company: From *Parkinson's Law* by C. Northcote Parkinson. Copyright © 1957 by C. Northcote Parkinson. From *The Law and the Profits* by C. Northcote Parkinson. Copyright © 1960 by C. Northcote Parkinson. Reprinted by permission of Houghton Mifflin Company.

Libertarian Press, Inc.: Passage reprinted from *The Anti-Capitalistic Mentality* by Ludwig von Mises with permission from Libertarian Press, Inc., Spring Mills, PA 16875.

Little, Brown & Company: From Edward Banfield's *The Unheavenly City Revisited*. Reprinted by permission of Little, Brown & Company.

New York University Press: Reprinted from *Power and Market: Government and the Economy* by Murray N. Rothbard. Copyright © 1977 by the Institute for Human Studies, Inc. Reprinted by permission.

Princeton University: From Robert Triffin, *The Evolution of the International Monetary System: Historical Reappraisal and Future Perspectives*, Study No. 12, 1964, Table 1. Reprinted by permission of International Finance Section.

Python (Monty) Pictures, Ltd.: Material (Apology) by Eric Idle/Monty Python. © Python (Monty) Pictures, Ltd. Used by permission.

Random House, Inc.: From *Systemantics: How Systems Work and Especially How They Fail* by John Gall, © 1975 by John Gall. Reprinted by permission of Times Books, a Division of Random House, Inc.

Regnery Gateway Inc: From *Fat City* by Donald Lambro. Reprinted by permission of Regnery Gateway, Inc.

Murray N. Rothbard: From *For a New Liberty* by Murray N. Rothbard. Published by Libertarian Review Foundation, New York City, 1985. Reprinted by permission of the author.

Professor Helmut Schoeck, M.D.: From *Envy: A Theory of Social Behavior* (New York, 1970). By permission of the author.

Silver & Gold Report: Dr. Franz Pick's Dow Jones Chart, © 1985 by Franz Pick, N.Y. By permission of Franz Pick.

Simon & Schuster: From *The Road Less Traveled* by M. Scott Peck, M.D. Copyright © 1978 by M. Scott Peck, M.D. From *Battle for Stock Market Survival* by Gerald M. Loeb. Copyright © 1971 by Gerald M. Loeb. Reprinted by permission of Simon & Schuster.

The Spotlight: Three charts from E. L. Anderson, *Upright Spike of '79 Doomsday for America*. Reprinted by permission.

Lyle Stuart, Inc.: From *The Rich and the Super-Rich* by Ferdinand Lundberg. Copyright © 1968. Published by arrangement with Lyle Stuart.

The Wall Street Journal: Excerpted from *Big Taxes, Big Profits*—January 1983, by Paul Craig Roberts. Reprinted by permission of Paul Craig Roberts.

Weiss Research, Inc.: From *The Great Money Panic* by Martin D. Weiss. Courtesy of Martin D. Weiss, editor of *Money & Markets*.

"John Galt" is a nom de plume of one who understands and loves freedom. The author is not connected to, nor is this book endorsed by, the Estate of Ayn Rand.

10 9 8 7 4 5 4 3 2 1

Library of Congress Cataloging-in-Publication Data
Galt, John.
    Dreams come due.

    1. Economic policy.   2. Trade regulation.
3. Laissez-faire.   4. Economics.   I. Title.
II. Title: Government and economics as if freedom mattered.
HD75.G35   1986   338.9   86-6472
ISBN: 0-671-61159-3

*Dedicated to those
who understand
and love freedom*

CONTENTS

Nothing is new except arrangement.

—WILL DURANT

It takes two to speak the truth,—one to speak, and another to hear.

—HENRY DAVID THOREAU

There is no new thing under the sun.

—ECCLESIASTES

Learning is finding out what you already know.

—RICHARD BACH
ILLUSIONS

WHAT THIS BOOK IS

Dreams Come Due is a book about economic laws and government. These laws are the result of human behavior and the ultimate law of compensation (see COMPENSATION). Economic laws (like physical laws) cannot be circumvented, except in the dreams (legislation) of politicians and other wishful thinkers, and a price must always be paid (by the people) for every attempt to do so. The bills for these dreams are now beginning to come due and will continue to do so for the foreseeable future.

The message of this book can be broken into three parts:

1. Government (with only a very few exceptions) is the enemy of mankind. It is instituted to do violence to its citizens and eventually tries to control everything but itself.

2. Democracies are successful not because of governments, but in spite of them. Today's democracies became great and powerful when governments were small. The economies of the Western world (with one or two exceptions) are now in slow decline because big and growing governments have bled (or are bleeding) them dry of freedom, prosperity, justice, money, capital, personal independence, incentive, morality, and hope and are giving them a transfusion of regulation, recession, "laws," currency, inflation, taxes, debt, welfare, corruption, and despair.

3. The decline could be reversed by adhering to the Natural Laws of Economics in this book, but it would require a much higher pain threshold from the electorates and a political courage that, to my knowledge, has never existed.

The chapters in this book are in alphabetical order. Each chapter is preceded by a set of historical quotations that set the tone for my thoughts on that particular subject. You can read any chapter in less than ten minutes. They do not have to be read in any particular order, except where suggested.

Believe nothing, no matter where you read it, or who said it, no matter if I have said it, unless it agrees with your own reason and your own common sense.

—BUDDHA

Toil, feel, think, hope; you will be sure to dream enough before you die without arranging for it.

—J. STERLING

Idealism [dreaming] is fine; but as it approaches reality, the cost becomes prohibitive.

—WILLIAM F. BUCKLEY, JR.

INTRODUCTION

"We believe easily what we fear or what we desire." With these words, La Fontaine captured the essence of the world's current political situation. Everyone desires to believe (i.e., dreams) that government is omnipotent; that it can and somehow will control spending and inflation, repay its debts, ensure freedom and prosperity, honor constitutions and treaties, and respect property rights. *I promise you now that it is not, it cannot, and it will not!* It will continue its irresponsible, needless, and wasteful spending growth; it will continue to try to inflate the supply of currency and credit; it will continue its assault against freedom, property rights, and thus prosperity by shredding constitutions and ignoring treaties. I do not have to prove these statements; history has proved them for me.

This book was written because not one person in fifty understands what has happened and is happening to the United States and the world in day-to-day political and economic affairs. In the words of Emerson, they do not understand that "you cannot do wrong without suffering wrong." Albert Jay Nock captured the reason for this lack of understanding in *Our Enemy, The State:*

> There appears to be a curious difficulty about exercising reflective thought upon the actual nature of an institution into which one was born and one's ancestors were born. One accepts it as one does the atmosphere; one's practical adjustments to it are made by a kind of reflex. One seldom thinks about the air until one notices some change, favourable or unfavourable, and then one's thought about it is special; one thinks about purer air, lighter air, heavier air, not about air. So it is with certain human institutions. We know that they exist, that they affect us in various ways, but we do not ask how they came to exist, or what their original intention was, or what primary function it is that they are actually fulfilling; and when they affect us so unfavourably that we rebel against them, we contemplate substituting nothing beyond some modification or variant of the same institution. Thus colonial America, oppressed by the monarchical State, brings in the republican State; Germany gives up the republican State for the Hitlerian State;

Russia exchanges the monocratic State for the collectivist State; Italy exchanges the constitutional State for the "totalitarian" State.

Washington politicians, economists, and other government worshippers, whose only concern is for the next election, have increasingly victimized and polarized our country through their envy-motivated dreams. They have sown the seeds of disaster with idiotic legislation that unceasingly robs the people of their freedom by placing more and more "law" above the rights of property. Now that these dreams are coming due at an ever increasing rate, they are pointing the finger at the *victims,* blaming them for the results, while continuing to pass new "laws" (i.e., compounding their crimes) that only assure us worse disasters in the future.

Generally, today's electorate has three problems:

1. It does not understand basic economics and (because of government policies) is increasingly dominated by envy instead of morality.
2. It does not understand the real purpose of government (or law) and cannot comprehend or control its scope and waste.
3. It is not aware of the Orwellian semantics game used by the politicians and bureaucrats in Washington to win support. There are significant differences between laws and justice, currency and money, needs and rights, government and freedom, government spending and private investment, demand and supply, inflation and rising prices, spending and saving, deficits and budgets, politicians and responsible individuals, political actions and economic results, and taxes and incentives.

To overcome this confusion, we must have and understand an objective set of laws that are as unchanging as the laws of physics. Read and grasp the following economic laws, based largely on the Ten Pillars of Economic Wisdom from the American Economic Foundation, and you will never again be confused or unknowingly cheated by government. When you have finished the economic laws, I suggest you read the sections Money, Currency, and Inflation before continuing the book.

So come and tour what governments have dreamed, from Accounting to Welfare, and the resulting disasters they have banked for present and future generations to endure.

The obscure we see eventually, the completely apparent takes longer.

—EDWARD R. MURROW

Common sense is genius dressed in its working clothes.

—RALPH WALDO EMERSON

Facts that are not frankly faced have a habit of stabbing us in the back.

—SIR HAROLD BOWDEN

THE NATURAL LAWS OF ECONOMICS

1. Nothing in our material world, regardless of the form of government, can come from nowhere or go nowhere, *nor can it be free*: everything in our economic life was produced by taking risks, and has a source, a destination, and a cost that must be paid by *someone* somewhere.
2. Government is never a source of goods. It is only a source of costs to society. *Everything* produced is produced by the people, and everything the government "gives" to one group of people, it must first take (plunder) from another group of people. Because of government's inherent inefficiency and waste, the amount given by government will always be much less than the amount taken.
3. The only revenue that government has to spend is that revenue taxed or borrowed out of people's earnings. When government decides to spend more than it has received from these sources, that extra, unearned revenue is created out of thin air, through the banks and printing presses, and when spent, takes on value *only by reducing the value* of all currency, savings, and insurance. (This is inflation.)
4. Wages (not profits) are the principal cost of everything, so real wages (wages adjusted for inflation) cannot be increased, unless there are increases in production and productivity.
5. Productivity is based on human energy (both physical and mental) and tools.
6. Tools are created and replaced by capital formation, which can come only from savings.
7. Savings, thus capital formation, can come only from profits or surplus. (Try to invest losses or deficits.) The greater the profits, the greater the possible savings and investment.
8. What a government taxes, such as work, savings, and investment, it gets less of. What a government subsidizes, such as unemployment, debt, consumption, it gets more of.
9. Debt is always paid, if not by the borrower, then by the lender.

Many lenders are about to discover this as their dreams (loans) come due.

10. History teaches that the most productive and the richest societies in the world with the most security have always had the most personal freedom (i.e., the smallest government), as well as the strongest property rights. (There are no human rights without property rights.)

ACCOUNTING

Accounting [measuring financial data with depreciating currency]
is much like looking at a bikini on a beautiful girl. What it
reveals is interesting, but what it conceals is vital.

—ABRAHAM J. BRILOFF

Accuracy is the twin brother of honesty; inaccuracy is a near kin
to falsehood.

—TRYON EDWARDS

The greatest of all gifts is the power to estimate things at their
true worth.

—LA ROCHEFOUCAULD

Since inflation (see INFLATION) is basically government-sanctioned destruction of wealth (government always realizes the greatest gains from inflation) through destruction of the currency, it renders most accounting figures meaningless. Depreciating currency (see CURRENCY) cannot be used as a standard measure of assets, liabilities, or income over any significant period of time. In terms of official government figures, today's dollar has lost more than 85 percent of its 1940 purchasing power (see CONSUMER PRICE INDEX), and in reality it has lost much more (see INFLATION, REAL).

The most important personal accounting in the United States takes place on April 15 of each year, and on that day the government makes the greatest gain from inflation via the progressive income tax. Here is what happened to an individual's tax liability if his taxable income kept pace with the Consumer Price Index (CPI) from 1940 to 1980 ($17,000 in 1940 purchasing power is equivalent to $100,000 in 1980):

YEAR	TAXABLE INCOME Dollars	FEDERAL TAXES Dollars	EFFECTIVE TAX RATE Percentage
1940	17,000	1,960	11.5
1980	100,000	42,142	42.1

You can see that the government's "take" on the same amount of purchasing power income increased a mere 367 percent in 40 years. A taxpayer who was allowed to keep 88.5 percent of his income in 1940 was allowed to keep only 57.9 percent of the *same* income in 1980, in spite of all the "tax cuts" (see TAX CUTS).

A similar situation occurs in the "welfare for the rich" section of the tax code known as *long-term capital gains*. Assume that an investor bought IBM in 1970 for $60 a share and sold it in 1980 for $75. The $15 "gain" could have been taxed at 28 percent, leaving the investor with $10.80 plus his $60 of capital. However, the dollar officially lost 53 percent of its purchasing power from 1970 to 1980; so even before the sale, the investor had lost 41 percent of his investment to currency inflation. To compound the loss further, the government demanded a tax of $4.80.

The stagnating price of stocks (see DOW JONES INDUSTRIAL AVERAGE) suggests that corporations suffer a similar fate, making it virtually impossible for a corporation to make a real profit (see PROFITS, CORPORATE) during an inflationary period. Because inventories must be replaced at higher currency prices, inventory "profits" are merely one-time inflation adjustments and have no relation to real (see REAL [REALLY]) operating profits. Moreover, depreciation, based on preinflationary, or historical, costs, is often understated (and thus profits overstated) as capital assets must be replaced at newly inflated prices. This effectively forces many corporations to pay income taxes on their capital. Even corporations who had the foresight to borrow long-term capital at low fixed rates by issuing bonds must eventually replace that capital with new debt at the then-prevailing interest rate (e.g., corporations that issued twenty-year bonds in 1964 at 4.5 percent would have had to pay 12.7 percent to replace this capital in 1984) (see INTEREST RATES).

To establish an estimate of real earnings for any particular corporation, it would be necessary to go through all assets and liabilities item by item, attempting to adjust each one for inflation. A shorter method gives a very good approximation. All major corporations report returns on stockholder equity. If a corporation reports a return on equity of 15 percent and inflation is 10 percent, then the real return is only 5 percent. Reported earnings can be adjusted by dividing reported return on equity by real return on equity (5 percent divided by 15 percent equals 33 percent; so real earnings were only 33 percent of reported earnings). With this in mind, let's see how some major companies fared during the most recent year of high inflation:

Corporate Earnings Adjusted for Inflation in 1980

COMPANY	PER-SHARE EARNINGS (Dollars)	RETURN ON EQUITY (Percentage)	INFLATION RATE (Percentage)	REAL RETURN ON EQUITY (Percentage)	REAL EARNINGS PER SHARE (Percentage)
AT&T	8.19	12.8	13.5	−0.7	−0.45
CBS	6.92	17.5	13.5	4.0	1.58
Exxon	6.50	25.3	13.5	11.8	3.03
GE	6.65	20.2	13.5	6.7	2.21
IBM	5.72	22.3	13.5	8.8	2.26
McDonald's	3.66	22.3	13.5	8.8	1.44
Sears	1.92	7.5	13.5	−6.0	−1.54
Xerox	7.33	18.7	13.5	5.2	2.04

The average return on equity for the eight companies shown is 18.3 percent before adjusting for inflation, but the real return is actually 4.8 percent. Thus the average real earnings of some of the largest and most successful corporations in our country are only about 26 percent of what they actually reported in 1980. Income taxes were paid literally on "paper profits." Perhaps now it is easier to understand why the stock market (see DOW JONES INDUSTRIAL AVERAGE) basically has been declining in real terms since 1966. The dream of measuring wealth and income with currency is slowly coming due.

AGRICULTURE

(Striking It Poor)

When we must wait for Washington to tell us when to sow and when to reap, we shall soon want bread.

—THOMAS JEFFERSON

A mortgage casts a shadow on the sunniest field.

—R. G. INGERSOLL

Worm or beetle—drought or tempest—on a farmer's land may fall,
Each is loaded full o' ruin, but a mortgage beats 'em all.

—WILL CARLETON

Has anyone ever heard of a farmer making any sacrifice of his own interest, however slight, to the common good? Has anyone ever heard of a farmer practising or advocating any political idea that was not absolutely self-seeking—that was not, in fact, deliberately designed to loot the rest of us to his gain?

—H. L. MENCKEN

The *demise* of the family farm has been one of the keys to America's economic growth. People who are busy growing food are not available to build houses, cars, or computers. Even a government economist should be able to understand this correlation.

In 1900, almost 50 percent of our work force was involved in farm or ranch labor. By 1981, only about 3.7 million people (or 4 percent of our labor force) were engaged in agriculture; yet this smaller number could produce enough food to make us the best-fed nation in the world, while also providing 90 percent of *all* world agricultural exports. Each American farmer (in spite of massive government interference in the agricultural economy) currently feeds an average of sixty-two people. In the Soviet Union, where there are both chronic food and chronic labor shortages, each farmer feeds seven people. In the other large "worker's paradise," China, each farmer feeds 1.3 people. (These figures for the Soviet Union and China absolutely refute socialism, in *any* form, as a system of government. They also demonstrate what happens when government "farms." In the Soviet Union, most tractors look like tanks, and they "farm" border areas like Poland. In China, on the other hand, tractors are disguised to look like peasants holding hand spades.)

In the past few years, the United States has experienced another "farm crisis." Farmers who chose to speculate and to go heavily into debt are going broke almost as fast as socialist governments (see DEBT, FOREIGN). After the farmers themselves, the greatest share of the blame can be confidently placed on Washington's doorstep.

During the 1970s farmers heard the government's message loud and clear and fell on it fast: Inflation will never be controlled, so borrow to the hilt to take advantage of rising land and crop prices. Don't farm; speculate. Farmers also "knew" that the government would continue to plunder the rest of society (to *whatever* extent was necessary) so that it could subsidize the industry through cheap loans, through paying farmers *not* to grow crops, or through purchasing crops farmers couldn't sell at a profit in the free market. The government lost more than $70 billion of American taxpayers' wealth trading farm commodities from 1933 to 1980. And yet since 1980, farm subsidies increased from $3 billion to more than $15 billion in 1985. But even this amount of "assistance" has not been enough to stave off financial disaster. And not even the U.S. government is willing to shoulder all the horrendous losses farmers have generated for themselves and their lenders.

H. L. Mencken was fond of saying that farmers are the worst speculators in the world (except for governments, of course); and our rapidly destabilizing economy is proving him right. The dream of highly leveraged farmers has now come due. The trend, as always, will be for the overextended and less efficient farmers to leave farming, while more efficient operators will survive and eventually prosper again.

In spite of the highly visible bankruptcies (which still have a long way to go), the farm industry, as a whole, is in solid financial condition with an equity-to-debt ratio of 4 to 1. It is farm income that is causing most of the financial problems. The following table reveals that gross farm income for 1984, adjusted for inflation (see CONSUMER PRICE

INDEX), was almost double the levels of 1940, but net farm income was only about half:

Farm Income Adjusted for Inflation
(1940 Purchasing Power, Billions of Dollars)

YEAR	GROSS INCOME (Current Dollars)	GROSS INCOME (1940 Dollars)	NET INCOME (Current Dollars)	NET INCOME (1940 Dollars)
1940	11.3	11.3	4.5	4.5
1945	25.4	19.8	12.3	9.6
1950	33.1	19.3	13.6	7.9
1955	33.5	17.5	11.3	5.9
1960	38.9	18.4	11.5	5.4
1965	46.5	20.7	12.9	5.7
1970	58.8	21.2	14.4	5.2
1975	100.6	26.2	25.6	6.7
1980	150.2	25.5	21.2	3.6
1983	151.4	21.7	16.1	2.3

This disparity between gross farm income and net farm income essentially had two causes:

1. Farm debt got out of control and then interest rates (see INTEREST RATES) got out of control. In 1970, farmers were financing $53 billion of debt at a prime rate of 7.9 percent for a debt service of $4.2 billion in interest against a net income of $14.2 billion. By 1983, farmers were financing $216.3 billion of debt at a prime of 10.8 percent for a debt service of $23.4 billion against a net income of only $16.1 billion. With interest costs rising over 550 percent, farm production expenses went from 75.7 percent of the gross income in 1970 to 89.4 percent in 1983. With this staggering increase in expenses, net income had to collapse—and it did.

2. Soon after the orgy of speculation through debt began, agricultural commodity prices crashed because, as a result of worldwide government farm subsidies, regulation, and other forms of interference in the free market, too many farmers were producing too much food (the law of supply and demand). (And once the

price of farm commodities began to decline, so did the price of farmland, which was usually purchased with very small equities that disappeared almost overnight.) (See REAL ESTATE.) Not surprisingly, in the United States, real farm income has actually fallen from $6.4 billion in 1975 to $2.3 billion in 1983, while the total expenditures for the Department of Agriculture's various "systems" (see SYSTEMS) have increased by more than 700 percent, from about $3 billion in 1975 to $22 billion in 1983.

But why does the government go to such lengths to try to protect the farmers, who, in spite of the huge increases in their subsidies, like most extortionists, can never be satisfied, who are continually threatening to strike, while rolling their tractors through Washington? With the memories of their most recent demonstrations (protesting mostly their own greed and gullibility) fresh in our minds, I offer a few illuminating comments from H. L. Mencken:

> He [the farmer] is, on the contrary, the pet above all other pets, the enchantment and delight, the saint and archangel of all the unearthly Sganarelles and Scaramouches who roar in the two houses of Congress. He is more to them, day in and day out, than whole herds of Honest Workingmen, Gallant Jack Tars and Heroic Miners; he is more, even, than a platoon of Unknown Soldiers. There are days when one or another of these totems of the statesman is bathed with such devotion that it would make the Gracchi blush, but there is never a day that the farmer, too, doesn't get his share, and there is many a day [currently everyday] when he gets ten times his share. . . . No session ever begins without a grand assault at all arms upon his hereditary foes, from the boll-weevil and the San José scale to Wall Street and the Interstate Commerce Commission. And no session comes to an end without a huge grist of new laws to save him from them [and the forces of the free market]—laws embodying the most subtle statecraft of the most daring and ingenious body of lawmakers [looters] ever assembled under one roof on the habitable globe.

These congressional agricultural "policies" have assured taxpayers of always being in a heads-they-win-tails-we-lose situation with regard to farmers. Bumper crops mean higher subsidies (i.e., taxes), and bad harvests mean higher prices. If the government would stop subsidizing farmers at taxpayer expense, the free market (as it does for all other businesses; see MARKETS, [FREE]) would determine who farms. And there is never a long-term shortage of product (food) or profits in a free market. We must get the government out of farming, and farmers and farm lobbies (along with all other special interest groups) out of government.

APOLOGY

The typical lawmaker of today is a man devoid of principle—a mere counter in a grotesque and knavish game. If the right pressure could be applied to him he would be cheerfully in favor of polygamy, astrology or cannibalism.

—H. L. MENCKEN

I have never made but one prayer to God, a very short one: "O Lord make my enemies ridiculous." And God granted it.

—VOLTAIRE

There is no more independence in politics than there is in jail.

—WILL ROGERS

About all I can say for the United States Senate is that it opens with prayer and closes with an investigation.

—WILL ROGERS

I never said all Democrats were saloon-keepers. What I said was that all saloon-keepers are Democrats.

—HORACE GREELEY

A good one (politician) is quite as unthinkable as an honest burglar.

—H. L. MENCKEN

They are decided only to be undecided, resolved to be irresolute, adamant for drift, all powerful for impotence.

—WINSTON CHURCHILL

Throughout this book, I may seem to be overly critical of the people who have usurped our freedom and placed this country in such a desperate situation—namely, our elected representatives (and others too humorous to mention). My intention is not to place these people in an *undeserved* bad light, so I will apologize in advance for any unwarranted insult, real or imagined, that might be inferred from this text. As Frank Hubbard was fond of saying, "Now and then an innocent man is sent t' th' legislature."

In this spirit, I borrow (with no intent to repay, just like socialist governments, or any government for that matter) an apology from the wit of Monty Python, with thanks to Eric Idle:

> I would like to apologize for the way in which politicians are represented in this book. It was never my intention to imply that politicians are weak-kneed political time-servers who are concerned more with their personal vendettas, private power struggles and payoffs for favorable legislation than with the problems of government, nor to suggest at any point that they sacrifice their credibility by denying free debate on vital matters in the mistaken impression that party unity comes before the well-being of the people they supposedly represent, nor to imply at any point that they are squabbling little toadies without any concept of freedom or without an ounce of concern for the vital social problems of today. Nor indeed do I intend that the reader should consider them as corrupt or crabby ulcerous little self-seeking vermin with furry legs and an excessive addiction to alcohol and drugs and [taking a (teenage) page from Congress] certain explicit bisexual practices which some people might find offensive.

I am sorry if this impression comes across.

AUTOMATION

Nothing increases the number of jobs so rapidly as labor-saving machinery, because it releases wants theretofore unknown, by permitting leisure.

—ISABEL PATERSON
THE GOD OF THE MACHINE

It is one of the greatest economic errors to put any limitation upon production. . . . We have not the power to produce more than there is a potential to consume.

—LOUIS D. BRANDEIS

. . . with each advance [of technology], a part of the work is entrusted to the forces of Nature, and there is a corresponding decrease in the labor that needs to be performed or to be remunerated. Now, every payment that is eliminated evidently represents a victory, not for the one who renders the service, but for the one who receives it, that is, for mankind.

—FREDERIC BASTIAT

Automation through new technology (see TECHNOLOGY) has always been a chief bogeyman of the labor union (see UNIONS). As if their wage demands, taxes, and government regulations weren't enough, the unions attempt to stifle modernization of American plants, insisting that they are trying to save jobs. True the "leadership" *is* trying to save jobs—their own jobs—and to preserve dues-payers, while the rank and file expect their jobs to be saved at the expense of American consumers. Meanwhile, they destroy our ability to compete in world markets and assure us a lower standard of living, all because union "leadership" and the rank and file are dominated largely by envy (see ENVY).

This envy-dominated mentality is perfectly described in Helmut Schoeck's book *Envy: A Theory of Social Behavior:*

There are two contrasting social processes in which the envious man plays a considerable role: inhibiting processes, which serve tradition by thwarting innovation, and the destructive processes of revolution. The ostensible contradiction disappears as soon as it is realized that in both cases envy is the motive for the same action: the sarcasm, sabotage and menacing Schadenfreude [resentment] towards anyone who seeks to introduce something new, and the gloating, spiteful envy with which revolutionaries seek to tear down the existing order and its symbols of success.

The dream of lifetime job security and ever increasing wages without serious competition (see COMPETITION) has started to come due with depressing results for union workers and the economy: declining productivity (see PRODUCTIVITY) and loss of markets and jobs, as products such as automobiles and electronics are increasingly being built in Japan in more efficient, automated plants, with cheaper labor.

If the union theory that automation causes loss of jobs were correct, then a good example should be agriculture, which is represented by no union and, probably only coincidentally, had a stupendous gain in productivity through automation and new technology during the past four decades. From 1940 to 1980, agriculture lost more than 7 million jobs, yet increased land cultivation by 11 million acres, and doubled crop yields, while holding currency price increases below the "official" rate of inflation (see CONSUMER PRICE INDEX).

According to union "logic," 7 million jobs were permanently lost. That is partially true: 7 million low-paying, dirty, menial jobs were lost. But from 1940 to 1980, the economy created over 51 million *new* jobs (although none so romantic as walking behind a horse twelve hours a day), and the "official" gross national product grew over twenty-six times in terms of currency (see CURRENCY). (It has been estimated that the Bell System, operating on the same level of automation used in the early 1900s, would have needed over 1 billion employees to handle the calls made in 1980. Would you like to pay part of that phone bill?)

Had unions been able to organize farm labor, I have no doubt there would have been a requirement that every tractor have a horse hitched to it and a man to tend it (similar to the American railroads, which are forced to pay coal firemen to ride around on diesel locomotives).

Robots are the current prime targets of organized labor. They have expressed no interest in Eddie "The Weasel" Lucciono's proposal that they join existing unions or organize their own and have feigned indifference to his proposal that they lend their pension money for construction of gambling casinos in Las Vegas and Atlantic City to help ease the current severe shortage.

Japan has already surpassed us in robot installation and the lead widens day by day, as union leaders and Congress plot an "industrial policy," new import duties (see TARIFFS), and "voluntary import quotas" (to protect consumers from better products at lower prices) and dream on.

BIBLIOGRAPHY

Books come at my call and return when I desire them; they are never out of humor and they answer all my questions with readiness. Some present in review before me the events of past ages; others reveal to me the secrets of Nature. These teach me how to live, and those how to die; these dispel my melancholy by their mirth, and amuse me by their sallies of wit. Some there are who prepare my soul to suffer everything, to desire nothing, and to become thoroughly acquainted with itself. In a word, they open the door to all the arts and sciences.

—PETRARCH

The real purpose of books is to trap the mind into doing its own thinking.

—CHRISTOPHER MORLEY

Employ your time in improving yourself by other men's writings, so that you shall gain easily what others have labored hard for.

—SOCRATES

Books open your mind, broaden your mind, and strengthen you as nothing else can.

—WILLIAM FEATHER

A man will turn over half a library to make one book.

—SAMUEL JOHNSON

There are many excellent books on economics and capitalism, but one of the best ones I have read is *The God of the Machine* by Isabel Paterson. It is quoted extensively in this book. Read it and understand what is happening to our country and the world, and why— and what happens when political dreams come due.

BONDS, GOVERNMENT

Words [currencies] pay no debts.

—WILLIAM SHAKESPEARE

Let us live in as small a circle as we will, we are either debtors or creditors before we have had time to look round.

—GOETHE

Let us all be happy, and live within our means, even if we have to borrow the money to do it with.

—ARTEMUS WARD

My favorite definition of a bond was coined by Franz Pick, when he proclaimed, "A government bond is a certificate of guaranteed confiscation." Never in history has there been a government bond that paid off in purchasing power equal to the original amount borrowed. If bonds were denominated in money (see MONEY), instead of currency (see CURRENCY), this would not be the case.

Adam Smith was well aware of this con game over two hundred years ago (1776) when he wrote *The Wealth of Nations*:

> When national debts [bonds] have accumulated to a certain degree, there is scarce, I believe, a single instance of their having been fairly and completely paid. The liberation of the public revenue, if it has ever been brought about at all, has always been brought about by a bankruptcy; sometimes by an avowed one, but always by a real one, though frequently by *pretended payment*. [The emphasis here is mine.]

The pretended payment Smith alluded to was payment in depreciated (i.e., near worthless) currency.

The following table illustrates what happened to any "investor" (speculator? unwitting philanthropist? victim?) with $1 million who placed his capital in ten-year government bonds, starting in 1960:

Real Return from a $1 Million Investment in Ten-Year Government Bonds After Adjusting for Inflation and Income Taxes
(Using Consumer Price Index (CPI) and Assuming 50% Tax Rate)

YEAR	BOND YIELD (Percentage)	INCREASE IN CPI (Percentage)	REAL BOND YIELD (Percentage)	AFTER-TAX YIELD (Percentage)	REAL PURCHASING POWER OF $1 MILLION (Dollars)
1960	4.12	1.6	2.52	0.46	1,004,600.00
1961	4.12	1.0	3.12	1.06	1,015,248.80
1962	4.12	1.1	3.02	0.96	1,024,995.10
1963	4.12	1.2	2.92	0.86	1,033,810.10
1964	4.12	1.3	2.82	0.76	1,041,667.10
1965	4.12	1.7	2.42	0.36	1,045,417.10
1966	4.12	2.9	1.22	−0.84	1,036,635.60
1967	4.12	2.9	1.22	−0.84	1,027,927.80
1968	4.12	4.2	−0.08	−2.14	1,005,930.20
1969	4.12	5.4	−1.28	−3.34	972,332.10
1970	7.35	5.9	1.45	−2.22	950,746.36
1971	7.35	4.3	3.05	−0.62	944,851.73
1972	7.35	3.3	4.05	0.38	948,442.17
1973	7.35	6.2	1.15	−2.52	924,541.42
1974	7.35	11.0	−3.65	−7.32	856,864.99
1975	7.35	9.1	−1.75	−5.42	810,422.91
1976	7.35	5.8	1.55	−2.12	793,241.94
1977	7.35	6.5	0.85	−2.82	770,872.52
1978	7.35	7.6	−0.35	−4.02	739,883.45
1979	7.35	11.3	−3.95	−7.62	638,504.33
1980	11.46	13.5	−2.04	−7.77	630,396.04
1981	11.46	10.4	1.06	−4.67	600,956.55
1982	11.46	6.1	5.36	−0.37	598,733.01
1983	11.46	3.2	8.26	2.53	613,880.96
1984	11.46	4.3	7.16	1.43	622,659.45

By the end of 1984, the investor had witnessed the following results from his "investment":

1. During the twenty-five years he owned bonds, his pre-tax yield, adjusted for inflation, was negative for seven years; his after-tax

yield (after adjustment for inflation) was negative for sixteen of those years.

2. More than $375,000 worth of purchasing power was embezzled from his original capital by government income taxes and inflation.

3. For the "privilege" of being ripped off by inflation, he had to pay over $1,300,000 in income taxes, assuming a 50 percent tax rate.

4. Even if no income taxes had been paid, the bonds would have provided a real compounded return of only 1.58 percent per year, although the average annual growth, without adjusting for currency depreciation, *appeared* to be 6.85 percent. (At 1.58 percent interest, principal doubles in *only* forty-four years!)

5. After income taxes and inflation adjustments, this investment showed a compounded *loss* of 1.88 percent a year for the twenty-five years the bonds were held. This means the government not only paid *no* interest on its debt, but actually charged the borrower for the privilege of lending it his wealth.

6. Had there been no inflation or income taxes (we can still dream) and assuming the same rates of interest, the $1 million of government bonds would have grown to more than $5.2 million (see COMPOUNDING).

Were government bonds sold by prospectus with full disclosure, as the Securities and Exchange Commission requires corporate bonds to be (and, just for fun, assuming the SEC were really interested in what happens to investors), the following statement would have to appear on the front page:

THESE SECURITIES INVOLVE A HIGH DEGREE OF RISK, AS THEY ARE DENOMINATED IN A CURRENCY THAT HAS LOST OVER 85 PERCENT OF ITS PURCHASING POWER SINCE 1940 AND ARE BACKED BY A GOVERNMENT THAT HAS BALANCED ITS BUDGET TWICE SINCE 1960. EVERY PRIOR INVESTOR IN THESE SECURITIES HAS SUFFERED REAL CAPITAL LOSSES, AND THE ISSUER HAS NO INTENT OF REPAYING ITS DEBTS, EXCEPT BY ISSUING MORE BONDS AND DEPRECIATING THE CURRENCY USED FOR REPAYMENT. THESE SECURITIES HAVE NOT BEEN APPROVED OR DISAPPROVED BY THE SECURITIES AND EXCHANGE COMMISSION.

BUREAUCRACY

I was never molested by any person but those who represented the state.

—THOREAU

Government means politics, and interference by government carries with it always the implication of coercion. We may accept the expanding power of bureaucrats so long as we bask in their friendly smile. But it is a dangerous temptation. Today politics may be our friend and tomorrow we may be its victims.

—OWEN D. YOUNG

Bureaucracy is a giant mechanism operated by pygmies.

—HONORÉ DE BALZAC

The trade of governing has always been monopolized by the most ignorant and the most rascally individuals of mankind.

—THOMAS PAINE

The worthless and offensive members of society [bureaucrats], whose existence is a social pest, invariably think themselves the most ill-used people alive, and never get over their astonishment at the ingratitude and selfishness of their contemporaries.

—RALPH WALDO EMERSON

He has erected a multitude of new offices, and sent hither swarms of officers [bureaucrats] to harass our people and eat out their substance.

—DECLARATION OF INDEPENDENCE

It is impossible to have big government without a massive and parasitic bureaucracy. These organizations are generally staffed by envious little demagogues who have traded their own freedom and self-worth for a meaningless, but overpaid "job" and the mirage of lifetime security. (Some life.) Having given up on their own lives, they seek to validate their choice and gain some measure of self-esteem by attempting to control or "legally" plunder (and eventually destroy) that which they can never possess: the lives and wealth of the producers who cannot be bought, but must support them.

Eric Hoffer gave us some excellent insight into why people are willing to surrender their individuality to a bureaucratic existence under the pretext of altruism in his classic book *The True Believer*:

> A man is likely to mind his own business when it is worth minding. When it is not, he takes his mind off his own meaningless affairs by minding other people's business. . . .
>
> The burning conviction that we have a holy duty toward others is often a way of attaching our drowning selves to a passing raft. What looks like giving a hand is often a holding on for dear life. Take away our holy duties and you leave our lives puny and meaningless. There is no doubt that in exchanging a self-centered for an [allegedly] selfless life we gain enormously in self-esteem. The vanity of the selfless, even those who practice utmost humility, is boundless.

The second half of the "bureaucrat equation" is the lust for power. Bureaucrats love their power to regulate, strangle, and suffocate. Charles Colton captured the essence of this love and its attraction to "government groupies" when he wrote:

> Power, like the diamond, dazzles the beholder, and also the wearer; it dignifies meanness; it magnifies littleness; to what is contemptible, it gives authority; to what is low, exaltation.

Many taxpayers are under the impression that most civil servants are not especially bright, but dedicated and loyal. With the exception of that assessment of their mental horsepower, nothing could be further from the truth. They are dedicated to becoming as powerful and highly paid as they possibly can and are loyal to the bureaucracy and the bureaucracy only! Their dreams are mainly of retirement.

To hear Washington tell it, we are on the verge of running out of bureaucrats because of low pay and poor working conditions. The fact is that there are almost ten applicants for every federal position, an average of 300,000 people a year trying to get government "jobs" (strange how many people will pursue such poor jobs). Fewer than 2 percent of these people are hired.

All salary surveys (other than Washington's) show that the average bureaucrat is overpaid by around 50 percent when compared to a worker in the private sector and that he is only half as productive (surprise, surprise). The bureaucrat also works shorter hours and cannot be fired (the dismissal rate is less than 0.2 percent). There are currently over 200,000 civil servants making $30,000 to $50,000 a year.

Pension plan? No problem! A government employee's benefits are equal to 55 percent of his salary (the private sector averages less than 30 percent), and he can retire at fifty-five. Naturally the pension is indexed for inflation losses (we can't have these people suffering for their sins even though most private pension plans are not adjusted for inflation). Since the bureaucrat puts less than two years of benefits into the plan, naturally taxpayers are required to make up the difference (currently there is an unfunded liability of at least $1 trillion that does not show up in the national debt figure), but we've got to do it or they might quit. (In case you haven't noticed, only bureaucrats in sensitive positions of monopoly such as police, firemen, teachers, or air traffic controllers ever strike or threaten to strike. Can you imagine the lack of concern and benefits that would come from a strike by the Department of Health, Education, and Welfare; the Department of Energy; the Department of Agriculture; the Securities and Exchange Commission; or the Federal Trade Commission?)

No information on the civil service would be complete without a view of its inner workings. The best description of the bureaucracy I have seen comes from Charles Peters (a former bureaucrat), in *How Washington Really Works* (he uses the term *works* very loosely; a better title would have been *How Washington Really Doesn't Work*):

> There is a permanent government in Washington that consists of people whose power does not depend on election results. It includes the courts, the military, and the foreign services. . . . But the largest part of the permanent government is the civilian employees. Ten times that number are funded by the taxpayers, either through government contracts, as employees of state, county, and municipal governments, or as members of the military. . . .
>
> What would happen if there were a dramatic reduction in the number of government employees? . . . Have you noticed any difference in the service you get from Washington bureaucrats during the last two weeks of December? Probably not, but did you know that in recent years absenteeism among Washington federal employees during that time has run as high as 60 percent?

Vice-admiral Hyman Rickover has echoed Peters's sentiments by repeatedly insisting that 50 percent of the civilian employees in the Pentagon could be fired without hurting "efficiency" (I think he must have meant inefficiency). Although efficiency, in this case, is a very poor choice of words, his point is well taken. Thanks to the following quote from P. H. Box's book *Three Master Builders and Another*, we don't have to wonder what would happen if there were a dramatic reduction in the number of bureaucrats:

Mussolini realised that Italy was suffering, in common with most Southern countries, from a plethora of officials and State employees. He began by amalgamating overlapping ministries and suppressing superfluous offices. A ruthless cutting of staffs in the various ministries was inaugurated, designed to discover the exact point at which the services could be maintained in a state of efficiency. In the six months ending 30th April, 1923, 17,232 men were dismissed from the railways, which since the war had become under the State management hopelessly overstaffed and inevitably insolvent. Notice was given that by the end of 1923 the staff must be reduced by another 300,000. The stupendous disorder of the State railways can be gauged by the fact that after these amputations, they increased in efficiency.

Peters offers the following insight into why government bureaucracy (see SYSTEMS) cannot and will not solve *any* of the world's problems:

The reason why bureaucrats like internal reorganization better than external action is easy to understand. Suppose you work in an antipoverty agency and you do your job so well that poverty is eradicated. Or suppose you work in the Department of Energy and the energy problem [which government created; see OIL AND GAS] disappears. What will happen to you? The bureaucrat can figure that out. If he takes real action, if he's truly effective, he'll be out of work, he won't survive. If, on the other hand, his action is make believe, poverty will not disappear, the energy problem will not be solved, and his job will be safe—he will survive. Now you understand the fundamental Washington equation:

Make believe = Survival

We can leave this section with one last quote from Box's book (which would be a dream come true for almost every country in the world if the rhetoric were actually followed by action):

We have had enough of the State railwayman, the State postman, and the State insurance official. We have had enough of the State administration at the expense of the Italian [U.S.] tax-payer, which has done nothing but aggravate the exhausted financial condition of the country. . . .

CAPITAL

Capital is to the progress of society what gas is to a car.

—JAMES TRUSLOW ADAMS

Labor can't prosper so long as capital lies idle. Capital can't prosper while labor is unemployed.

—DEWITT M. EMERY

Capital is not a free gift of God or nature. It is the outcome of a provident restriction of consumption on the part of man.

—LUDWIG VON MISES

If you divorce capital from labor, capital is hoarded, and labor starves.

—DANIEL WEBSTER

Capital is one of the two key elements necessary for production (men is the other). Capital accumulation (both financial and intellectual) through profits (see PROFITS, CORPORATE) and saving (see SAVING) is the only path to a higher standard of living. The only reason mankind has been able to advance materially is because it has benefited from the capital accumulated and passed down by prior generations.

Government is the natural enemy of all capital (see GOVERNMENT). The following list contains a general description of some of the methods that governments use to destroy capital or prevent its formation:

1. Taxation of production and existing wealth: This is the direct expropriation of a portion of private property without permission or compensation.
2. Inflation (see INFLATION) of currency: This is a process of destroying currency and financial capital by diluting its value, but, as we saw in the Accounting section, it also causes the inadvertent destruction of capital by causing people to confuse it with income.

When inflation equals the pretax rate of return on a capital "investment" (see INVESTMENT), people trying to live on their savings are devouring their capital, not living on income. Currency depreciation forces capital into speculation (see SPECULATION) and into static investments such as gold, silver, and collectibles (instead of production) that may preserve purchasing power, but produce no further wealth.

3. Directly blocking the free movement of capital: In most countries of the world, including such notable "free countries" as America, Great (?) Britain, France, Australia, Mexico, and Brazil (as well as *all* communist countries, naturally), a citizen is not allowed to move *his* currency freely across international borders. All governments block the free movement of human capital through immigration laws. They also (to a greater or lesser extent) block the free movement of goods and services between countries with tariffs (see TARIFFS) and other forms of import restrictions.

4. The uncertainty of the law (see LAW, THE): Government growth (see GOVERNMENT GROWTH) and the consequent destruction of property rights (see PROPERTY RIGHTS) either immobilizes capital because of the confiscatory tax consequences of selling existing investments with large inflationary (i.e., illusory) "gains," drives it from the country to areas of greater freedom, or forces it into the underground economy (see UNDERGROUND ECONOMY).

5. Direct expropriation: This is merely taxation at the 100 percent rate. The Mexican government (to cite only one of an unlimited number of examples) nationalized (i.e., stole) all domestic oil and gas production (almost entirely discovered and developed with American capital) in the early 1900s.

The first law of capital is that it *must* be maintained, but the U.S. government and most other governments in the world are currently on a capital consumption binge of epic proportions (see MOMENTUM). In her brilliant book *The God of the Machine*, Isabel Paterson explained the disastrous consequences of this course of action:

If war [or government] takes more than the surplus production over a given length of time, even an unbroken series of victories [or new welfare programs] must bring the nation ever nearer to irremediable defeat [or bankruptcy], on the ultimate cessation of supplies.

The mistake of a nation which makes war [or allows government growth; see GOVERNMENT GROWTH] at capital cost, thinking to win before its reserves are exhausted, is that it has undertaken an incalculable expenditure from a limited quantity [of capital]. It has cut off the dynamo and is running on the battery; but the power in a battery is a fixed quantity, while the future time a war [or government growth] will last, and the consequent expenditure of energy it will call for through time, *can never be known in advance*. The one certainty is the ratio which such calculations ignore, the fact that if capital is being depleted, more energy taken from the circuit than it produces in surplus, it is a losing formula; the nation must constantly become weaker.

The political dream of prosperity through capital consumption will always come due.

COMPENSATION

To suppress a truth is to give it force beyond endurance.

—CHINESE PROVERB

They have habitually assumed that each proposed good would, if secured, be a pure good, instead of being a good purchasable only by submission to some evil which would else have been remedied; and, making this error, have injuriously diverted men's labor.

—HERBERT SPENCER

No evil is without its compensation. The less money, the less trouble; the less favor, the less envy. Even in those cases which put us out of wits, it is not the loss itself, but the estimate of the loss that troubles us.

—SENECA

There is nothing so well known as that we should not expect something for nothing—but we all do and call it Hope.

—EDGAR WATSON HOWE
COUNTRY TOWN SAYINGS
THE STORY OF A COUNTRY TOWN

"Compensation" by Ralph Waldo Emerson is perhaps the greatest essay ever written. The amount of wisdom contained in those thirteen pages, more than enough to govern any nation, is simply staggering. While studying Emerson's thoughts (which were largely the inspiration for this book), I became aware that most of governments' problems (which invariably become mankind's problems) stem from the fact that they do not abide by this "law of laws."

Emerson summarized the law of compensation with the words "You cannot do wrong without suffering wrong." He correctly perceived that "Justice is not postponed. . . . Every secret is told, every crime is punished, every virtue rewarded, every wrong redressed, in silence and certainty." Various aspects of the law of compensation have been restated in countless proverbs: You get what you pay for (or in government's case, you don't get what you pay for, and in most cases, thank goodness); give and it shall be given you; nothing ventured, nothing gained; and measure for measure. But since government has not passed this law (see LEGISLATION), it cannot possibly understand how the law can affect it. Emerson chronicles the endlessly pathetic history of government (see GOVERNMENT) with the following passage:

> The ingenuity of man [government] has always been dedicated to the solution of one problem—how to detach the sensual sweet, the sensual bright, etc., from the moral sweet, the moral deep, the moral fair; that is, again, to contrive to cut clean off this upper surface so thin as to leave it bottomless; to get a one end, without an other end. . . .

In keeping with this exercise in futility, government is constantly trying to find a way to have unlimited creation of currency and credit without inflation, unlimited spending and deficits without economic ruin, unlimited national debt without repayment, and unlimited growth of power and plunder (regulation and taxation) without revolt. And what is the result of government attempts to ignore the law of compensation? It is utter chaos preceding predictable and resolute failure. For Emerson discovered a law without loopholes (a trick Congress and most tax lawyers thought was impossible):

> This dividing and detaching is steadily counteracted. Up to this day it must be owned no projector [government] has had the smallest success. The parted water reunites behind our hand. Pleasure is taken out of pleasant things, profit out of profitable things, power out of strong things, as soon as we seek to separate them from the whole. We can no more halve things and get the sensual good, by itself, than we can get an inside that shall have no outside, or a light without a shadow. . . .
>
> Life invests itself with inevitable conditions, which the unwise [governments] seek to dodge, which one and another brags that he does not know, that they do not touch him; but the brag [legislation] is on his lips, the conditions are in his soul. . . . So signal is the failure of all attempts to make this separation of the good from the tax, that the experiment would not be tried—since to try it is to be mad [which government most certainly is]—but for the circumstance that when the disease began in the will, of rebellion and separation, the intellect is at once infected, so that the man [government] ceases to see God whole in each object, but is able to see the sensual allurement of an

object and not see the sensual hurt; he sees the mermaid's head but not the dragon's tail, and thinks he can cut off that which he would have from that which he would not have. . . .

And what are the results of government abandoning the functions for which it was established and mutating into a malignant force (see SYSTEMS) whose sole purpose is the unsurpation of power from the people? What are the results of government ignorance, fraud, immorality, plunder, and waste? Emerson gives us the answer:

Whilst I [governments] stand in simple [honest and moral] relations to my fellow-man [citizens], I have no displeasure in meeting him. We meet as water meets water, or as two currents of air mix, with perfect diffusion and interpenetration of nature. But as soon as there is any departure from simplicity and attempt at halfness, or good for me that is not good for him; his eyes no longer seek mine; there is war [revolt] between us; there is hate in him [citizens] and fear in me [government].

The law of compensation cannot be set aside except in political dreams. That it has been ignored by crowds and politicians, who are consumed by greed and envy (see ENVY) and guilt, explains why so many of the bad dreams discussed in this book are coming due. Government can pass no law (see LAW, THE) that exempts it from its just deserts or absolves the people from their legitimate responsibilities (see RESPONSIBILITY) because, as Emerson correctly perceived,

This law [not governments] writes the laws of cities and nations. It is in vain to build or plot or combine against it [as government does each and every day]. Things refuse to be mismanaged for long. . . . Though no checks to a new evil [government, law or government program] appear, the checks exist, and will appear. [Advice for dictators:] If the government is cruel, the governor's life is not safe. [Advice for Art Laffer (see LAFFER CURVE):] If you tax too high, the revenue will yield nothing. [Advice for Congress and the IRS:] If you make the criminal [tax] code sanguinary, juries will not convict. [Advice for the criminal courts:] If the law is too mild, private vengeance comes in.

COMPETITION

All through man's history, there has been a competition between the safe and the adventurous; the fully informed and the to-be-informed; between the "pattern set for all men" and the glimmer of a gleam for men to follow.

—HARRY A. OVERSTREET

Competition, as the "life" of trade, surely is a tremendous spur to progress. Is it not the pursued man or business that advances through persistent effort to keep ahead? The constant striving to maintain leadership ever involves new ways and means of accomplishing more efficiently and thus it is the "pursued is the progressive man."

—W. D. TOLAND

And while the law (of competition) may be sometimes hard for the individual, it is best for the race, because it ensures the survival of the fittest in every department.

—ANDREW CARNEGIE

Though the many who revile competition strangely ignore the enormous benefits resulting from it—though they forget that most of the appliances and products distinguishing civilization from savagery, and making possible the maintenance of a large population on a small area, have been developed by the struggle for existence—though they disregard the fact that while every man, as producer, suffers from the under-bidding of competitors, yet, as consumer, he is immensely advantaged by the cheapening of all he has to buy—though they persist in dwelling on the evils of competition and saying nothing of its benefits. . . .

—HERBERT SPENCER

Competition is the driving force behind all improvement in our standard of living. It springs from freedom (i.e., the freedom to choose; see FREEDOM) and the thought that service, innovation, and excellence will be rewarded. But it is correctly perceived as a major disadvantage to certain special interests.

Politicians, unions, and business (which see competition as a great benefit to every industry except theirs) all pay lip service to the virtues of competition until it begins to make inroads into their own areas of interest (such as the auto industry, steel industry, textiles, airlines, or trucking), it then becomes "unsafe," "suicidal," "cutthroat," "unfair," "wasteful duplication of service," "dumping," or "monopoly" (see DIC-TIONARY OF GOVERNMENT EUPHEMISMS). When an entity, foreign or domestic, begins to compete "too successfully" or attempts to start a new service, government is "forced" to impose tariffs (see TARIFFS) or regulation (see REGULATION), to ask for "voluntary import quotas," to provide subsidies, or to call on the "antitrust laws" (see MONOPOLY) to penalize success. (The envious never want to compete; they would much rather limit or destroy competition.)

There are only two forms of economic competition available to mankind: healthy and unhealthy. We are going to have to decide which one we want. The first can exist only in a free society; it leads to progress and prosperity and allows for improvement, innovation, and greater production and service at lower prices. This type of competition is based on ability and performance and is blocked to some extent by all forms of government (see POSTAL SERVICE) and virtually eliminated by communism and socialism. (In fact you could say that a major function of the coercive monopoly of government is shielding itself and various other favored entities, such as the local phone company or postal service, from competition.) And in any form of government (see GOVERNMENT, FORMS OF), when growth reaches a certain point, it begins, like a cancer, to destroy the productive segment of the economy (see GOVERNMENT GROWTH). Healthy competition (and a rising standard of living) is soon replaced by unhealthy competition, in which *privilege* is rewarded. All see how little they can work or how corrupt they can become (i.e., to what level of government or influence they can rise, so they can live from plunder or seize the law; see LAW, THE). At this point, threat or coercion replaces incentive, and society (see SOCIETY) starts a long, inevitable decline (see MO-MENTUM) as it shifts from gainful production to regulation, corruption, and plunder.

If we do not work to restore freedom from government—and therefore healthy competition, competition to produce and serve—we will have to relearn the wisdom of Frederic Bastiat's warning in *The Law*:

> They will come to learn in the end, at their own expense, that it is better to endure competition for rich customers than to be invested with monopoly over impoverished customers.

COMPOUNDING

But I know that the eighth wonder [of the world] is compound interest [compounding].

—BARON DE ROTHSCHILD

...for compound interest on compound interest is the rate and usage of this exchequer.

—RALPH WALDO EMERSON

Baron de Rothschild once called compound interest (compounding), "the eighth wonder of the world," and, were it not for government, it could be. The wonderful thing about compound interest is what it can do for you if you accumulate capital. The horrible thing about compounding (which, like a double-edged blade, cuts two ways) is what it can do to you (and ultimately to the lender) if you compound debt, foreign loans to socialist governments (see DEBT, FOREIGN), expenditures, or losses. It then becomes the "eighth horror of the world." (You can pick any seven governments to complete the first part of that list.)

In the United States and the world today, government (an old compounder from way back) is compounding three things: debt, taxes, and inflation. (And unfortunately, income taxes and inflation have made it virtually impossible for the private sector to compound anything but depreciating currency; see CURRENCY.) This could be classified as "negative compounding" because each of the three entities government compounds is ultimately disastrous for the economy. Government's negative compounding (of debts, taxes, and inflation) always begins slowly, then accelerates, and finally reaches a point where it is increasing at an exponential or infinite rate. In the stock or commodity market, this is known as a *blow-off formation*. Since we live in a finite world, nothing can increase at an infinite rate (not even government stupidity), and a collapse *must always* occur. The most recent example of this was the silver market of 1979–80, which ended with a crash of over 90 percent.

Several years ago an economic collapse was predicted for October 1979 based on the following charts showing the national debt, federal budget, and Consumer Price Index from 1913–79:

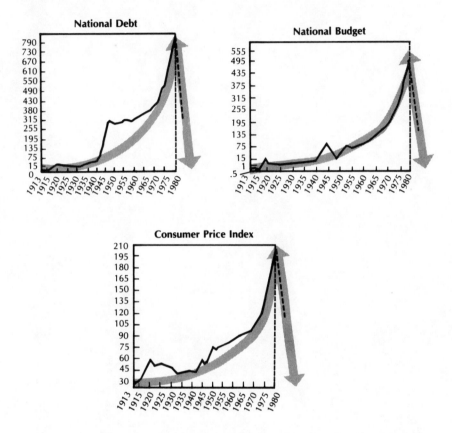

Notice that each chart exhibits an exponential curve that is very close to reaching an infinite rate of increase. This *should have* signaled an economic collapse, indicated by the shaded arrow. The man who developed the theory made just one mistake. He forgot that the national debt and budget are measured in constantly depreciating currency and thus, for the most part, are meaningless indicators of impending doom. The national debt (see DEBT, NATIONAL), adjusted for inflation (see CONSUMER PRICE INDEX), actually decreased from 1945 to 1980. The one chart that has some relevance today is the Consumer Price Index, which shows the collapse of our currency. A recurrence of the exponential increase of this index *could* mean one of two things: the end of the dollar (runaway inflation) or the end of inflation (a deflationary collapse; see DEFLATION). But even if neither occurs in the near future, something has eventually got to give. The dream of "negative compounding" will come due.

CONSUMER PRICE INDEX

(CPI)

Delusions, errors and lies are like huge, gaudy vessels, the rafters of which are rotten and worm-eaten, and those who embark in them are fated to be shipwrecked.

—BUDDHA

Beware lest you lose the substance by grasping at the shadow.

—AESOP

Under certain conditions, men respond as powerfully to fiction as they do to realities, and in many cases, they help to create the very fictions to which they respond.

—WALTER LIPPMAN

The Consumer Price Index (CPI) is one of the more insidious statistics developed by our government because it directs the hostility of the inflation-weary public toward business and the marketplace instead of toward the cause: government mismanagement of currency and credit. The CPI uses prices to measure inflation, but currency price increases are only *symptoms* of inflation (see INFLATION) and not necessarily an accurate measure of its rate (see INFLATION, REAL). *Real prices are not going up! The value of currency* (see CURRENCY) *is going down* (as it always does). Government has tricked the general population into thinking that "prices" are increasing, but, in reality, all that is increasing is the supply of currency and credit. People are encouraged to watch the prices at the supermarket, not the rate of growth in the Federal Reserve's "money supply" (currency supply) figures.

I have constructed an index which is much more representative of what is really happening. I call it the *Dollar Depreciation Index* (or *Government Rip-off Index*). It traces the purchasing power of the dollar from 1940, using government CPI figures (which are very understated) converted to reflect what is really happening: declining currency value, not "rising consumer prices." This index will be used as the correction factor every time we adjust currency figures in this book:

Dollar Depreciation Index (DDI)

YEAR	PURCHASING POWER IN 1940 CONSTANT DOLLARS (Percentage)
1940	100.00
1945	77.90
1950	58.26
1955	52.29
1960	47.36
1965	44.49
1970	36.09
1975	26.04
1980	17.00
1984	13.31

As you can see, the dollar, like government and politicians, continues to make less and less cents.

Using the DDI figures, we can now see what 1984 prices represent when adjusted to 1940 purchasing power (i.e., 1940 prices) by multiplying the 1984 price by the 1984 DDI (13.31 percent):

ITEM	1984 PRICE (Dollars)	1940 PRICE (Dollars)
Personal Estate	1,000,000.00	133,100.00
House	200,000.00	26,620.00
Salary	100,000.00	13,310.00
Car	20,000.00	2,662.00
Television	1,000.00	133.10
Man's suit	500.00	66.55
Dinner for two	50.00	6.66
Movie for two	10.00	1.33
Hamburger	2.00	0.266
Gallon of gas	1.20	0.16
Loaf of bread	1.00	0.133
Cup of coffee	0.50	0.066
Newspaper	0.25	0.033
Phone call	0.25	0.033

Still think prices are going up? Still long for the good old days? The good old days are gone because we have substituted unbacked currency for money (see MONEY). The prices shown are proof that consumer prices measured in constant purchasing power have not increased at all. If you accept the more realistic inflation figures shown later in this book, you will find that the prices shown here have actually declined in terms of constant purchasing power. This is exactly what you would expect from an economy that had progressed as far as ours had (in spite of government) in forty-four years.

CORRUPTION

(An Honest Government Official Is One Who Has Not Had a Good Enough Offer)

Now the sole remedy for the abuse of political power is to limit it; but when politics corrupt business, modern reformers invariably demand the enlargement of the political power.

—ISABEL PATERSON
THE GOD OF THE MACHINE

Experience constantly proves that every man who has power is impelled to abuse it.

—MONTESQUIEU

How invariably officialism becomes corrupt every one knows.

—HERBERT SPENCER

Force always attracts men of low morality.

—ALBERT EINSTEIN

It is discouraging how many people are shocked by honesty and how few by deceit.

—NOËL COWARD

Corruption, the most infallible symptom of constitutional liberty...

—EDWARD GIBBON

France fell because there was corruption without indignation.

—ROMAIN ROLLAND

Among a people [or government] generally corrupt liberty cannot long exist.

—EDMUND BURKE

⊠ The words *corruption* and *government* are as inseparable as *politicians* and *taxes*, or *federal budgets* and *deficits*. Currently, two American public officials are indicted on charges of corruption every day of the year (and even this represents only the small percentage ever caught). We have often seen scandals reach all the way to the White House.

Corruption is always a *geometric* function of the size of government. (Thus it is much more prevalent in countries on the verge of total breakdown, as any visitor to Mexico and Russia can attest.) Large government can come only from increasing confiscation of private wealth and freedom. Wealth and freedom severed from their rightful owner draw looters and thieves, as a body severed from life draws vultures and flies.

To understand why government is permeated by corruption, it is first necessary to understand what type of people are drawn to careers (crime sprees) of power over their fellow men. Leo Tolstoy offered us the following insight into these "public servants":

> In order to obtain and hold power a man must love it. Thus the effort to get it is not likely to be coupled with goodness, but with the opposite qualities of pride, craft and cruelty.

Ferdinand Lundberg gave us a painfully accurate and detailed description of the more amateurish of these public parasites in his book *The Rich and the Super-Rich*:

> Lest the sheltered reader, tucked away in his bower, think that Senator Clark, [a former United States senator, from Pennsylvania, who wrote a very damning book titled *Congress: The Sapless Branch*] here delivers himself of an extravagant opinion or resorts to hyperbole, it is a settled conclusion among seasoned observers that, Congress apart as a separate case, the lower legislatures—state, county and municipal—are Augean stables of misfeasance, malfeasance and nonfeasance from year to year and decade to decade and that they are preponderantly staffed by riffraff or what police define as "undesirables," people who if they were not in influential positions would be unceremoniously told to "keep moving." Exceptions among them are minor. Many of them, including congressmen, refuse to go before the television cameras because it is then so plainly obvious to everybody they are what they are. Their whole demeanor arouses instant distrust in the intelligent. They are, all too painfully, type-cast for the race track, the sideshow carnival, the back alley, the peep-show, the low tavern, the bordello, the dive. Evasiveness, dissimulation, insincerity shine through their false bonhomie like beacon lights.

(And as we all know only too well—thanks to certain *former* Congressmen—it is even worse on the FBI's television cameras.)

In commenting on the collective makeup and "morality" of the various state legislatures, Lundberg continues:

> As to other legislatures, Senator Estes Kefauver found representatives of the vulpine Chicago Mafia ensconced in the Illinois legislature, which has been rocked by one scandal of the standard variety after the other off and on for seventy-five years. What he didn't bring out was that the Mafians were clearly superior types to many non-Mafians.
>
> Public attention, indeed, usually centers on only a few lower legislatures—Massachusetts, New York, New Jersey, California and Illinois—and the impression is thereby fostered in the unduly trusting that the ones they don't hear about are on the level. But such an impression is false. The ones just mentioned come into more frequent view because their jurisdictions are extremely competitive and the pickings are richer. Fierce fights over the spoils generate telltale commotion. Most of the states are quieter under strict one-party quasi-Soviet Establishment dominance, with local newspapers cut in on the gravy. Public criticism and information are held to a minimum, grousers are thrown a bone and not many in the low-level populace know or really care. Even so, scandalous goings-on explode into view from time to time in Florida, Texas, Louisiana, Oklahoma, Missouri and elsewhere—no state excepted. Any enterprising newspaper at any time could send an aggressive reporter into any one of them and come up with enough ordure to make the Founding Fathers collectively vomit up their very souls in their graves.

There is an old saying that if you wish to know what a man is, place him in authority. Haven't we seen enough? As long as government continues to grow like fungus on stale bread (see GOVERNMENT GROWTH), government corruption will continue to grow even faster. Sooner or later, it will eventually permeate our whole society (see SOCIETY). The politician's answer to this problem will be more legislation (see LEGISLATION) on "government ethics," but the one and only way to reduce the amount of corruption is to reduce the size and power of government. When you remove the ability to dispense stolen wealth and special government privileges, the corruption will end automatically. Since it is virtually impossible even to arrest the growth of government (much less to reduce its size; see GOVERNMENT GROWTH), the dream of "honest" theft and "mutual assured plunder" will come due.

CROWDS

A mob is a society of bodies voluntarily bereaving themselves of reason and traversing its work. The mob is man voluntarily descending to the nature of the beast. Its fit hour of activity is night. Its actions are insane, like its whole constitution. It persecutes a principle; it would whip a right; it would tar and feather justice, by inflicting fire and outrage upon the houses and persons of those who have these.

—RALPH WALDO EMERSON

When the mass acts on its own, it does so only in one way, for it has no other: it lynches.

—JOSÉ ORTEGA Y GASSET

If it had to choose who is to be crucified, the crowd will always save Barabbas.

—JEAN COCTEAU

And what politician, when he incites the masses to envy, asks himself whether his object is power and its concomitant privileges...

—HELMUT SCHOECK
ENVY: A THEORY OF SOCIAL BEHAVIOR

There is no telling to what extremes of cruelty and ruthlessness a man will go when he is freed from the fears, hesitations, doubts and the vague stirrings of decency that go with individual judgement.

—ERIC HOFFER
THE TRUE BELIEVER

In 1895, Gustave Le Bon wrote a classic book called *The Crowd*. It was followed in 1930 by José Ortega y Gasset's *The Revolt of the Masses*. Like all great truths, the themes in these books are timeless and even more appropriate in today's world of "megagovernment" than when they were first written. They both provide extensive insight into crowd behavior and thus explain what Ortega y Gasset called "hyper-democracy," (unlimited government with "property rights" determined by the envy and greed of the majority; see PROPERTY RIGHTS), that is so prevalent in today's world.

Le Bon explains the most important aspect of a crowd:

> Whoever be the individuals that compose it, however like or unlike be their mode of life, their occupations, their character, or their intelligence, the fact that they have been transformed into a crowd puts them in possession of a sort of collective mind which makes them feel, think and act in a manner quite different from that in which each individual of them would feel, think and act were he in a state of isolation.

This crowd mind usually sinks to a uniformly low level (say about government-high) in intellect and morality. Much as a chain can be no stronger than its weakest link, a crowd seems to assume the intellect and emotion of its lowest members (which means that it is easily influenced by envy; see ENVY). All successful despots (and politicians), such as Hitler, Stalin, and Mao Tse-tung, have been well aware of this trait as well as others that Le Bon discusses:

> The masses have never thirsted after truth . . . whoever can supply them with illusions is easily their master; whoever attempts to destroy their illusions is always their victim. . . . A crowd is impressed by excessive sentiments . . . to exaggerate, to affirm, to resort to repetitions and never attempt to prove anything by reasoning . . .
>
> So far as the majority of their acts are considered, crowds display a singularly inferior mentality. . . .

In *The True Believer* Eric Hoffer, amplifying on Le Bon's quote, gave us an excellent view of the mindless men and doctrines that make up these "mass movements."

> All active mass movements strive, therefore, to interpose a fact-proof screen between the faithful and the realities of the world. They do this by claiming that the ultimate and absolute truth is already embodied in their doctrine and that there is no truth nor certitude outside it. The facts on which the true believer bases his conclusions must not be derived from his experience or observation but from holy writ.

As government and its plunder grow, so does envy. As society (see SOCIETY) becomes more envious, it is increasingly fragmented into special interest groups (crowds) who attempt to seize control of the law (see LAW, THE) for their own benefit. Once crowds and their "laws" of envy begin the inevitable devastation of an economy, there finally comes a point when it can no longer generate enough wealth to satisfy the demands for plunder. Then control of the law will no longer suffice. When "laws," property rights, and morality are finally exhausted, only force (and its death and destruction) remains as the final arbitrator. At this point the official government collapses or is overthrown, as in most so-called "developing countries," and the societies degenerate into crowds in a state of continual civil war that Helmut Schoeck characterizes as permanent revolution (i.e., a government run by crowds that merely count guns instead of votes). (Lebanon is the current trend setter in this form of government, with Central America closing fast.)

Ortega y Gasset explains the eventual decline of freedom and thus civilization as crowds come to rule more and more governments:

> The mass believes that it has the right to impose and to give force of law to notions born in the café. I doubt whether there have been other periods of history in which the multitude has come to govern more directly than in our own. . . .
>
> The characteristic of the hour is that the commonplace mind, knowing itself to be commonplace, has the assurance to proclaim the rights of the commonplace and to impose them wherever it will. . . . The mass crushes beneath it everything that is different, everything that is excellent, individual, qualified and select. . . . Here we have the formidable fact of our times, described without any concealment of the brutality of its features.

No individual can stand against the government of crowds, and *no one* is immune from its irrationality, envy, or plunder. A mob of looters "voting" the property of others to itself is merely the ultimate form of democracy (see DEMOCRACY). As Lord Acton wrote in *The History of Freedom in Antiquity:*

> It is bad to be oppressed by a minority, but it is worse to be oppressed by a majority. For there is a reserve of latent power [envy] in the masses which, if it is called into play, the minority can seldom resist.

But from the absolute will of an entire people [or lynch mob] there is no appeal, no redemption, no refuge....

Tennyson delivered a remarkable prophecy for our time when he said, "the individual withers, and the world [the state] is more and more."

CURRENCY

(Is That All There Is?)

Only government can take perfectly good paper, cover it with perfectly good ink and make the combination worthless.

—MILTON FRIEDMAN

Permit me to control the money [he meant currency] of a nation, and I care not who makes its laws.

—BARON DE ROTHSCHILD

If you want to remain the slaves of the bankers and pay the costs of your own slavery, let them continue to create money [he meant currency] and control the nation's Federal Reserve credit.

—SIR JOSIAH STAMP
President of the Bank of England

Whoever controls the volume of money [he meant currency] in any country is absolute master of all industry and commerce.

—JAMES A. GARFIELD

Currency: paper in circulation that *substitutes* for money.

Daniel Webster once said, "A disordered currency is one of the greatest political evils." What Mr. Webster did not understand is that *all* currencies eventually become "disordered" (i.e., inflated; see IN-FLATION).

Paper currency always begins with some tie (no matter how tenuous) to money (see MONEY). But as the definition indicates, currency simply substitutes, or is a receipt, for money. Currency itself is no more money than is a deed, a house, or some land. As government's desire (not need) for revenue begins to outdistance its courage to pass direct taxes, currency's ties to money are gradually cut. As this happens, paper currency begins to seek its intrinsic value. (Paper has a current intrinsic value of eighty dollars per ton no matter how many zeroes are printed on it!)

Today, not one currency in the world is backed by gold or silver (and thus no currency in the world can perform the *function of money.*) Never in the history of mankind has there been one currency that did not lose its value once it was divorced from its gold and silver backing. (The Swiss franc has generally been considered the strongest and most desirable currency in the world, but from 1950 to 1980, it lost more than *60 percent* of its purchasing power.) Yet the government and news services insist on reporting "increases in prices" such as the consumer price index (CPI), instead of the declining value of U.S. currency (DDI). The blame is placed on the marketplace, which, so the accusation goes, "raises prices." Blame should fall on the government, which *consistently regulates* the value of the currency downward by increasing its supply. The power of government fraud in its legal tender monopoly makes any other form of profitable endeavor pale by comparison. The profit margin on printing currency is close to 100 percent. Each Federal Reserve note (regardless of its denomination) costs about a penny, but the government sells it for whatever number they print on it. With that kind of incentive, the continuing oversupply of currency and credit is assured. (Inflation will never be stopped by government.)

Webster made the definitive statement on unbacked, paper currency in the following quote:

> It undermines the virtues necessary for the support of the social system, and encourages propensities destructive to its happiness. It wars against industry, frugality, and economy, and it fosters the evil spirits of extravagance and speculation. Of all the contrivances for cheating the laboring classes of mankind, none has been more effectual than that which deludes them with paper money. ... Ordinary tyranny, oppression, excessive taxation, these bear lightly on the happiness of the mass of the community, compared with fraudulent currencies and the robberies committed by depreciated paper.

All governments have issued paper notes backed by its "full faith and credit" (i.e., backed by nothing) and called them "legal tender," but we do not have to sanctify their fraud by calling it "money."

DEBT, FOREIGN

Lend not to him who is mightier than thou, or if thou lendist, consider thy loans as lost.

—OLD ADAGE OF FLORENTINE BANKERS

A small loan makes a debtor; a great one, an enemy.

—PUBLILIUS SYRUS

Some people [all governments] use one-half their ingenuity to get into debt, and the other half to avoid paying it.

—GEORGE D. PRENTICE

Creditors have better memories than debtors.

—BENJAMIN FRANKLIN

It is characteristic of our present manners ... that if anyone repays a debt, it must be regarded as an immense favor.

—TERENCE

The old saying holds: Owe your banker 1,000 pounds and you are at his mercy. Owe him one million [or a few billion] and the position is reversed.

—JOHN MAYNARD KEYNES

The idea that banks and governments (i.e., taxpayers) of the West can lend capital to socialist governments (who will then "invest" it and repay the loan from "profits") is one of the most grandiose dreams currently coming due. The following list identifies most of the players:

Foreign Debt 1982

COUNTRY	DEBT (Billions of Dollars)
Brazil	$90.0
Mexico	82.0
Argentina	44.0
South Korea	36.0
Venezuela	28.0
Israel	26.7
Poland	26.0
USSR	23.0
Indonesia	22.0
Egypt	19.2
Philippines	16.6
East Germany	14.0
Peru	11.5
Romania	9.9
Nigeria	9.3
Hungary	7.0
Zaire	5.1
Zambia	4.5
Bolivia	3.1

Notice that, although the geography is diverse, the flow of loans is always from the more free economies that can generate the surplus capital to the less free economies that cannot generate even the interest payments on the loans. They all also share several other fundamental characteristics that the bankers chose to ignore:

1. They are economies dominated by huge or growing governments (see GOVERNMENT GROWTH) that in turn are dominated by envy: Five of the countries on the list are communist and therefore need no comment on the size of government, but even in Brazil, which has the smallest government and thus would certainly be classified as one of the more free countries on the above list, the twenty largest corporations in the country are owned by the state. Had any banker cared to look at the Mexican government's share of gross domestic product, he would have noticed that from 1970 to 1979, it had grown at a compounded rate of 5.17 percent per year. This rate of growth would have made any totalitarian government proud.

2. Rampant inflation or currencies with no value in the West: Argentina was experiencing inflation at an annual rate of more than 800 percent in 1982, and Mexico's rate was more than 100 percent. The currencies of the USSR, East Germany, Romania, and Hungary are worthless in the West, and Poland, which has its currency printed in England, was unable to pay even the printing bill for a shipment of notes in 1982.

3. Political corruption on an unimaginable scale: Reliable estimates place the personal fortune of the president of Zaire in excess of $4 billion. Since Zaire's debt is "only" $5.1 billion, it appears that the "beloved" Mr. Mobutu has "amassed" the only borrowed fortune in history. Now all that remains is for his "loyal" subjects (all the "disloyal" subjects have been slaughtered by the army) to repay it.

4. The few, if any, "property rights" are subject to government whim: Many Mexicans attempted to protect *their* assets from the government by moving capital out of Mexico and into dollars. Supreme Looter (President) Portillo, who considers all capital to be the property of the state, responded hysterically (and predictably) to this act of self-preservation with the following statement: "They have already looted us. They will not loot us again." To keep "them" from further "looting" the country of *their* capital, he nationalized the banks and converted over $10 billion of dollar-denominated accounts into worthless pesos, thereby proving "them" absolutely right for moving *their* assets out of *his* reach.

5. Severe restrictions on foreign capital infusions and trade: In Mexico there are businesses that do nothing but locate "partners" for foreign entities wishing to start ventures in the country. For supplying only their citizenship, they must by law receive 50 percent of the equity. By closing the door on foreign equity capital, governments force their economies to seek debt financing.

Although loans to governments (i.e., sovereign debt) may look safe, they are always very dangerous as we saw in the section on Bonds. Most governments use loans strictly for consumptive spending, but even when they don't, they can no more invest capital for profit than they can balance a budget. Looters (politicians and bureaucrats) cannot become productive even when supplied with "free" capital. (They always seem to use it to build pyramids and other useless monuments to their egos.) Herbert Spencer made the following comment long ago (and governments have never tired of proving it): "Countless facts prove the Government to be the worst owner, the worst manufacturer, the worst trader [investor]: in fact, the worst manager, be the thing managed what it may." The following list gives some recent examples of Spencer's observation:

1. In Brazil, the state corporations pay sixteen months of wages for eleven months of "work," while the government gives massive credits to farmers at less than 25 percent of the government's borrowing costs.

2. Mexico, after carefully reviewing the lack of profitability and noting the huge, worldwide surplus of production capacity in iron and steel, decided it needed its own steel industry anyway to instill pride in its starving population and to hedge against the potential prosperity threatened by its oil and gas discoveries. The new mills are operating at less than 40 percent of capacity (surprise, surprise) and in spite of their newer technology, very cheap labor, and taxpayer subsidies, they will never be competitive in world markets.

3. Argentina chose to invest a considerable sum of borrowed wealth in real estate—namely the Falkland Islands. They fell behind on their payments, and the property was repossessed (at a total loss) by Britain. This forced Argentina to recall its generals to correct some dangerous defects in the political and military workmanship.

4. In Poland, the cost of mining coal exceeds the price at which it is sold by more than 10 percent. (Presumably, the government makes up the loss on volume sales.)

5. Zaire (with the U.S. Department of Energy acting as technical adviser) spent over $1 billion to build a dam to supply electric power to a province that was already self-sufficient in electricity. This was the largest (or stupidest) "power failure" in history at that time. (The United States, by supreme effort, later recaptured the title with its WPPSS [Washington (State) Public Power Supply System (muni bonds)] $2.25 billion bond default. The head of this utility was quoted as saying he felt the title belonged here.)

Isabel Paterson long ago summarized the problems and *certain outcome* of loans from government to government (or loans from anyone to government) in the following passage from *The God of the Machine*:

Loans made by one government to another do not answer to any of the proper conditions of credit. The money [currency] lent belongs to the people of the lending nation, not to the officials who grant the loan; and it becomes a charge upon the people of the borrowing nation, not upon the officials who negotiate the loan and spend the money [currency]. There is no collateral, and no means of collection by civil action. If the debt is not paid, war or the threat of war is the only recourse. Meantime private production is wrecked; the economy of the lending nation has to meet the capital loss; while the economy of the borrowing nation is loaded with the dead weight of government projects (buildings, armies, etc.) for which the money [currency] is spent. It is an infallible formula for disaster.

As Ms. Paterson predicted, most of the capital from these foreign "loans" is gone forever. (Some bankers will see their life flash before them as they read the preceding statement because it also means that ten of the largest banks in the United States could be gone with it.) Taxpayers, who have already been forced to guarantee large portions of these debts directly, will now be forced to bail out the banks. The world economy and these debts are now almost totally at the mercy of politicians. Can there be any doubt about how this dream will turn out?

DEBT, NATIONAL

The first step in debt is like the first step in falsehood, involving the necessity of going on in the same course, debt following debt, as lie follows lie.

—S. SMILES

Debt is the secret foe of thrift, as vice and idleness are its open foes. The debt-habit is the twin brother of poverty.

—T. T. MUNGER

Blessed are the young, for they shall inherit the national debt.

—HERBERT HOOVER

Not only has the nation to pay the interest [on the national debt], it has lost the principal also.

—HERBERT SPENCER

The people will be crushed under the burden of taxes; loan after loan will be floated; after having drained the present, the state will devour the future.

—FREDERIC BASTIAT

Speak not of my [the national] debts unless you mean to pay them.

—KIN HUBBARD

Debt is the worst poverty.

—THOMAS FULLER

There has been an incredible amount of wailing and moaning about Congress's most recent revelation, the national debt. Politicians never realized that continual deficits (see DEFICITS) have to be financed by (gasp) debt! I have never seen our self-proclaimed "leaders" so worried and concerned about one subject. (Not worried enough to cut spending, balance the budget, or begin paying off the debt, but they are worried.)

The national debt is a disaster, but not for the government: only for the people and institutions that have loaned the government their wealth (see BONDS) and the taxpayers who must now service it at real interest rates (see INTEREST RATES). The reality is that there is no government debt. There is only debt incurred by the government that must be repaid by the taxpayers through higher taxes or by the *lender* through higher inflation. Also remember that the debt is measured in currency, not in money (see MONEY). The following table shows the federal debt adjusted by the Dollar Depreciation Index and gives some idea of the amount of purchasing power that has been embezzled by the government:

Gross Federal Public Debt
(Billions of Dollars)

YEAR	CURRENCY DOLLARS	CONSTANT DOLLARS (1940)	DEBT AS PERCENTAGE OF GROSS NATIONAL PRODUCT
1940	43.0	43.0	43
1945	258.7	201.5	122
1950	257.4	150.0	90
1955	274.4	143.5	69
1960	286.3	135.6	57
1965	317.3	141.2	46
1970	370.9	133.9	37
1975	544.1	141.7	35
1980	914.3	155.4	35
1984	1,663.0	221.3	45

As you can see from the table, the national debt in terms of purchasing power really increased only 9.8 percent from 1945 to 1984. As a percentage of GNP, the debt declined from 90 percent in 1950 to 45 percent in 1984.

Now perhaps the "heartless" Republicans with their "drastic spending cuts," $200 billion deficits, and the relatively new high real rates of interest, actually can substantially increase the debt in real terms (that would certainly accelerate many dreams that must come due). But the free market will probably continue to mark down the purchasing power of the debt just as fast as the politicians can increase it in terms of currency.

The real potential for disaster, as far as the taxpayers and lenders (not the government) are concerned, is a deflation (see DEFLATION) that would suddenly turn the illusion of a federal debt into an unbelievably painful and unpayable reality. Only time will tell us the eventual outcome for this compounding monster.

The best solution would be to cut spending (laughter) and pay the bond holders what is left of their purchasing power. But that's not going to happen; so let's get a bill in Congress to raise the national debt ceiling to the unofficial limit—infinity—officially (after all, it's only currency). They could then use the time they have been wasting on a foregone conclusion to debate about the century in which they are going to "mandate" a balanced federal budget. I am sure that the more responsible conservatives in Congress will never stand for raising the permanent limit on the national debt to infinity, but perhaps a compromise could be worked out that would raise the temporary limit to that level.

In terms of great bargains for government, the national debt has already been the crime of the century. But as we have seen, the government prefers to make its *lenders* repay the entire debt (instead of just 90 percent). Why repay when you can inflate away!

DEFENSE

Wars are caused by undefended wealth.

—DOUGLAS MACARTHUR

Whoever thinks over earnestly and objectively this question of a general disarmament, and considers it in its remotest contingencies, must come to the conviction that it is a question which cannot be solved so long as men are men, and States are States.

—THEOBOLD VON BETHMANN-HOLLWEG

There is no kind of peace which may be purchased on the bargain counter.

—CAREY McWILLIAMS

Before all else, be armed.

—MACHIAVELLI

We love peace, but not peace at any price. There is a peace more destructive of the manhood of living man, than war is destructive of his body. Chains are worse than bayonets.

—DOUGLAS JERROLD

For the foreseeable future, America must maintain a superior strategic defense over the Soviets (who, like all malevolent forces, are persuaded only by power). But since Congress (with the "help" of all its special interests) sets expenditure levels, and the Department of Defense (a typically efficient government bureaucracy) is in charge of spending, a minimum of 33 percent of the defense budget is certain to be fraud and pure waste (see WASTE). (In the 1982 budget, the 33 percent minimum was more than $71 billion.) To add insult to injury, the American taxpayer is also forced to pay over $100 billion a year defending Europe, Japan, and South Korea.

The defense budget for 1983 totaled about $260 billion, but $106 billion of this went to general-purpose forces, $44 billion to general personal activities, and only $24 billion (less than 10 percent) to strategic weapons systems. (Naturally, this is the area where the liberal politicians focused their attempted cuts.)

The crying need of the Department of Defense aside from cutting congressionally mandated waste like pork-barrel defense contracts and military bases (of the 4,000 military installations in the United States, only 312 are considered significant by the Pentagon) is an overhaul of what is (humorously) referred to as its weapons procurement programs. These programs have reduced the large defense contractors to corporate welfare cases. Because they refuse to recognize that, in the long run, government business is nearly always a disaster for a company, and not an opportunity, they have voluntarily sold out to government dependency. Moreover, with huge bureaucracies and contracts that provide fixed profits that *increase* with costs, these programs waste billions of dollars while furnishing our forces with junk weapons that not only fail to work, but can and have cost American lives. Although such weapons as the M-16 rifle, the F-111 fighter plane, the Lockheed C5A cargo plane (some might remember what happened to the guy who blew the whistle on that program), and the M-1 tank have all been produced, truly innovative ideas like Northrop's B-49 Flying Wing Bomber are killed by petty politics in Congress and the Pentagon, only to be "rediscovered" three decades later.

The system of weapons acquisition that has furnished these "wonder weapons" (wonder why they were built?), that has hopelessly crippled American defense contractors and keeps us fully prepared to fight the last war, was installed in 1963. Prior to 1963, only six years was required to turn an idea into a *viable* weapons system. It now takes an average of sixteen years for a bad idea to become a worse weapons system.

Governmental incompetence in defense (or any other field) is nothing new. Armies have always gone to war with at least some inferior or obsolete equipment, as this passage from Herbert Spencer's essay, "Over-Legislation" (written in 1853) clearly shows:

Suppose that it [the government] had rationally equipped its troops, instead of giving them cumbrous and ineffective muskets, barbarous grenadier-caps, absurdly heavy knapsacks and cartouche-boxes, and clothing colored so as admirably to help the enemy's marksmen; suppose that it organized well and economically instead of salarying an immense superfluity of officers, creating sinecure colonelcies of 4,000 pounds

sterling a year, neglecting the meritorious and promoting incapa-
bles. . . .

Even though it has bungled in everything else, had it in one
case done well—had its naval management alone been efficient—the
sanguine would have had a colorable excuse for expecting success in a
new field. Grant that the reports about bad ships, ships that will not
sail, ships that have to be lengthened, ships with unfit engines, ships
that will not carry their guns, ships without stowage, and ships that
have to be broken up, are all untrue; assume those to be mere slanders
who say the Megoera [a naval ship] took double the time taken by a
commercial steamer to reach the Cape; that during the same voyage
the Hydra [a naval ship] was three times on fire, and needed the pumps
kept going day and night . . . let all these, we say, be held groundless
charges, and there would remain for the advocates of much government
some basis for their political aircastles, spite of military and judicial
mismanagement.

We can get some insight into the current workings of our defense
bureaucracy from a paper written by Thomas Amlie, former director
of the Navy Weapons Center at China Lake:

The DOD (Department of Defense) has all the symptoms of being
corrupt, incompetent and incestuous, and is so to an alarming degree.
This is not because of some sinister plot. . . . Many of the players are
aware that things are going badly and are unhappy because they do not
have meaningful jobs where they can contribute. They are not, in the
main, dishonest or incompetent [Want to bet?], just caught in a very
bad situation [in which they chose to remain]. . . . The bureaucrat soon
learns that he who does nothing has a simple life and he who tries to
do something gets in trouble. Even if the doer succeeds, he is seldom
rewarded. All pressures are to maintain the status quo and not rock the
boat because the Congress and Administration are willing to put up
the money every year, *independent of the results* [my emphasis]. . . .

The basic reason for the problem is incredibly simple and will be
incomprehensible to one who has not spent time in the system [see
SYSTEMS]: there is no profit and loss sheet [just losses]. Thus, there
is no competition or incentive to produce. The goal of every good
bureaucrat is to get an exclusive franchise on whatever it is he is doing.
If nobody else is doing it, no one can measure how well or poorly he
is doing it. . . . The only requirements are to stay busy, generate paper
and make no mistakes [How could they?].

In spite of the obvious inefficiencies, waste, and other disadvantages,
we must rebuild our defense because the one lesson of history (which

our politicians and the nuclear freeze proponents refuse to learn) is that the USSR (as with all communist countries) *cannot* be trusted. A complete list of their broken promises would be too long to give here, but among the most recent are their repudiations of the nuclear test ban treaty during Khrushchev's regime, the Helsinki Final Accord, and their horrible violation of the 1972 Geneva Convention's ban on the use, testing, and stockpiling of biological weapons. Yet, we continue to lose vital ground by trying to make new arms limitation treaties with them because "the next time it will be different." As Will Rogers used to say, "The United States never lost a war or won a conference." Sad, but true.

As expected, a lot of liberal politicians are crying about the arms spending necessary to rebuild our forces. Yet, these are many of the same politicians who helped denude our defense program in the 1970s by cutting its budget by 45 percent, then channeling those and other revenues into the skyrocketing transfer payments (see WELFARE) portion of the budget, an area that increased by 265 percent between 1963 and 1983.

U.S. Defense Spending and Transfer Payments As Shares of the Federal Budget

YEAR	DEFENSE (Percentage)	TRANSFER OF PAYMENTS (Percentage)
1963	43.2	18.2
1965	38.8	19.2
1969	42.2	26.5
1970	39.2	28.5
1971	35.2	33.1
1972	32.4	35.1
1973	29.6	37.1
1974	28.8	39.5
1975	26.0	41.8
1976	24.0	43.9
1977	23.7	43.9
1978	22.8	42.1
1979	23.3	42.5
1980	22.9	43.3
1981	24.3	46.4
1982	24.2	48.1
1983	25.6	48.3

Since these "defenders of democracy" seem to be able to find the time and resources to fund every program *except* the legitimate functions of government, perhaps they should be reminded of a quote from Sir John Slessor:

> It is customary in democratic countries to deplore expenditure on armaments as conflicting with the requirements of the social services. There is a tendency to forget that the most important social service that a government can do for its people is to keep them alive and free.

The dream that we could neglect defense spending in the face of a massive Soviet buildup has now come due, and the people (as always) will have to pay the price through much higher defense spending for the rest of the 1980s. I suggest that those "born-again-budget-balancers" in Congress who spend all their time decrying Pentagon spending focus their attention and cuts on that part of the budget where the greatest amount of wealth is being spent—and largely wasted (see WELFARE)—and that's not defense. There is *no* welfare in the USSR, and there can be no welfare in the United States without national security.

DEFICITS

(Or Here We Grow Again)

There are no necessary evils in government. Its evils exist only in its abuses.

—ANDREW JACKSON

A billion here and a billion there, and before you know it, you are talking about real money [currency].

—SENATOR EVERETT DIRKSEN

I place economy among the first and most important virtues, and public debt [caused by deficits] as the greatest of dangers....

—THOMAS JEFFERSON

Bring your desires down to your present means. Increase them only when your increased means permit.

—ARISTOTLE

Most powerful is he who has himself in his own power.

—SENECA

Putting off an easy thing makes it difficult; putting off a hard one [balancing the budget] makes it impossible.

—GEORGE H. LORIMER

It is no use saying, "We are doing our best." You have got to succeed in doing what is necessary.

—WINSTON CHURCHILL

We know the United States has had trouble balancing its budget, but how do the rest of the governments in the world measure up? Want to hazard a guess? The following table will end the suspense:

"Balanced Budgets"
Around the World

COUNTRY	NUMBER OF FISCAL YEARS	NUMBER OF BALANCED BUDGETS
Argentina	12	0
Australia	21	0
Brazil	21	8
Canada	21	1
Finland	21	7
France	21	5
Germany	21	1
India	18	0
Ireland	21	0
Italy	21	0
Israel	20	0
Japan	20	2
Mexico	15	0
New Zealand	16	0
Norway	17	0
Philippines	21	5
South Africa	21	0
Spain	19	1
Sweden	21	7
Switzerland	21	7
Turkey	13	0
United Kingdom	21	3
United States	21	2
Venezuela	20	10

Of the twenty-four countries shown, eleven were not able to balance their budget even once. The champion of "fiscal responsibility" was Venezuela with half of its budgets in balance. For the 464 years in the table, budgets were balanced a total of 59 years, or 12.7 percent of the time. (And remember that many budgets that "appear" balanced or have only small deficits are, in fact, in huge deficit because of "off-budget items" that governments can hide from the public; see SOCIAL SECURITY.) This record is despicable, but totally expected from any entity as irresponsible and amoral as government (see GOVERNMENT).

Deficits do not result from taxes that are too low, but from spending that is too high, and the one certainty you can count on is the bigger the government, the bigger the deficit. The U.S. federal expenditures grew from 2.5 percent of gross national product in 1929 to more than 24 percent in 1982, and yet we now have the largest deficits in our history (excluding World War II). Government is continually developing new "needs" (see NEEDS) that must be met by destroying old rights (see PROPERTY RIGHTS). In addition to these needs, governments have never been able to stop spending wealth on any program, no matter how ridiculous, so don't expect future budgets to be in balance even 10 percent of the time. Note that the current debate in Washington is only on the size of the deficit (it's *too* large), not whether or not there is going to be one. That is now an accepted and acknowledged fact.

The lesson of history is that no matter how much wealth government takes, it has never been "enough" and it will never be "enough" (just as with any other extortionist), so it is up to the people to draw the line on government and its plunder (and fortunately some people *are* starting to draw that line: see TAX REVOLT).

DEFLATION

Panics, in some cases, have their uses; they produce as much good as hurt. Their duration is always short; the mind soon grows through them and acquires a firmer habit than before. But their peculiar advantage is, that they are the touchstone of sincerity and hypocrisy, and bring things and men to light, which might otherwise have lain forever undiscovered.

—THOMAS PAINE

Experience is a jewel, and it had need be so, for it is often purchased at an infinite rate.

—WILLIAM SHAKESPEARE

Deflation: a contraction in the volume of available currency and credit resulting in a decline of the general price level.

Deflation is the opposite side of the inflation coin (see INFLATION). It is the inevitable result of an inflation that strangles itself by crippling the entire economy. Inflation breeds rampant debt, speculation (see SPECULATION), and illiquidity (see LIQUIDITY), which eventually leads to a panic and crash in some sector of the economy. (In 1929 it was the stock market that had moved to unprecedented highs and then crashed. My "crash candidate" for the next deflation is the real estate market because it has been the major beneficiary of this inflation cycle; see REAL ESTATE.) There has never been a hangover that was not preceded by a drunk, and there has never been a deflation that was not preceded by an inflation.

The most famous deflation, *to date*, occurred during the depression of the 1930s (following a period of inflation, debt accumulation, and speculation), when the value of the dollar *increased* (imagine that if you can) by about 40 percent. Cash was king and debt was shunned. Every other form of investment (with the exception of gold, which was manipulated higher by government) suffered a ruinous decline.

Politicians fear deflation as liars fear truth. Deflation invariably causes a majority of former "statesmen" to look for more suitable employment. (Perhaps as used car salesman? No, the moral standards are too high. It would have to be as lawyers or lobbyists.)

After fifty years of almost uninterrupted inflation, there seems to be a popular myth pervading most people's thinking, that deflation will not occur because government just won't allow it to happen. They will *always* be able to reflate the economy. If the government had such power over markets (see MARKETS [FREE]), gold would still be thirty-five dollars an ounce, oil would be three dollars a barrel, the prime rate would be 6 percent, and unemployment (see UNEMPLOYMENT) would be frozen at 3 percent.

History demonstrates that we must be very cautious of events that can't possibly happen. The longer a trend (especially a destructive trend) has been in force, *the more suspect it becomes* (not the more certain). The real question is not whether deflation will occur again, but how long the various markets will allow inflation to continue before they bring on deflation with their collapse. Markets can reduce the value of assets much more rapidly than government can create currency and credit. (We are currently seeing some very ominous signs against further inflation in the declines in commodities markets and crude oil and the rally in the bond market.)

Just as a hangover does not cure drunkenness, deflation does not "cure" inflation. It just brings on a different set of extremely unpleasant consequences. Deflation is not only the opposite of inflation: it is also the opposite of prosperity.

DEMOCRACY

(Go Left at Prosperity)

There never was a democracy that did not commit suicide.

—SAMUEL ADAMS

The main stream which has borne European society towards Socialism during the past 100 years is the irresistible progress of Democracy.

—SIDNEY WEBB

There is no antithesis between authoritarian government and democracy. All government is authoritarian; and the more democratic a government is the more authoritative it is; for with the people [crowd] behind it, it can push its authority further than any Tsar or foreign despot dare do.

—GEORGE BERNARD SHAW

It is a besetting vice of democracies to substitute public opinion for law. This is the usual form in which masses of men exhibit their tyranny.

—JAMES FENIMORE COOPER

Democracy means simply the bludgeoning of the people by the people for the people.

—OSCAR WILDE

Make the people sovereign and the poor will use the machinery of government to dispossess the rich.

—C. NORTHCOTE PARKINSON

The state represents violence in a concentrated and organized form. The individual has a soul, but as the state is a soulless machine, it can never be weaned from violence to which it owes its very existence.

—MAHATMA GANDHI

◩ The history of governments can be broadly categorized as monarchy, oligarchy, democracy, and dictatorship. Of the four systems of government, democracy does the best job of ensuring the rights of the individual, but it has one fatal defect that guarantees its eventual self-destruction: All democracies in the world today are in the process of mutating into some form of economic anarchy (i.e., plunder by seizing the "law") because their constitutions cannot protect private property against the unlimited demands of crowds (who are dominated by envy; see ENVY) for unearned benefits. (As John Randolph once said, "You may cover whole skins of parchment with limitations, but power alone can limit power.") These benefits have been provided by "legal" government plunder (see LAW, THE) because "law" has been placed above the rights of property (see PROPERTY RIGHTS).

Demands for the property of others can *temporarily* be met because the state has *unlimited* power to tax the productive efforts and wealth of its citizens. (The federal government's share of GNP had increased from 3 percent in 1930 to 24.0 percent in 1984; see GOVERNMENT GROWTH). But, as government grows and the economy moves up the Laffer curve (see LAFFER CURVE), the price is always loss of economic freedom and property rights, which invariably leads to a stagnant or dying economy (see UNDERGROUND ECONOMY) and more government. A study of history indicates that this process is as irreversible as aging.

The general stages of the political cycle of a country that achieves democracy are as follows:

1. Monarchy (or oligarchy)
2. Revolution (or war)
3. Democracy and some form of capitalism
4. Prosperity (possible world leadership)
5. Creeping socialism (decay)
6. Totalitarian government

Note the prophecy in the following statement and try to guess when it was said and by whom: "Democracy, as practiced in Western Europe today, is the forerunner of Marxism. In fact, the latter would not be conceivable without the former. Democracy is the breeding ground in which the bacilli of the Marxist world pest can grow and spread."

The author was Adolph Hitler in the 1930s, and the source not withstanding, this statement has proved to be very accurate. Communists wield considerable power in France and Italy, while Great Britain leads both in socialism and decay.

Democracy could be made to work only if government could somehow be chained down (i.e., *permanently* limited to a *small* fixed percentage of the gross national product) to prevent it from continually placing more and more "law" above the rights of property—but that is impossible. (It would not really matter if the budgets of the world governments were somehow balanced, because even if they continue their current growth rates, eventual disaster is assured.)

Until the productive efforts and property of the people are fully protected from the unlimited demands of crowds acting through the government, the observation of the British historian Thomas Macaulay, will be the rule and not the exception:

> The day will come when (in the United States) a multitude of people will choose the legislature. Is it possible to doubt what sort of a legislature will be chosen? On the one side is a statesman preaching patience, respect for rights, strict observance of public faith. On the other is a demagogue ranting about the tyranny of capitalism and users and asking why anybody should be permitted to drink champagne and to ride in a carriage while thousands of honest people are in want of necessaries. Which of the candidates is likely to be preferred by a workman?... When Society has entered on this downward progress, either civilization or liberty must perish. Either some Caesar or Napolean will seize the reins of government with a strong hand, or your Republic will be as fearfully plundered and laid waste by barbarians in the twentieth century as the Roman Empire in the fifth; with this difference, that the Huns and vandals who ravaged the Roman Empire came from without, and that your Huns and vandals will have been engendered within your country, by your own institutions.

Since democracies have proved beyond doubt that they are unable to protect the rights of property by limiting the size of government, they have placed themselves on the road to oblivion. This road of dreams is long, slow, painful, and certain (see MOMENTUM). The British are almost there, while America and many other democracies are just a decade or two behind. Carolina Maria de Jesus captured the essence of this inevitable decline in *Child of the Dark: The Diary of Carolina Maria de Jesus*:

> You had faith, and now you don't have it anymore?
> No, my son, democracy is losing its followers. In our [every]

country everything is weakening. The money [she meant currency] is weak. Democracy is weak and the politicians are very weak. Everything that is weak dies one day.

Democracy is born with the dream of freedom to produce and prosper and dies with the dream of freedom from work and personal responsibility.

DEPRESSION, THE GREAT

Every achievement is foreshadowed in fancy; every major disaster is the result of inadequacy, error, or perversion of intelligence.

—ISABEL PATERSON
THE GOD OF THE MACHINE

In times of great stress, in times of depression, the public mind loses its balance and becomes the victim of the catchword.

—SIR HENRY THORNTON

The energies released by a crisis usually flow toward sheer action and application.

—ERIC HOFFER

Under the Federal Reserve Act panics are scientifically created: the present one [the Great Depression] is the first scientifically created one worked out as we figure a mathematical problem.

—CHARLES A. LINDBERGH

The Great Depression is a "great" example of a government-induced disaster in the economy, and, as could be expected, the blame was placed on free enterprise. Were it not for World War II, we would probably still be in the depression because the government would still be trying to "help" us out of it.

This depression started, as they all do, with an inflationary credit expansion. From 1921 to 1929, the money supply (back then we still had money; see MONEY) expanded at an annual rate of 7.7 percent (this figure is above even current Federal Reserve Bank growth targets, which are subject to change whenever elections or recessions are approaching). Prices did not increase over this period, but remember that increasing prices are a *symptom* of inflation, whereas an increase in the supply of currency or credit not backed by gold *is* the inflation (see INFLATION and INFLATION, REAL). Had it not been for this credit expansion, most prices would have fallen during this period and consumers would have benefited greatly.

The credit expansion alone ensured the stock market of having its dream of continuing credit creation come due (with predictable consequences), but the government was not finished yet.

The Republicans (the friends of big business and free enterprise) had established tariffs (see TARIFFS) as part of their platform in 1928. They were finally able to ram the Smoot, Hawley Tariff Act through Congress in 1930 (it was signed into law by President Hoover the same year), and with it came the largest tariffs in United States history.

The purpose of this tariff bill was ostensibly to protect American producers in "select" industries, but the final bill covered more than eighteen thousand "critical" items, such as cashews from India, which had a 1,000 percent increase (America did not produce *any* cashews at this time). Our trading partners retaliated by placing tariffs on American goods, and a worldwide depression was thus guaranteed.

Now that "free enterprise" had "failed," it was time for "positive government action" (see DICTIONARY OF GOVERNMENT EUPHE-MISMS). As economic activity collapsed and government panic (i.e., spending and taxes) increased, "their share," at all levels of government, of the gross national product rose from 9.9 percent in 1929 (the last year of single-digit government share of GNP) to 18.3 percent in 1932. In other words, just when government should have been cutting spending back to hold their percentage of a declining GNP, at worst, constant, they were, in fact, doubling the government burden on a very sick economy.

Since government spending was going up as the economy declined, deficits in the federal budget were assured. After 1930, the federal budget ran a deficit every year until 1949. Hoover was convinced the budget must be balanced, and being a politician, saw only one way to do it (and it wasn't to cut spending). Taxes had to be raised.

In 1932, "the party of the rich" raised taxes in the four thousand dollar bracket from 1 to 4 percent (a 400 percent increase), and the top bracket was increased from 25 to 63 percent. Roosevelt (friend of the working man) in following through on his New Deal program of "tax and tax, spend and spend, elect and elect," took the bottom rate to 23 percent (remember, the top rate in 1931 was 25 percent) and the top rate to a "modest" 94 percent in 1944 (see INCOME TAX).

So much for the failure of capitalism.

DEVALUATION

(Stopping Payment on the Cash)

The people never give up their liberties but under some delusion.

—EDMUND BURKE

Never believe anything political unless it is officially denied.

—OLD BRITISH ADAGE

Devalue: to deprive of value (i.e., steal); reduce the value of; to fix a lower "legal" value on (a currency).

A devaluation of a currency occurs when one government is able to out-inflate the government of one of its trading partners. (Every currency in the world is being inflated, thus keeping this "international debasement competition" very spirited; see INFLATION). It is a form of government bankruptcy in which every holder of the currency is defrauded, but it is always hailed by governments as a way to increase exports and thus secure a great economic victory. There have been over fifteen hundred "official" devaluations decreed since 1945 (and probably triple this number of market devaluations). This is how the governments of the world use their legal tender monopoly to "repay" the trust and dependence of the people who hold their currencies.

Since it is virtually impossible to isolate a country's economy from the world economy, the after-effect of a devaluation is always a rise in the domestic prices in the devaluing country by the amount devalued. If the currency is devalued 25 percent, the internal prices will rise by an additional 25 percent (plus the inflation rate). Since import prices are immediately "increased" to offset the new lower value of the de-valued currency, it is much more difficult, if not impossible, for consumers to choose products from the more efficient international markets.

Devaluations are a disaster for a country just as a bankruptcy is for a business. They invariably stimulate the growth of government (see GOVERNMENT GROWTH), not the economy. If you need a recent example, look at the wonders it has worked for Mexico and France. If devaluations helped the balance of trade, Japan and West Germany (who revalued their currencies upward in the 1970s) would have run huge trade deficits, and the United States and Great Britain would have had large trade surpluses. Instead, the exact opposite was true.

A peso for your thoughts.

DICTIONARY OF GOVERNMENT EUPHEMISMS

(Making the World Safe for Hypocrisy)

Half the work that is done in this world is to make things appear what they are not.

—E. R. BEADLE

Political chaos is connected with the decay of language ... one can probably bring about some improvement by starting at the verbal end.

—GEORGE ORWELL

If you call a tail a leg, how many legs has a dog? Five? No, calling a tail a leg don't make it a leg.

—ABRAHAM LINCOLN

A man that should call everything by its right name would hardly pass the streets without being knocked down as a common enemy.

—SIR GEORGE SAVILE

An important art of politicians is to find new names for institutions which under old names have become odious to the public.

—CHARLES MAURICE DE TALLEYRAND-PERIGORD

The slovenliness of our language makes it easier for us to have foolish thoughts.

—GEORGE ORWELL

It is much easier for government (see GOVERNMENT) to do violence to the rest of us if they can pervert or blur the meaning of words. Objective becomes subjective and cause can be confused with effect. The more meanings a word has, the more meaningless and inflammatory it becomes.. The Soviet Union proclaims the virtues of their type of "freedom" and "democracy" just as loudly and often as the United States. Lewis Carroll, as a speech writer, could have written the following statement for any politician, dictator, or other type of villain, as easily as he did for Humpty Dumpty in *Through the Looking Glass:*

> "When I use a word," Humpty Dumpty said in a rather scornful tone, "it means just what I choose it to mean—neither more nor less."

But thinking men and women must ask the same question as Alice: "The question is," said Alice, "whether you can make words mean so many different things."

With the liberties that government and its supporters take with the meanings of words, there is really not much point in trying to understand anything they say. But if you have a desire for this kind of entertainment, you must be able to translate the Orwellian language (Newspeak) they use. So come now to the never-never land of "firmly tentative," "bold caution," "inconsistent consistency," and "interim final rules"; where currency becomes money, laws become justice, plunder becomes taxes, and inflation becomes price increases; where, to quote Orwell's *1984*, "WAR IS PEACE; FREEDOM IS SLAVERY; IGNORANCE IS STRENGTH"; where, as Eric Hoffer wrote in *The True Believer:*

> There is thus an illiterate air about the most literate true believer [politician or bureaucrat]. He seems to use words as if he were ignorant of their true meaning. Hence, too, his taste for quibbling, hairsplitting and scholastic tortuousness.

In this spirit, the following *partial* list of definitions is presented:

abusive tax shelters: abusive taxes
affirmative action: government-imposed quotas (reverse discrimination)
ally (friend): former or future enemy (China or Soviet Union)
antitrust laws: unintelligible "laws" that limit the freedom and economic efficiency of large corporations (Malice in Legalland)
austerity: higher taxes and more government spending and regulation (austerity for the people, never for the government)

balanced budget: bigger deficits (what every politician is going to give us once he is elected; there's no time like the future!)

barbarous relic: gold (i.e. money)

big: something that is always bad (such as big corporations) unless it is a government

big deficits: big government

bipartisan legislation: "legal" plunder (organized injustice), which is supported by both political parties because the take is shared equally

black market: free market

bond: "certificate of guaranteed confiscation"—Franz Pick

brain drain: freedom drain (movement of the most talented and productive people to countries with more freedom)

budget cuts: a slight decrease in the rate of increase of government spending

budget process: deficit process (Ready. Fire. Aim!)

bureaucrat: parasite or broker of plunder ("professional profligate"— Alan Abelson)

campaign contributions: auction market for future legislation (speculating in legislation futures)

campaign platform: what a political party lies (stands) for

campaign promises: liar's poker

capital gain: a gain that the IRS considers automatic for any investor

capital gain tax: a tax paid on a currency gain that usually amounts to a purchasing power loss

capital loss: a loss on an "investment" that, according to the tax code, never happens (the IRS may demand to share part of your capital gain that is in reality a capital loss, but they want no part of your capital losses, real or otherwise)

capitalism: socialism

cease-fire: halftime for war

civil servant: an individual who "works" for the government and is neither civil nor servile

commissions: parking places for problems (such as Social Security) until after the next election (politicians always hope a problem will go away if they ignore it long enough)

common good: individual bad

compassion: apathy or vicarious generosity

competition: regulation

compromise: more spending and higher taxes (being *slightly* pregnant) *conservative:* anyone opposed to higher taxes and spending unless it benefits him or his constituents (organized hypocrite or confused liberal)

conservative campaign: any political campaign that is hard-up for bad ideas

consumer price index: dollar depreciation index

contingent: absolute or certain (as in contingency tax)

contribution: extortion (for example, a Social Security "contribution")

cost-of-living escalator: currency depreciation compensator

credibility gap: lies and deceit

crisis: problem created by government

cure: a proposed political solution, to a problem caused by government, that always makes things worse, such as price controls to stop inflation (the cure is always worse than the disease)

currency: government-issued notes that always lose their value (currency bears the same relation to money as a car title does to a stolen car)

cutthroat competition: healthy competition (lower prices or better products for consumers)

cutting red tape: creating new regulations that apply to old regulations

debt rescheduling: tactic employed by bankrupt socialist governments that cannot pay even the interest on their loans to banks of industrialized countries in the hope they can borrow more now and default later, or, If you don't have it, flaunt it ("Broke but negotiating"— Richard Russell)

defection: emigration (emigration has become so popular in communist countries that people are literally dying to get out)

defector: any citizen (victim) who escapes from his government's oppression

defense: aggression

defensive weapon: Russian bomber in Cuba

deficit: mandatory part of any government budget

democracy: the right to choose the government that plunders you (the bludgeoning of the people by the people for the people)

Department of Energy: OPEC's Washington Office (agency that administers the U.S. foreign aid program for the Arabs)

depression: government-inflicted wound on the economy

destructive competition: healthy competition

détente: unilateral disarmament by the United States

devaluation: bankruptcy resulting from a country's government being able to out-spend and out-inflate one of its trading partners (ring around the dollar)

develop: corrupt or destroy (i.e., developing the economy)

developing countries: stagnating countries or socialist countries that are being pushed (kicking and screaming) or are trying to borrow their way into the nineteenth century

dialogue: capitulation

dictator (left-wing): a criminal (such as Castro) who oppresses the people, admires Stalin, and embraces communism (synonym: an enemy of the United States)

dictator (right-wing): a criminal (such as Samosa) who oppresses the people, admires Hitler, and embraces fascism (synonym: a "friend" of the United States)

diplomacy: bribery, extortion, or threats, or, the ability to say "nice doggey" until you can find a big rock

diplomats: spies and terrorists

disarm: rearm

discrimination: progressive income tax

distributive justice: theft or redistribution of stolen property ("legal" plunder)

downpayment on the deficit: higher taxes, spending, and deficits

dumping: process by which other countries become "wealthy" by selling their products below their cost (bargain prices for consumers on imported products)

easy "money": more currency and credit (inflation) (synonym: all government revenue)

economic democracy: elimination of property rights (socialism)

economic forecast: political forecast (attempt to guess how much government interference will be inflicted on the economy during a given period of time)

economic policy: government growth, inflation, and stagnation (stagflation)

economic pressure groups: looters who pant and pine for someone else's property

election: "advance auction of stolen goods"—H. L. Mencken

embassy: spy headquarters

enemy: former or future friend (Soviet Union or China)

energy crisis: political crisis (regulatory crisis)

ethics: something that must never interfere with politics

entitlement programs: the "orderly transfer" (theft) of wealth earned by a producer to someone who the government says is somehow "entitled to" it ("legal" plunder)

equal rights: desires, needs (equal rights to someone else's property)

equality: all people are equal, but some (mostly members of government) are more equal than others (synonym: what you desire from your superiors)

essential: superfluous (luxury we can't afford)

fact-finding tour: trip for government officials so they can see firsthand how badly they have screwed something up (all-expense-paid vacation)

fair: unfair

federal debt: taxpayer debt incurred by the government

Federal Reserve Bank: engine of inflation, or "we make 'money' the new-fashioned way: we print it"

Federal Reserve note: currency that bears the same relationship to money that a car title does to a stolen car

fine-tuning the economy: massive government disruption and ultimate destruction of the economy

fiscal dividend: gain in government revenue from inflating taxpayers into progressively higher tax brackets

fiscal policy: deficits

flexible: submissive or self-sacrificial

foreign aid: yearly auction sale primarily between the United States and the USSR to buy next year's "friends" and "allies" (recent brilliant U.S. purchases were South Viet Nam, Iran, and Nicaragua, while Russia got a great buy on Pakistan and Syria and is currently negotiating to pick up Iran)

foreign debt: perpetual loans with perpetual rescheduling (they would just as soon owe us as default)

foreign policy: "perpetual war for perpetual peace"—Charles A. Beard

forgotten man: anyone who attempts to be productive (taxpayer)

free country: a country like America where government owns a third of all the land (and rents us the rest), consumes more than 40 percent of the GNP, and has embezzled 85 percent of the value of its citizens' currency since 1940; where each citizen must report and pay up to half his income to Big Bro—the government—each year; where the government keeps more than fifteen separate files on each of its citizens; where every overseas phone call and telex is monitored by the National Security Agency (Thought Police); where no citizen is permitted to take more than ten thousand dollars of his depreciating currency out of the country without government permission

free market prices: prices freely set by buyers and sellers (i.e., the market) that politicians consider unfair (for example, those for oil and gas)

free trade: tariffs, "voluntary" import quotas, and subsidies

good government: more government

government: "association of men who do violence to the rest of us" —Tolstoy

Government Accounting Office (GAO): agency charged with seeing that government spending programs do not waste taxpayers' wealth, or chaplain of the whorehouse

government aid: waste

government debt: taxpayer debt incurred by the government

government estimate: wrong

government guarantee: taxpayer guarantee

government investment: loss (guaranteed loss for the taxpayer and the economy)

government loan: gifts (forty-one thousand current and retired federal employees have defaulted on $65 million of student loans)

government worker: parasite; diligent loafer

Great Society: Old Deal

hard-core unemployed: politicans, bureaucrats, and welfare loafers

helping the poor: plundering the productive

high interest rates: currency interest rates

high prices: falling real prices denominated in depreciating currency

hoarding: saving

honor: diseased egos

human rights: the right to choose or flee the government that oppresses you

improving compliance: more threats and coercion (people volunteer when they are threatened and/or forced)

independence: dependence

indexing: system used to adjust the salaries and pensions of all government employees so they won't have to suffer from the inflation they cause (method of treating the symptom instead of the disease)

industrial policy: causing companies (for example, Lockheed, Penn

Central and other railroads, and Chrysler) to fail and then investing in them

inflation: too many politicians chasing too few votes by creating currency and credit (unarmed robbery)

inflexible: occasionally not willing to sell out your constituents (opposing higher spending and taxes); or standing on principles

insurance: lottery

Internal Revenue Service: supplier of a "service" (to whom?) providing relief from prosperity

International Monetary Fund: agency that props up failing socialist economies (there is no other kind) with taxpayers' wealth so that U.S. and other Western banks will not have to pay for their stupidity

interpretation: rationalization

investment: rank speculation (like government bail-outs of bankrupt cities and corporations that no bank would touch with a five-foot pole and no private investor with a ten-foot pole)

jobs bill: a "law" to create "jobs" out of thin air with the taxpayers paying the bill

justice: organized, or majority-supported, injustice

Keynesian: someone who believes you create wealth by continually spending more than you steal or printing more zeroes on a piece of paper

law: any legislation that government legalizes by voting (organized, or majority-supported, injustice)

leadership: maintenance of the status quo (a long, slow decline) by means of the Gallup Poll (followership)

legal tender: something that continually loses value because its intrinsic worth is nil unless given value by "law" (value by force, or In inflation we trust)

legislation: political malpractice (lawyers' law)

legislators: special-interest errand boys

lender of last resort: U.S. taxpayers (victim of last—or is it first?—resort), borrower of last resort

less developed countries: less free countries

liberal: government worshipper

long-term capital gain: long-term capital loss caused by inflation that the government insists on taxing (but at lower rates) *long-term policy:* plan in use until the next election or Gallup Poll, whichever comes first

majority rule: one grunt, one vote (tyranny of the majority or mutual plunder)

manageable: unmanageable (a "manageable" national debt)

managing: mismanaging, interfering, or disrupting

market failure: government interference in the free market (political failure)

meaningful debate: meaningless rhetoric (for instance, meaningful debate on arms control)

military aid: see *foreign aid*

military government: permanent revolution

minimum wage law: legislation to prohibit gainful employment of unskilled labor (price controls on human beings)

modest: in terms of cutting government, such as "modest spending cuts": nonexistent cuts in spending; in terms of increasing the size of government, such as "modest spending increases": gargantuan increases

monetary policy: inflation (currency depreciation; government embezzlement)

money: continually depreciating paper currency (checks, notes, and slugs)

money supply: supply of currency and credit, increased at the whim of the Federal Reserve Bank (supply of "zeros" for currency and bookkeeping)

monopoly: any large company that provides outstanding service to consumers and thus gains a "large" market share

mutual: unilateral

national debt: $420 billion: "permanent" national debt limit; $2.1 trillion: "temporary" national debt limit; infinity: future "temporary" national debt limit

nationalization: armed robbery

necessary: unnecessary

needs: desires or expectations

negotiation: surrender (defeat with honor)

New Deal: socialism

no: the word no politician can say

nonaligned country: a socialist or fascist country shopping for the best foreign aid deal from the United States or the Soviet Union (or, better yet, a country getting aid from both at the same time)

"nonproductive" assets: assets like gold and silver coins that help protect people from government inflation

nuclear freeze movement: group that wishes to stop the United States from building new nuclear weapons so that the Soviets can get further ahead (they wonder what's wrong with the B-29 that dropped the bombs on Japan, or a B-52 that's older than the pilot who flies it)

objective: subjective

obscene profits: inflation-bloated currency figures (figments of Jimmy Carter's overworked imagination)

off-budget financing: fraud, or "cooking the books"; the set of books taxpayers don't get to see (spending government wants to hide from the taxpayers: out of sight, out of mind; or underground government)

offensive weapon: a Soviet bomber in Russia

offshore: private property that is (temporarily) out of governments' reach

open society: a society (like the United States) completely open to government intervention in every facet of its citizens' lives

paternalism: parasitism or slavery

peace-keeping force: furnishing U.S. troops for target practice

peace plan: surrender plan

peace with honor: surrender with dishonor

permanent: temporary as "permanent" national debt limit

police action: war without nuclear weapons (mass murder)

political crisis: not getting reelected

positive government action: "more inflation"—Henry Hazlitt

predatory prices: bargain prices for consumers

price controls: a way to transfer the blame and the consequences of government inflation to the private sector

principle: expediency ("Something that politicians must rise above" —H. L. Mencken)

problem: condition

promise: a firmly tentative *maybe*

property taxes: rent paid to the government for property you own

public interest groups: groups attempting to seize the law for their own purpose (personal interest groups or groups interested in obtaining a share of the public treasury)

public property: government property

public servant: public master (a person on the public payroll acting in his own interest)

rationing: attempting to equalize a shortage caused by government

Reaganomics: higher government spending and bigger deficits

real: a necessary adjective for every government financial figure denominated in currency when adjusted for inflation

realism: socialism (more government)

recession: economic downturn that occurs every four years, and is sponsored by government incompetence

redistribution: "fencing" stolen wealth in exchange for votes

reform: business as usual, such as "tax reform" (i.e., no real change)

regulation: strangulation

reindustrialization: government policy of subsidizing failure or investing in yesterday

rent control: heads, government wins; tails, the property owner loses (Why buy the cow when you set the price for the milk?)

revenue enhancement (They've got to be kidding!): tax increases

revenue hemorrhage: expenditure hemorrhage

revenue shortfall: out-of-control spending

revolution: a civil war that replaces a bad government with a worse one

rights: needs or desires (demands)

selfish: anyone who covets the fruits of his own labor

social change: more government (less freedom)

Social Security: world's largest chain letter that provides "security" for the elderly by bankrupting the U.S. economy

socially responsible: subservient or submissive

society: a social system for the benefit of government

sovereign debt: government-guaranteed default such as the Polish debt

speculators: people who receive all the blame for the destructive nature of government policies because they attempt to protect themselves by profiting from them

spending cuts: slight decrease in the rate of increase of spending

spending program: wasting program (Congress never met one it didn't like)

stabilization: involuntary subsidy paid by taxpayers to keep prices above or below the free market price that has the long-term effect of totally destabilizing the market

statesman: someone who is unable to attain elected office

stimulating the economy: creating currency and credit from thin air

strong currency: a currency that is being inflated at a slower rate than the other currencies of the world

supply management: government restriction of supply or production (greater wealth through lower production)

supply-side economics: supplying the economy with higher government spending and tax increases while calling them government spending reductions and tax cuts

target: taxpayer

tariff: government restraint of trade (corporations accused of this act are drawn and quartered by the Department of "Justice")

tax audit: guilty until proved innocent of violating a law you cannot understand

tax-base erosion control: a longer, more confusing word for *revenue enhancement* (tax increase)

tax benefits: the thanks you owe a burglar for the benefits of not being robbed

tax cut: a slight decrease in the rate of increase of taxes

tax-free: subject only to the inflation tax

tax haven: freedom haven (any country with low tax rates and a semblance of property rights)

tax loophole: government economic distortion (i.e., creating demand for real estate investment at the expense of investment in plant and equipment)

tax protestor: someone under the mistaken impression that the Constitution is the supreme law of the land and that it will be upheld by the courts

tax reform: tax increase

tax return: signed confession

taxation: theft by "law"

taxpayers: victims (stand still, little sheep, and be shorn)

temporary: permanent (like the "temporary" withholding tax on income instituted during the second world war)

tight "money": slower *growth* in the amount of currency and credit

trade: increasing exports and decreasing imports

transfer payments: wealth taken from people who work for a living and given to people who vote for a living ("legal" plunder) *treaty:* agreement that is made to be broken

trust fund: betrayal fund (Social Security)

underground economy: free economy

unemployment: voluntary or gainful idleness

unearned income: government revenues (income from savings and "investments" that usually disappears after adjusting for inflation)

unfair competition: healthy competition (better products or more efficient service)

unpatriotic: someone who does not believe in self-immolation

verifiable: unverifiable

voluntary: compulsory (for example, the voluntary income tax)

voluntary import quotas: extortionary restraint of trade

voluntary taxation: one who fails to volunteer is fined and put into jail

voodoo economics: reducing government spending and taxes ("legal" plunder)

voting: choosing the greater of two evils

war of national liberation: war of national enslavement

war on poverty: war on freedom, property rights, and prosperity

waste: any and all government programs

wasteful duplication of services: healthy competition

welfare: vicarious generosity of liberals and politicians

windfall profits tax: an "inflationfall" excise tax on oil that has absolutely no relation to profits (a windfall for the government)

work experience: pay for play

World Bank: the only bank that knowingly makes "loans" that won't ever be repaid (world's largest involuntary charity)

zero-based budgeting: contest to see which politician can add the most zeros to government spending programs

DOW JONES INDUSTRIAL AVERAGE

Don't gamble! Take all your savings and buy some good stock and hold it 'til it goes up, then sell it. If it don't go up, don't buy it.

—WILL ROGERS

October. This is one of the peculiarly dangerous months to speculate in stocks. The others are July, January, September, April, November, May, March, June, December, August and February.

—MARK TWAIN

With an evening coat and a white tie, anybody, even a stockbroker, can gain a reputation for being civilized.

—OSCAR WILDE

No one can say that the Dow Jones Industrial Average (DJIA), a financial average of the stock prices of thirty of the largest U.S. corporations, has fared very well since 1966, but the accompanying chart portrays an even grimmer story than might be imagined. The upper line on the chart represents the DJIA's *currency* value, but the lower line represents the average's purchasing power, or *real* value, when adjusted by the Dollar Depreciation Index (which badly *understates* real inflation; see INFLATION, REAL).

As you can see, in real terms, the DJIA actually peaked at 436 in 1966 (strangely enough, with real corporate profits for that decade: see PROFITS, CORPORATE) and finished 1984 at about 162. Today it would take a price of more than 3,200 for the DJIA to exceed its 1966 price in constant purchasing power. (Now you know the source from which *part* of the value of the currency and credit created by the government, since 1940, was embezzled.) The current rally of 1550 is largely the result of the Reagan administration's tax relief (not tax cuts; see TAX CUTS) that improved corporate profits; so, although

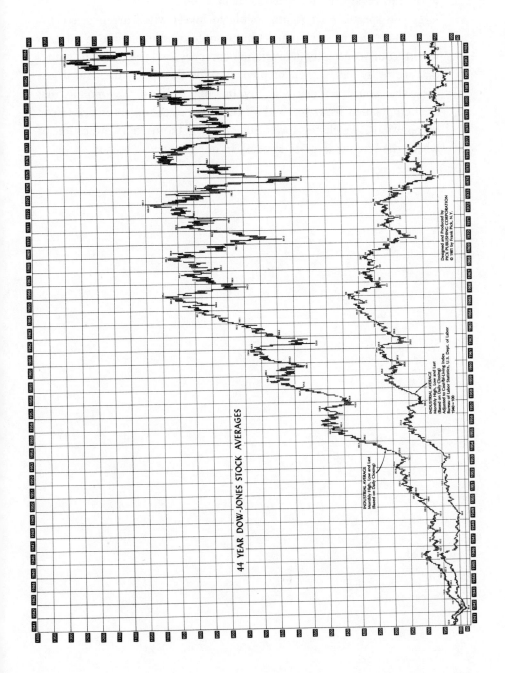

44 YEAR DOW-JONES STOCK AVERAGES

INDUSTRIAL AVERAGE
Monthly High, Low and Last
(Based on Daily Closing)

INDUSTRIAL AVERAGE
Monthly High, Low and Last
(Based on Daily Closing)
Adjusted to Cost-Of-Living Index
Bureau of Labor Statistics, U.S. Dept. of Labor
1940 = 100

Designed and Produced by
PICK PUBLISHING CORPORATION
© 1981 by Frank Pick, N.Y.

exciting and profitable for the bulls, the DJIA still has a long way to go just to regain the level achieved in 1966.

If you speculate (it is impossible to invest with currency; see INVESTMENT) in the stock market but want to continue to live in a dream world, count constantly depreciating currency, and pay taxes on "gains" that are really losses, then keep your eye on the upper line. But if you care what your currency will buy and like to know the amounts that are being stolen from you and all the other stockholders in American corporations, watch the lower line. It will be the true indication of where the "free enterprise system" in our country is headed.

ECONOMISTS

There is nothing more frightful than ignorance in action.

—JOHANN WOLFGANG

I pass with relief from the tossing sea of Cause and Theory to the firm ground of Result and Fact.

—WINSTON CHURCHILL

Every cause produces more than one effect.

—HERBERT SPENCER

The ideas of economists and political philosophers, both when they are right and when they are wrong, are more powerful than is commonly understood. Indeed the world is ruled by little else.

—JOHN MAYNARD KEYNES

Whence it follows that the bad economist pursues a small present good that will be followed by a great evil to come, while the good economist pursues a great good to come, at the risk of a small present evil.

—FREDERIC BASTIAT

Those who criticize the most [i.e., economists and politicians] are the ones who create nothing.

—HELMUT SCHOECK
ENVY: A THEORY OF SOCIAL BEHAVIOR

In current economic theory, we stand roughly where astronomy stood in the sixteenth century when Galileo declared that the Earth was not the center of the universe. This *fact* did not agree with the Catholic Church's view of our solar system (and who would know better than they), so Galileo was forced to "reconsider." For the "sin" of a lifetime of invaluable work, discovery, and dedication to truth, he spent his remaining years under the supervision of small-minded hypocrites of the Church.

Vauvenargues [1715–47] captured the essence of many of the world's (and Galileo's) problems when he said, "There is nothing that fear or hope does not make men believe." Playing on this fact, socialist economists (the only kind governments hire) gave the crowds (who are incapable of complex thought) what they desired: absurd economic theories that seemed so easy because they were based on envy (see ENVY), force, and legalized plunder (see LAW, THE). Government would magically create prosperity by plundering the few for the benefit of the many and by spending more than it taxed. Now that those dreams have come due, the same economists are using fear of their consequences as a platform for even more destructive policies. As they implement various "new" economic theories based merely on greater use of envy, force, and "legal" plunder, we watch our freedom decline, "law" by "law." To paraphrase Abraham Maslow, "If the only tool you have is a hammer [Keynesian economist], you [governments] tend to see every problem as a nail [monetary and fiscal policy]."

Today, the few free market voices, if heard at all, are ignored. Although history, as well as current facts and figures, proves the free market theory correct beyond a doubt, the establishment does not wish to give up its power by returning our freedom. Herbert Spencer had a similar complaint about economists in the nineteenth century:

> The facts cannot get recognized as facts. As the alchemist attributed his successive disappointments to some disproportion in the ingredients, some impurity, or some too great temperature, and never to the futility of his process or the impossibility of his aim; so, every failure of State-regulations the law-worshipper [economist] explains away as being caused by this trifling oversight, or that little mistake: all which oversights and mistakes he assures you will in future be avoided. Eluding the facts as he does after this fashion, volley after volley of them produce no effect.

The following excerpts from *U.S. News & World Report* (31 January 1983) typify the "wisdom" of several Nobel laureate economists. They all have a plan (more government) that is shielded from reality by Hoffer's "fact-proof screen." And all of their recommendations for ending our current economic difficulties have one point in common: they have previously failed time after time because none includes the one element that would ensure prosperity—freedom (see FREEDOM).

I have taken the liberty of decoding their Orwellian advice for the benefit of the readers who are not economics professors. In spite of their awards, these men, like most economists, have a lot to be modest about.

Paul Samuelson, Nobel laureate in 1970, had these comments:

Given our spending propensities, we have become an undertaxing nation.

[Given Congressional spending propensities, we will have to do with less so politicians and bureaucrats can plunder and waste more.]

Furthermore, the numbers (for the deficits) could be worse. If we stick to the game plan and begin indexing the tax system in 1985, we will cease to collect an extra fiscal dividend from inflation itself. That means we'll be even more of an undertaxed nation down the line.

[Furthermore, the deficits will be worse if we don't continue to rip-off producers by inflating them into higher tax brackets. You probably think you are overtaxed, but you are not fit to judge because you are not an economist. Notice there is no mention of the concept of, God forbid, cutting spending. Surely you don't expect Congress to live under the same constraints as the people who earn the wealth they squander.]

I disagree with zealots who say that we shouldn't settle for anything less than zero inflation. That goal reflects a doctrinaire ideologue's paranoia about inflation. To pursue it, as some in Washington want, could give us in 1989, when we look back on the decade, a very dismal record. Since the U.S. is fully one fourth of the world economy, that would be a drag on other nations, both developed and advanced.

[He disagrees with people who have the audacity to want no currency depreciation. The people who desire no inflation after watching the government steal more than 85 percent of the value of their currency are merely irrational paranoids. If we don't create more currency and credit out of thin air, the world will have a depression, so let's have "one more drink for the road."]

James Tobin, Nobel laureate in 1981, draws similar conclusions:

We need, above all, an expansionary monetary policy—one that will bring real interest rates down to reasonable levels, where they were during most of the post–World War II period.

[We need above all, more inflation because that will bring down real interest rates—look how low interest rates are in Brazil and Argentina. Everyone knows you can control interest with printing presses.]

To say you're afraid that an expansionary monetary policy at this stage would touch off an acceleration of inflation is to say that you don't want a recovery, because recovery can't occur without a further relaxation of monetary policy. That kind of knee-jerk reaction to an easier-money policy dooms us to no recovery at all.

[We can't have prosperity without inflation. People who don't want inflation don't want recovery. Presumably, there are no disadvantages to inflation and we can put off the inevitable consequences of this policy of distorting our economy by continuing to print currency and create credit. Just ignore any problem long enough and it will finally go away.]

An easier money policy will stimulate demand, production and increased capital investment as markets expand.... And I cannot emphasize too strongly that the energy for recovery here can be supplied only by the monetary policymakers.

[More inflation will stimulate more demand for inflation hedges and uneconomic tax shelters whose only contribution to the economy is to shelter taxes and will increase distortions of capital markets and capital investment. And I cannot emphasize too strongly that the energy for "recovery" here can be supplied only by the Federal Reserve. You probably thought the energy for recovery came from the productive segment of our economy.]

We can say that depression and double-digit unemployment have gone on long enough, to the point where the world is in serious danger. In that case, we will adopt a recovery strategy even at some risk of continued inflation.

[We can pretend that the economic pain we are currently suffering is enough to atone for forty years of government economic misman- agement and attempt to avoid further pain by using a "recovery strategy" consisting of creating currency and credit from thin air with the absolute guarantee of worse inflation and economic dislocations in the near future.]

Henry Hazlitt, one of a small minority of rational economists (who coincidentally has not won a Nobel Prize), gave us an answer to the prevailing economic wisdom in his excellent book *Economics in One Lesson*:

It would not occur to anyone unacquainted with the prevailing economic half-literacy that it is good to have windows broken and cities destroyed; that it is anything but waste to create needless public projects; that it is dangerous to let idle hordes of men return to work; that machines which increase the production of wealth and economize human effort are to be dreaded; that obstructions to free production and free consumption increase wealth; that a nation grows richer by forcing other nations to take goods for less than they cost to produce; that saving is stupid or wicked and that squandering brings prosperity. . . .

But lesser men [economists] get lost in complications. They do not re-examine their reasoning even when they emerge with conclusions that are palpably absurd. . . . It is certainly true, however, that a little economics can easily lead to the paradoxical and preposterous conclusions we have just rehearsed, but that depth in economics brings men back to common sense. For depth in economics consists in looking for all the consequences of a policy instead of merely resting one's gaze on those immediately visible.

My own suggestion for the disposition of the geniuses who prescribe more government, inflation, taxation, and debt for an economy that is dying from government, inflation, taxation, and debt is that they all be given a printing press and deported to a small, deserted island where they could establish their own "ideal" society. Instead, they receive Nobel Prizes, the responsibility for "educating" our youth, and exposure in national magazines that showcase their absurd theories. No matter what their ultimate disposition, let's follow Frederic Bastiat's advice in *The Law*:

> Away, then with the quacks and the planners! . . . Away with their artificial methods! Away with their social workshop, their phalanstery, their statism, their centralization, their tariffs, their universities, their state religion, their interest-free credit or bank monopolies, their regulations, their restrictions, their moralization, and their equalization by taxation!

Ludwig von Mises once issued a warning about government worshippers that everyone should emblazon in his memory: "If they were not potential dictators, they would not ask the government to interfere." As with all dictators (both potential and real), their dream of wealth and prosperity through insanity is fast coming due. The economy is not only more complex than they think: it is more complex than they can think.

EDUCATION, PUBLIC

Learning without thought is labor lost; thought without learning is perilous.

—CONFUCIUS

Only the educated are free.

—EPICTETUS

The public school system...although founded with the highest and most altruistic goals in mind, remains in a state of chronic failure because it violates the human principle of spontaneity.

—JOHN GALL
SYSTEMANTICS

The foundation of every state is the education of its youth.

—DIOGENES

Education has now become the chief problem of the world, its one holy cause. The nations that see this will survive, and those that fail to do so will slowly perish....

—G. STANLEY HALL

In large states public education will always be mediocre, for the same reason that in large kitchens the cooking is usually bad.

—FRIEDRICH NIETZSCHE

A tax-supported, compulsory educational system is the complete model of the totalitarian state.

—ISABEL PATERSON
THE GOD OF THE MACHINE

The dream of compulsory, "free" public education is losing its appeal, as parents are forced to relinquish control of their children's schools to egalitarian bureaucrats who (like all government employees) consistently demand greater resources but continue to produce worse results. The quality of our schools has collapsed almost as fast as our currency. (Maybe it's only coincidence.) The evidence is everywhere: Scholastic Aptitude Test (S.A.T.) average scores have declined from 958 in 1967 to 890 in 1980 (thus showing that equality of almost anything, but most especially education, occurs at a uniformly *low* level; see EQUALITY). Only 74 percent of today's high school students graduate, and this doesn't take into consideration the depreciation (inflation?) in the value of today's high school degree, handed out by increasingly apathetic teachers and administrators to students who cannot even read. (Currently one-third of high school graduates cannot read at a fifth-grade level.)

It seems that we cannot fully appreciate things that are *perceived* to be free, such as education. Even bureaucrats should be able to understand (not that they would care) that we can *pay* for public schools, but we cannot *buy* an education for someone who isn't interested (i.e., no one can force a child to learn, especially when his curriculum includes large doses of brainwashing on such fascinating subjects as "government"). As Edward Banfield noted in his book *The Unheavenly City Revisited*:

> That some children simply cannot be taught much in school is one example of a fact that the American [government] mind will not entertain. Our cultural ideal requires that we give every child a good education whether he wants it or not and whether he is capable of receiving it or not. If at first we don't succeed, we must try, try again. And if in the end we don't succeed, we must feel guilty for our failure. To lower the school-leaving age would be, in the terms of this secular religion, a shirking of the task for which we were chosen.

Education, in a truly free country, simply would not and cannot be compulsory (or state-supported). It, like health, is initially a parental responsibility (see RESPONSIBILITY), but ultimately a personal responsibility. Experience has proved time and again that the lack of a formal education doesn't necessarily prevent people from being successful, anymore than an expensive or forced education can ensure one's success.

Isabel Paterson captured the essence of the near monopoly of government schools in the following quotation from *The God of The Machine*:

There can be no greater stretch of arbitrary power than is required to seize children from their parents, [try to] teach them whatever the authorities decree they shall be taught, and expropriate from the parents [and innocent bystanders with no children] the funds to pay for the procedure. If this principle really is not understood, let any parent holding a positive religious faith consider how it would seem to him if his children were taken by force and taught an opposite creed.

In a country based on freedom, people would only have to support public education if they chose to use its services—and many would not. Most, if not all, public schools (like every government "service") could not compete in a free market environment without their involuntary tax subsidies.

Isabel Paterson has captured what would be the predictable reaction among increasingly militant public school teachers to the elimination of state education, and what the public would answer in turn.

The most vindictive resentment may be expected from the pedagogic profession for any suggestion that they should be dislodged from their dictatorial position; it will be expressed mainly in epithets, such as "reactionary," at the mildest. Nevertheless, the question to put to any teacher moved to such indignation, is: Do you think nobody would *willingly* entrust his children to you or pay you for teaching them? Why do you have to extort your fees and collect your pupils by compulsion?

It is time to begin deregulating our children and their minds by deregulating *their* schools.

ELECTIONS

That the politicians are permitted to carry on the same old type of disgraceful campaign from year to year is as insulting to the people as would be a gang of thieves coming back to a town they had robbed, staging a parade, and inviting citizens to fall in and cheer.

—EDGAR WATSON HOWE

Vote for the man who promises least; he'll be the least disappointing.

—BERNARD BARUCH

There are no morals in politics; there is only expedience.

—V. I. LENIN

Since a politician never believes what he says, he is surprised when others believe him.

—CHARLES DE GAULLE

Public office is the last refuge of a scoundrel.

—BOIES PENROSE

If you have a weak candidate and a weak platform, wrap yourself up in the American flag and talk about the Constitution.

—MATT QUAY

Great men, till they have gained their ends, are giants in their promises, but, those obtained, weak pygmies in their performance.

—PHILIP MASSINGER

If of ten men nine are recognisable as fools, which is a common calculation, how, ... in the name of wonder, will you ever get a ballot-box to grind you out a wisdom from the votes of these ten men?

—THOMAS CARLYLE

The government consists of a gang of men exactly like you and me. They have, taking one with another, no special talent for the business of government. They have only talent for getting and holding office. Their principal device to that end is to search out groups who pant and pine for something they can't get and to promise to give it to them. Nine times out of ten that promise is worth nothing. The tenth time it is made good only by looting A to satisfy B. In other words, government is a broker in pillage and every election is a sort of an advance auction sale of stolen goods.

At each election we vote in a new set of politicians, insanely assuming that they are better than the set turned out. And at each election we are, as they say in Motherland, done in.

—H. L. MENCKEN

(What if they gave an election and nobody came?)

EMIGRATION

(Voting With Your Feet)

An oppressive government is more to be feared than a tiger.

—CONFUCIUS

Again, a situation may arise in which talent is driven out of a country by social and economic controls which are basically envy-motivated, to take refuge in a region offering considerably better means for its effective employment.

—HELMUT SCHOECK
ENVY: A THEORY OF SOCIAL BEHAVIOR

The emigration of a country's most productive and creative population—popularly known as "the brain drain"—is the surest sign that a government has taxed away too much freedom (of productive effort or property rights). Although it does not present a problem for most communist governments (who not only "own" all the physical capital in their countries but the human beings as well), it is one of the chief problems of the "less developed socialist countries" (i.e., less free countries). While crying out for more foreign aid (see FOREIGN AID) or foreign loans, their envy-motivated governments (see ENVY) literally block, suppress, or drive the country's most important resource—its entrepreneurial and intellectual capital—from its borders (in addition to preventing the formation or importation of financial capital).

But people fleeing oppressive governments are able to improve their situation only in a relative sense. The number of countries where they are welcome and the number of people any country will receive is severely limited by other "freedom-loving" governments (who establish quotas or tariffs on the movement of human beings). Even if these people can overcome the bureaucratic maze and red tape and settle in another country, they are only moving from areas of little or no freedom to areas of at least some freedom (see FREEDOM).

It is a sad comment that most of the world's population desiring to emigrate want to come to the United States, where 42 percent of the gross national product is consumed by government. Still, we are considered one of the most free countries in the world. But for those in America who desire more freedom, there is really no other place to go except the underground economy (see UNDERGROUND ECONOMY).

If the trend toward bigger government continues—and history suggests that it will (see GOVERNMENT GROWTH)—this migration between countries is nothing more than men crawling up the side of a sinking ship.

ENVY

If envy were an illness, the world would be a hospital.

—GERMAN PROVERB

Envy is more implacable than hatred.

—LA ROCHEFOUCAULD

Envy is a beast that will gnaw its own leg if it can't get anything else.

—GERMAN PROVERB

The envious man thinks that if his neighbour breaks a leg, he will be able to walk better.

—GERMAN PROVERB

There is perhaps no phenomenon which contains so much destructive feeling as moral indignation, which permits envy or hate to be acted out under the guise of virtue.

—ERICH FROMM

Envy is one of the oldest and most destructive of all human emotions. Few people can begin to comprehend the central role it plays in every facet of their daily lives and the power it exercises over government.

As mankind has advanced through the centuries, envy has come to be almost as much at home in prosperous nations (who prosper only because they have been able to limit the influence of envy in their societies, yet feel unjustifiable guilt for their productivity) as in impoverished ones. The fear of envy may explain why the countries with more freedom (i.e., the most prosperous countries; see JAPAN, A MODEL) always seem to self-destruct through economic (redistributive) anarchy. Although envy is never absent from any society, it becomes most pervasive and counterproductive when it gains control of government and then of the "law" (see LAW, THE), which subsequently sets itself above the rights of property (see PROPERTY RIGHTS). As laws of envy (redistribution of wealth through "legal" plunder, such as the progressive income tax; see INCOME TAX) multiply, so does the emotion, because like all forms of neurosis envy cannot be satisfied. Various envious entities continually find new "inequalities" (see EQUALITY) that must be rectified by more government plunder, and thus less individual freedom (see FREEDOM) and security (see SECURITY).

As envy becomes institutionalized in government, it destroys incentives to produce, and the economy begins to stagnate or contract. A sickening economy and the additional envy it generates are the most powerful forces behind the growth of government, which eventually leads to socialism and communism. Government growth always leads to the growth of inequity. As the economy shifts from production to plunder, the gap widens between the rich and/or politically powerful and the poor. (In socialist countries, such as the USSR, the differential between maximum and minimum incomes approaches 50:1, but rarely exceeds 15:1 in any Western industrial country.) Greater inequity leads to the growth of envy, which leads to more government growth; it is a self-perpetuating nightmare that finally consumes itself.

The process of establishing a system of government based on an emotional sickness is well described by Helmut Schoeck in his penetrating book *Envy: A Theory of Social Behavior*:

> The various forms of socialism have always recruited a large proportion, if not the majority, of their important supporters and theoreticians from among those people who were deeply troubled by the problem of envy in society. These were mostly people in good, if not excellent, circumstances, who suffered from the idea that they gave cause for envy. Their concern was directed equally towards those who were envied like themselves and toward those who were envious. . . . The impulse given to socialism by this viewpoint is primarily towards a form of society in which there will be neither envied nor envious. In socialist economists such as Abba P. Lerner, we find the envy-motive used indirectly, appearing now as a social virtue. Thus, a progressively rising income tax is proposed on the grounds that, for the psychological good of the collective, the appeasement of envy in the normal wage-earner—on witnessing the penalties of the highly paid—was quantitatively more important and beneficial than the discomfiture of the few, despoiled by the state for the benefit of the envious.

A free economy (i.e., an economy that controls envy through custom, religion, and law) ensures hope for the future and ever greater prosperity as people work voluntarily to expand and share an ever growing pie. This constantly improving standard of living helps keep envy from becoming a devisive and counterproductive force. Everyone has a chance to improve his own situation, and no one is plundered by "law." But once an economy begins to receive "help" and "direction" (i.e., socialism) from a government that has surrendered to envy, it begins an inevitable decline, and positive feelings are supplanted by worry, despair, fear (see FEAR), hatred, and even greater envy. The question of how to divide (read: plunder) an ever shrinking economic pie becomes an overriding concern as various "public interest" groups fight to seize control of the government and/or the "law" for their own purpose. Since an impersonal, "altruistic" government, which has become the main source of "security" (through special privileges and monthly checks) for millions of people, cannot be attacked; it is the productive individuals who *can* retain all or part of their wealth who become the subject of hatred and persecution (i.e., envy). Schoeck expounds upon this feeling with the following quote from the *London Times*:

> There is no vice, of which a man can be guilty, no meanness, no shabbiness, no unkindness, which excites so much indignation among his contemporaries, friends and neighbours, as his success. This is the unpardonable crime, which reason cannot defend, nor humility mitigate. . . . The man who writes as we cannot write, who speaks as we cannot speak, labours as we cannot labour, thrives as we cannot thrive, has accumulated on his own person all the offenses of which man can be guilty. Down with him!

The chief goal of government seems to be the total elimination of envy from society. The message of Schoeck's book and history is that this goal is unattainable and incredibly destructive to those countries who pursue it. So how is envy to be treated? Schoeck answers:

> The capacity to envy is a fact. . . . The degree of the questioner's self-estimation will determine which ensues, envy or guilt. . . . It cannot be conjured away by social reforms. The only liberation from this useless and destructive sense of guilt comes from the realization that there is no way of eliminating what causes one to be envied. Envy's culture-inhibiting irrationality in a society is not to be overcome by fine sen-

timents or altruism, but almost always by a higher level of rationality, by the recognition, for instance, that more (or something different) for the few does not necessarily mean less for the others: this requires a certain capacity for calculation, a grasp of larger contexts, a longer memory; the ability, not just to compare one thing with another, but also to compare very dissimilar values in one man with those in another.

Today we can state on a better empirical basis than would have been possible fifty or a hundred years ago that the world cannot belong to the envious, any more than the causes of envy can be eradicated from society. The society devoid of all traces of class or status, and similar refuges for wits'-end thinking and uncomfortable feelings, should no longer be considered worthy of serious discussion. . . .

Even those who have never taken seriously utopias of classless societies and pure socialism have been seduced in the course of the last hundred years into falsely concluding that the critical role in society is the prerogative of envious dispositions whom a single concession would supposedly placate. Of course there is much social stupidity that can and must be avoided. There is no virtue in rubbing salt into a wound. But historical observation and rules deducible from basic human behavior would seem to suggest that there is something like a hardening towards exaggerated sensitivity to envy. Francis Bacon had already realized that nothing is more calculated to exasperate the envious man and to feed his discontent than irrational action, an abdication from a superior position with the removal of his envy in view. The time has surely come when we should stop behaving as though the envious man was the main criterion for economic and social policy.

Well said! The dream of placating envy and relieving guilt through irrational acts will soon come due.

EQUALITY

All men have an equal right to the free development of their faculties; they have an equal right to the impartial protection of the state; but it is not true, it is against all the laws of reason and equity, it is against the eternal nature of things, that the indolent man and the laborious man, the spendthrift and the economizer, the imprudent and the wise, should obtain and enjoy an equal amount of goods.

—VICTOR COUSIN

That all men are equal is a proposition to which, at ordinary times, no sane individual has ever given his assent.

—ALDOUS HUXLEY

Those who attempt to level never equalize. In all societies some description must be uppermost. The levellers, therefore, only change and pervert the natural order of things; they load the edifice of society by setting up in the air what the solidity of the structure requires to be on the ground.

—EDMUND BURKE

If by saying that all men are born free and equal, you mean that they are all equally born, it is true, but true in no other sense; birth, talent, labor, virtue, and providence, are forever making differences.

—EUGENE EDWARDS

All animals are equal but some animals are more equal than others.

—GEORGE ORWELL

Equality is one of the most consummate scoundrels that ever crept from the brain of a political juggler—a fellow who thrusts his hand into the pocket of honest industry or enterprising talent, and squanders their hard-earned profits on profligate idleness or indolent stupidity.

—JAMES KIRKE PAULDING

■ "We hold these truths to be sacred and undeniable; that all men are created equal. . . ." This famous declaration by Thomas Jefferson has been perverted beyond recognition by the forces of envy. The equality to which Jefferson referred was an individual's equal right to protection from force and fraud, not the equal right of the envious to use government (see GOVERNMENT) and the law (see LAW, THE) for the mutual plunder of the property of others. Equality, in the words of Helmut Schoeck, is the "equal protection to the unequal achievements [i.e., inequality] of the members of the community. . . ."

In the current political climate, *equality* and *justice* have become interchangeable. But if men are to remain free, equality cannot and must not be confused with justice. If you think these words are synonymous, go to the Soviet Union or China (the world capitals of "equality"), where there is no freedom, equality, or justice.

Equality has one defect that makes it the universal and eternal demand of envy: people desire it only with their superiors. But even if universal equality were possible, it would not begin to satisfy envy. As Helmut Schoeck wrote:

> Envy is ineluctable, implacable and irreconcilable, is irritated by the slightest differences, is *independent of the degree of inequality* [my emphasis], appears in its worst form in social proximity or among near relatives, provides the dynamic for every revolution, yet cannot of itself produce any kind of coherent revolutionary programme.

Max Scheler penetrated the disguise of envy masquerading as a demand for "equality" (i.e., uniformity at the level of the crowd) when he wrote *Das Ressentiment im Aufbau der Moralen (Resentment in the Structuring of Ethics)*:

> Modern egalitarian doctrine generally—whether it takes the form of a statement of fact, a moral demand, or both of these things—is, however, clearly the product of *resentment* [envy]. It is surely obvious that, without exception, the apparently innocuous demand for equality—of whatever kind, whether sexual, social, political, religious or material—in fact conceals only the desire for the *demotion*, in accordance with a selected scale of values, of those having more assets, and those who are in some way *higher up*, to the level of those lower down. In any struggle for power, however great or petty, no one feels that the scales are weighted in his favour. Only the one who fears he *will lose*, demands it as a *universal principle*. The demand for equality is always

a speculation on a falling market. For it is a law according to which people can only be equal in respect of those characteristics having the *least value*. "Equality" as a purely rational idea can never stimulate desire, will or emotion. But resentment [envy], in whose eyes the higher values never find favour, conceals its nature in the demand for "equality"! In reality it wants nothing less than the destruction of all those who embody those higher values which arouse its anger.

But, before "equality" can be demanded and implemented, there is still one essential requirement. The envious man cannot let the world know that it is his envy that must be placated; he must arouse the crowd and its "room-temperature I.Q." by using a twisted form of altruism as his motive, which turns free men into sacrificial animals. Kierkegaard was very close to this truth when he wrote:

> In order that levelling can really take place, a phantom [that comes to life as a crowd dominated by envy] must first be brought into being, its spirit a monstrous abstraction, an all-embracing something that is Nothing [initially], a mirage—that phantom is the Public [good]...."

The greater number of natural rights (see RIGHTS) we surrender to the envious in the name of "equality" and the elimination of envy, the more envy we will create. The closer we come to the kind of "equality" demanded by envy under the guise of needs (see NEEDS), the closer we come to the ultimate disaster of a socialist world. Richard Cotten made a perfect summary of the subject of equality when he warned, "Freedom is not free, free men are not equal, and equal men are not free!"

FEAR

Fear always springs from ignorance!

—RALPH WALDO EMERSON

Our tragedy today is a general and universal physical fear so long sustained by now that we can even bear it. . . . The basest of all things is to be afraid.

—WILLIAM FAULKNER

Fear is the main source of superstition, and one of the main sources of cruelty.

—BERTRAND RUSSELL

Fear is like fire: If controlled it will help you; if uncontrolled, it will rise up and destroy you.

—JOHN F. MILBURN

No power is strong enough to be lasting if it labors under the weight of fear.

—CICERO

Fear is an acid which is pumped into one's atmosphere. It causes mental, moral and spiritual asphyxiation, and sometimes death; death to energy and all growth.

—HORACE FLETCHER

In no other period of history has fear pervaded our world as it does today. This trend is reflected worldwide by the rise of terrorism, and in the United States by the crime statistics.

As government grows, it must increase its "legal" plunder (see LAW, THE) at the expense of freedom and property rights. Currency must substitute for money (see MONEY), guaranteeing inflation (see IN-

FLATION) and setting into motion the destabilization of society. As government spending (plunder) and inflation gain momentum, so do uncertainty, insecurity, and finally, fear. Soon people realize that there are no limits to what government will spend and thus tax, or inflate, away from their productive efforts and savings (see SAVING). They struggle in vain for some measure of security (see SECURITY) that cannot come as long as it is denominated in paper currency, backed only by a politician's promise and guaranteed by "laws" that are changed at the whim of each new legislature.

Fear is best characterized by Emerson in his essay "Compensation":

Fear is an instructor of great sagacity and the herald of all revolutions. One thing he teaches, that there is rottenness [of government and currency?] where he appears. . . . He indicates great wrongs which must be revised.

Fear is the antithesis of hope. The greater the fear in a society, the less hope there can be. In *The True Believer*, Eric Hoffer describes the benefits of hope and the disasters that occur when hope is lost:

It is true of course that the hope released by a vivid visualization of a glorious future is a most potent source of daring and self-forgetting. . . . When today is all there is, we grab all we can and hold on. We are afloat in an ocean of nothingness and we hang on to any miserable piece of wreckage as if it were the tree of life. On the other hand, when everything is ahead and yet to come, we find it easy to share all we have and to forego advantages within our grasp. The behavior of the members of the Donner party when they were buoyed by hope and, later, when hope was gone [and replaced by fear] illustrates the dependence of co-operatives and the communal spirit on hope. Those without hope are divided and driven to desperate self-seeking. Common suffering by itself, when not joined with hope, does not unite nor does it evoke mutual generosity. The enslaved Hebrews in Egypt, "their lives made bitter with hard bondage," were a bickering, back-biting lot. Moses had to give them hope of a promised land before he could join them together. The thirty thousand hopeless people in the concentration camp of Buchenwald did not develop any form of united action, nor did they manifest any readiness for self-sacrifice. There was there more greed and ruthless selfishness than in the greediest and most corrupt of free societies. [I have never known of a truly free society that was corrupt.]

Fear, regardless of the source, is the enemy of freedom. Fear nearly always results in a decline in morality and an increase in government's size and force. As Hoffer discerned:

Hitler imposed himself upon the world both by promoting Nazism and by forcing the democracies [through fear] to become zealous, intolerant and ruthless. Communist Russia shapes both its adherents and its opponents in its own image.

Currently, Congress is afraid of the rising trade and budget deficits, the tax revolt (see TAX REVOLT), and the underground economy (see UNDERGROUND ECONOMY), so, instead of helping the situation by cutting spending and taxes, they increase spending, taxes (thus increasing the deficits; see LAFFER CURVE), and the penalties for non-payment of taxes and add to the number of tax collectors. Such action merely increases the fear in society, and a society cannot survive indefinitely in a climate of increasing fear: the emotional drain is too great. Currently, Central America, Mexico, and the Middle East are graphic examples of this tendency. Ultimately, the United States will be no exception.

FOREIGN AID

(Nothing for Something)

The record seems to show that free enterprise is the only system of government in the world that is not on trial. If it is on trial, why is America being called upon to save the world from economic chaos?

—WALTER S. GIFFORD

The ultimate result of shielding men [countries] from the effects of folly [government] is to fill the world with fools.

—HERBERT SPENCER

A gift much expected is paid, not given.

—GEORGE HERBERT

When money, credit, and goods are handed to the static [socialist] economies for nothing, whether as gift or by allowing default, the result is certain, a world war on a commensurate scale, with increased and hopeless oppression of the people of the static economy.

—ISABEL PATERSON
THE GOD OF THE MACHINE

There can be no greater error than to expect or calculate upon real favors from nation to nation. It is an illusion [dream?] which experience must cure, which a just pride ought to discard.

—GEORGE WASHINGTON

Foreign aid has been an immoral, giant sewer for the wealth of American taxpayers since 1946. Although the Constitution (which has been only of *historical* interest to the U.S. government) grants the government no authority to tax American citizens for the benefit of foreign entities, the total amount of foreign aid, including interest on what we borrowed to give away, is estimated at over $1 trillion dollars (equal to a large portion of the national debt). In addition to this incalculable amount of wealth wasted, the results of our "generosity" have actually been detrimental to the United States. Our government simply cannot understand ingratitude generated by foreign aid programs. Helmut Schoeck describes this ingratitude with truth and wisdom in *Envy: A Theory of Social Behavior*:

> Almost a hundred years later Nietzsche gave a very similar interpretation of ingratitude, but our own age, obsessed by the desire to do good to the most distant nations and peoples, is unwilling to admit that the recipients of its welfare, for reasons that are obvious, deeply envy and hate the givers and, in extreme cases, live only in the hope of the latter's destruction. . . . No one admits publicly, and hence public opinion does not admit, that ingratitude is the norm. It is astounding that countless benefactors allow themselves to be persuaded over and over that ingratitude with the resultant hatred is a rare and special case.

Scan the following *partial*, most recent list of recipients (no one in Washington seems to know the current amounts or how to obtain them) and see the "goodwill" (ingratitude) we have bought in exchange for our wealth (help). America has certainly never been guilty of supporting a government that won a civil war. The list includes such "leaders" as Chiang Kai-shek, President Diem of Viet Nam, the Shah of Iran, and the freedom-loving General Somoza (and is soon to include some "leader" of El Salvador, Guatemala, or Honduras):

U.S. Foreign Aid, 1946 to 1972
(In Billions of Dollars, Not Including Interest)

Afghanistan	0.4	Italy	5.5
Argentina*	0.3	Japan	3.5
Australia	0.6	Jordan	0.8
Belgium–Luxembourg	1.8	Korea	10.0
Brazil*	2.7	Kuwait	0.03
China, Republic of	5.1	Laos	1.5
Denmark	0.9	Libya	0.2
France	7.0	Mexico*	0.5
Germany and West Berlin	3.7	Netherlands	2.0
Greece	3.7	Nicaragua	0.2
India	8.0	Nigeria	0.4
Indochina	1.5	Norway	1.2
Indonesia	1.4	Pakistan	4.5
Iran	2.0	Peru	0.5
Israel	1.0	Philippines	2.0

Poland*	0.5	United Arab Republic	0.8
Saudi Arabia	0.2	United Kingdom	7.5
Spain	2.0	Venezuela*	0.3
Thailand	1.6	Viet Nam	15.5
Turkey	5.7	Yugoslavia*	2.5

*Get ready to add huge amounts of American bank "foreign aid" to these figures as some of these countries reschedule (default on) their loans.

Poverty is not the reason that these countries need aid. Aid, for the most part, has only worsened poverty by increasing the size of government and wasting scarce resources on idiotic programs that would fail immediately if they were not subsidized. These countries "need" aid because their governments and laws (see LAW, THE) are dominated by envy, and thus hostile to freedom, capitalism, and prosperity. The people of these countries are not impoverished citizens, but economic prisoners of "their" governments, victims of "legal" plunder on a massive scale. As Frederic Bastiat wrote in *The Law*:

> Which nations are the happiest, most moral, and most peaceful? Those among which the law intervenes the least in private activity; where the government makes itself felt the least; where individuality has the most scope....

If the "poor" countries of the world had free economies (capitalism), and thus stable governments, private industry and capital investment (which, when offered, are currently rejected as "exploitation" amid screaming for more aid and loans) would flow into them. Their standard of living would increase almost immediately, and long-term prosperity would be assured. But the lessons of empty government promises and endless expropriation of foreign assets have not been lost on multinational corporations.

The solution to this problem is simple: abolish all foreign aid. Let's see how socialist economies function without the prop of Western wealth. Once our government discovers the lessons of history—that friends cannot be bought and envy cannot be assuaged—there will be massive outrage and an exodus of many of our former "comrades" to the Soviet camp. The "defection" of these statist governments would suit our ultimate goals perfectly. They can bleed the anemic Soviet economy dry a lot faster than the economy of the United States. Let these countries seek aid from the pathetic socialist economies they have chosen to emulate!

FREEDOM

Where the State begins, individual liberty ceases, and vice versa.

—MIKHAIL A. BAKUNIN

Man is born free, and everywhere he is in chains.

—JEAN JACQUES ROUSSEAU

The war for freedom will never really be won because the price of freedom is constant vigilance over ourselves and over our Government.

—ELEANOR ROOSEVELT

Liberty has never come from Government. Liberty has always come from the subjects of it. . . . The history of liberty is a history of limitations of governmental power, not the increase of it.

—WOODROW WILSON

What is freedom? Freedom is the right to choose: the right to create for oneself the alternatives of choice. Without the possibility of choice and the exercise of choice a man is not a man but a member, an instrument, a thing. —ARCHIBALD MACLEISH

Freedom is the absence of coercion or constraint in all choice or action that does not inflict force or fraud on another. This means it is the antithesis of government (see GOVERNMENT), because government, no matter how small, can only come from some amount of "legal" plunder (see LAW, THE) because it always separates its "services" from the payment (e.g., as with the postal service, the consumer is never allowed to choose). Plunder (taxation) is a diminution of property rights (see PROPERTY RIGHTS) through the power of coercion, which always results in a reduction of freedom. George Washington was well aware that government could only grow by destroying freedom when he wrote, "Arbitrary power is most easily established on the ruins of liberty abused to licentiousness."

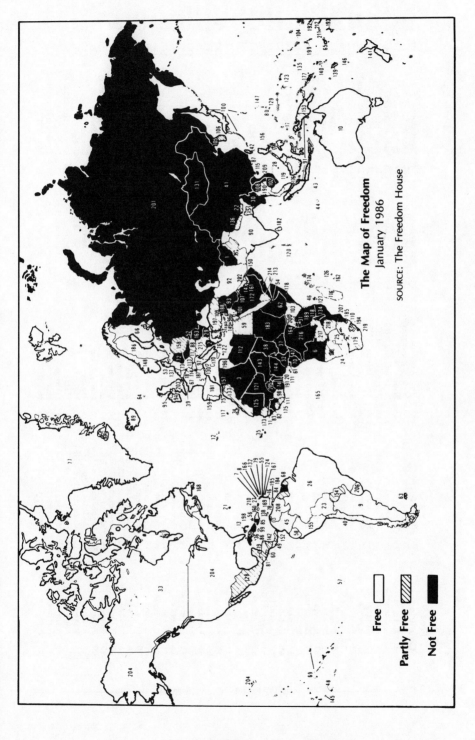

The Map of Freedom
January 1986

SOURCE: The Freedom House

Free
Partly Free
Not Free

Free Countries

#	Country
8	Antigua & Barbuda
9	Argentina
10	Australia
11	Austria
13	Bahamas
16	Barbados
18	Belgium
19	Belize
23	Bolivia
25	Botswana
26	Brazil
33	Canada
45	Colombia
49	Costa Rica
51a	Cyprus (G)
53	Denmark
55	Dominica
56	Dominican Republic
58	Ecuador
65	Fiji
66	Finland
67	France
73	Germany (W)
76	Greece
78	Grenada
86	Honduras
89	Iceland
90	India
94	Ireland
96	Israel
97	Italy
99	Jamaica
100	Japan
104	Kiribati
114	Luxembourg
126	Mauritius
135	Nauru
137	Netherlands
141	New Zealand
148	Norway
153	Papua New Guinea
155	Peru
159	Portugal
166	St. Kitts-Nevis
167	St. Lucia
169	St. Vincent
177	Solomons
181	Spain
186	Sweden
187	Switzerland
195	Trinidad & Tob.
199	Tuvalu
203	United Kingdom
204	United States
206	Uruguay
208	Venezuela

Related Territories

#	Territory
4	Amer. Samoa (US)
7	Anguilla (UK)
12	Azores (Port)
17	Belau (US)
21	Bermuda (UK)
27	Br. Vir. Is. (UK)
34	Canary Isls. (Sp)
36	Cayman Isls. (UK)
157a	Ceuta (Sp)
39	Channel Isls. (UK)
48	Cook Isls. (NZ)
63	Falkland Isls. (UK)
64	Faroe Isls. (Den)
75	Gibraltar (UK)
77	Greenland (Den)
95	Isle of Man (UK)
113	Liechtenstein (Sw)
117	Madeira (Port)
123	Marshall Isls. (US)
127	Mayotte (Fr)
157b	Melilla (Sp)
129	Micronesia (US)
132	Montserrat (UK)
138	Ne. Antilles (Ne)
139	New Caledonia (Fr)
145	Niue (N.Z)
147	N.Marianas (US)
160	P'rto Rico (US)
165	St. Helena (UK)
168	S.Pierre-Mi (Fr)
170	San Marino (It)
198	Turks & C. (UK)
210	Virgin Isls (US)

Partly Free Countries

#	Country
14	Bahrain
15	Bangladesh
22	Bhutan
28	Brunei
40	Chile
42	China (Taiwan)
51b	Cyprus (T)
59	Egypt
60	El Salvador
71	Gambia
81	Guatemala
84	Guyana
88	Hungary
91	Indonesia
92	Iran
98	Ivory Coast
101	Jordan
103	Kenya
106	Korea (S)
107	Kuwait
109	Lebanon
110	Lesotho
111	Liberia
116	Madagascar
119	Malaysia
120	Maldives
122	Malta
128	Mexico
133	Morocco
136	Nepal
142	Nicaragua
151	Pakistan
152	Panama
154	Paraguay
156	Philippines
158	Poland
161	Qatar
173	Senegal
175	Sierra Leone
176	Singapore
179	So. Africa
182	Sri Lanka
185	Swaziland
190	Thailand
193	Tonga
194	Transkei
196	Tunisia
197	Turkey
200	Uganda
202	United Arab Emirates
140	Vanuatu
212	W. Samoa
213	Yemen (N)
215	Yugoslavia
217	Zambia
218	Zimbabwe

Related Territories

#	Territory
5	Andorra (Fr-Sp)
24	Bophuthatswana (South Afr.)
43	Christmas Is. (Austral.)
44	Cocos Isls. (Austral.)
57	Easter Is. (Ch)
68	French Guiana (Fr)
69	French Polynesia (Fr)

Not Free Countries

#	Country
1	Afghanistan
2	Albania
3	Algeria
6	Angola
20	Benin
29	Bulgaria
205	Burkina Faso
30	Burma
31	Burundi
102	Cambodia
32	Cameroon
35	Cape Verde Is.
37	Central African Republic
38	Chad
41	China (Mainland)
46	Comoros
47	Congo
50	Cuba
52	Czechoslovakia
54	Djibouti
61	Equatorial Guinea
62	Ethiopia
70	Gabon
72	Germany (E)
74	Ghana
82	Guinea
83	Guinea-Biss.
85	Haiti
93	Iraq
105	Korea (N)
108	Laos
112	Libya
118	Malawi
121	Mali
125	Mauritania
131	Mongolia
134	Mozambique
143	Niger
144	Nigeria
150	Oman
163	Romania
164	Rwanda
171	Sao Tome & Principe
172	Saudi Arabia
174	Seychelles
178	Somalia
183	Sudan
184	Suriname
188	Syria
189	Tanzania
191	Togo
201	USSR
209	Vietnam
214	Yemen (S)
216	Zaire

Related Territories

#	Territory
79	Guadeloupe (Fr)
80	Guam (US)
87	Hong Kong (UK)
115	Macao (Port)
124	Martinique (Fr)
130	Monaco (Fr)
146	Norfolk Is. (Aus)
149	Occupied Ters. (Isr)
162	Reunion (Fr)
180	SW Africa (Namibia) (SA)
192	Tokelau Isls. (NZ)
211	Vatican (It)
	Wallis and Futuna (Fr)

Related Territories

#	Territory
219	Ciskei (SA)
207	Venda (SA)

Freedom is the most expensive commodity in the world because of its universal demand and increasingly government limited supply. There are only a few places on earth where people will not risk their lives or fortunes for a chance at greater freedom. (The United States is *not* one of them; see TAX REVOLT and UNDERGROUND ECONOMY).

Contrary to what most politicians would have you believe, freedom is not the right to choose (or escape) the government that plunders and oppresses you. It is the right to produce and retain the fruits of honest labor, and to choose, or *not choose*, a government that provides protection from force or fraud. This protection, *if it is desired*, is government's *only possible* legitimate function.

If you study the accompanying map, you will see *that because of government only*, the world is not free (and becomes less so each year). But even this map doesn't conform to the real definition or concept of freedom, which is always the possession of absolute property rights that are not subject to changes in the law. Any country in which government at all levels (federal, state, and local) takes more than 15 to 20 percent of its citizens' production is socialist at best, not free. By this measure, the United States, West Germany, Canada, Australia, Great Britain, France, and a host of lesser countries are not free (although they certainly have less coercion than communist countries).

All other factors being equal, the most accurate way to measure a country's freedom is by the size of government (i.e., the amount of inflation and taxation). Since freedom and prosperity are inseparable, it also follows that the smaller the government and the less it grows, the faster prosperity can grow. If a government is not growing any faster than the private sector (a very rare occurrence; see GOVERNMENT GROWTH), a country's official economic growth (excluding the underground economy) and stability almost perfectly correlate with the size of its government, as shown in the following table:

National Governments' Share of Official Gross National Product for 1979 or 1980

COUNTRY	SHARE OF GNP (*Percentage*)
Brazil (1979)	9.03
Switzerland (1980)	9.69
Japan (1980)	13.99
Spain (1979)	14.40
Germany (1980)	15.24

South Korea (1980)	18.46
Venezuela (1979)	20.84
France (1980)	21.82
United States (1980)	22.87
Canada (1980)	23.34
Finland (1979)	25.07
Australia (1980)	28.12
Italy (1980)	35.71
Great Britain (1980)	38.58
Sweden (1979)	43.75

Government is and always has been a cancer growth on the freedom of mankind, and cancer never limits its growth except by destroying its victim. Since this entity and its growth are the sources of most of our problems, the *only* solution to these problems is the restoration of our freedom. The only way this can be done is to *reverse* (not stop) the growth of government.

Isabel Paterson understood that freedom is a *necessity* for the survival of mankind and that America is its greatest repository and last line of defense. She incisively described America's "alternative" to freedom in *The God of the Machine*:

> Then if the free economies cut their own energy circuits internally by imposing the political power on production [i.e., plunder], from what source are they to draw the necessary energy to function and to fight? The United States cannot borrow, beg, copy, embezzle, or loot from any other nation in the world, whether for peace or for war. How then can America imitate the "totalitarian" nations? The thing is impossible. Freedom for Americans is not a luxury of peace, to be "sacrificed" in wartime. It is a necessity at all times. . . .

Frederic Bastiat understood the futility of surrendering freedom to governments that promise utopia and offered in his book, *The Law*, some very good advice to politicians and government worshippers (which they will never voluntarily implement because it would mean surrendering power).

> And now that the legislators and do-gooders have so futilely inflicted so many systems upon society, may they finally end where they should have begun: May they reject all systems, and try liberty; for liberty is an acknowledgement of faith in God and His works.

GOLD

Some lasting thing that men might keep without spoiling, and
that by mutual consent men would take in exchange for the truly
useful, but perishable supports of life.

—JOHN LOCKE

That is gold which is worth gold.

—GEORGE HERBERT

Gold was not and is not given value by fiat, any more than
cheese or cotton or leather were given value by fiat. It has value
because it serves a vital need. *Nothing can be given value by
fiat.*

—ISABEL PATERSON
THE GOD OF THE MACHINE

An almost hysterical antagonism toward the gold standard is one
issue which unites statists of all persuasions. They seem to sense
that gold and economic freedom are inseparable.

—ALAN GREENSPAN

When we have gold we are in fear; when we have none we are
in danger.

—JOHN RAY

Gold is the only commodity that can fulfill the definition of
money (see MONEY). It is the only truly international medium of
exchange, and over any significant period of time it will prove to be
the best store of value. Despite any government pronouncements to
the contrary, there are over twenty-five hundred years of history to
back these statements.

Gold is the only circulating medium of exchange that does not
represent a liability to its issuer. Unbacked currency (such as Federal

Reserve notes) is always a dubious asset to its holder and a decreasing liability (through inflation) to its issuer. Gold is an asset only to its owner. In short, gold is money, the ultimate medium of exchange. It is the measure of all other prices (especially currency).

People who buy gold today are merely practicing a form of tax revolt by avoiding the inflation tax and the income tax on currency-denominated investments that "earn interest" (see INTEREST RATES). They are willing to hold gold and forfeit "interest income" because (as we saw in BONDS, GOVERNMENT) they know that there is usually no real income from currency interest rates, even before it is further decimated by confiscatory progressive income taxes.

Gold prices can give some indication of how understated government inflation figures really are (see INFLATION, REAL). According to the Dollar Depreciation Index (which was constructed from official government CPI figures using 1940 as the base year), the dollar of 1980 is worth seventeen cents. But using the $35 gold price of 1940 and a 1980 free market price of $420, the dollar of 1980 was worth only 8.3 cents in terms of gold. So, although the dollar has depreciated at an "official" rate of 4.33 percent a year since 1940, in terms of gold, it has depreciated at a rate of 6.02 percent (almost 40 percent higher than the official rate) while prices relative to gold have continued to fluctuate since 1980 (as they always do). These figures indicate that prices (in terms of gold) have actually *fallen* continually as increases in capital formation, productivity, and technology have improved our standard of living. The history of the gold standard supports this fact, as shown in the following table prepared by Robert Triffin for his study "The Evolution of the International Monetary System: Historical Reappraisal and Future Perspective":

Wholesale Price Indexes, 1814 to 1913
(1913 = 100)

YEAR	UNITED STATES	BRITAIN	GERMANY	FRANCE
1814	178	178	129	132
1849	80	90	71	96
1872	133	125	111	124
1896	67	76	71	71
1913	100	100	100	100

While prices did fluctate, the long-term result in each country was *falling* prices over the 100 years on the gold standard. (Imagine 100 years of falling prices if you can.)

Politicians continually tell us we no longer need gold to back our currency, and then they go out and prove that we do. We need gold for the same reason we need locks on our homes and bank vaults— to secure our wealth. Gold is a discipline for elected officials who wish to give away everything that isn't nailed down. It's a guarantee of honest currency, and as long as government believes it can add to the money supply by creating bank credit and printing pieces of paper, it will be necessary to have gold as money. Here are the advantages derived from using gold as the foundation of our currency:

1. Gold makes government inflation impossible because it provides a slowly increasing stock of currency. Thus the value of currency is no longer at the mercy of the Federal Reserve and the politicians.

2. Gold forces government to balance its budget (i.e., cut spending) or to raise direct taxes (which voters can see and understand) instead of using inflation (the creation of currency and credit) as a tax. Since we have seen time and again, through our constant deficits, that no politicians have the nerve to tax us at the level of their spending, a gold-backed currency would effectively lower taxes.

3. Since gold backing provides a stable, honest currency, it tends to provide stable long-term capital markets with low interest rates, and a prosperous economy where production and saving are rewarded and speculation and debt are discouraged.

George Bernard Shaw once gave the following bit of advice to people who must choose between currency and gold:

> You have to choose (as a voter) between trusting to the natural stability of gold and the natural stability of the honesty and intelligence of the members of the government. And, with due respect to these gentlemen, I advise you, as long as the capitalist system lasts, to vote for gold.

To that I would add, don't ever forget the second most important golden rule: "Them that has the gold makes the rules."

GOVERNMENT

The State claims and exercises the monopoly of crime.... It forbids private murder, but itself organizes murder on a colossal scale. It punishes private theft, but itself lays unscrupulous hands on anything it wants, whether the property of citizen or of alien.

—ALBERT JAY NOCK

All government, of course, is against liberty.

—H. L. MENCKEN

To hear some men talk of the government, you would suppose that Congress was the law of gravitation, and kept the planets in their places.

—WENDELL PHILLIPS

Force always attracts men of low morality.

—ALBERT EINSTEIN

Things in our country [or any country] run in spite of government, not by aid of it.

—WILL ROGERS

In general, the art of government consists in taking as much money [currency] as possible from one class of citizens to give to another.

—VOLTAIRE

Government is an association of men who do violence to the rest of us.

—LEO TOLSTOY

Although those in power (in government) would strongly disagree, Tolstoy says everything you need to know about governments, except why they plunder each other and the people they are supposed to protect. The mystery is solved when you view government from the viewpoint of a psychiatrist. Governments, as we shall see, exhibit all the traits of a psychopath. Governments are, for the most part, insane.

M. Scott Peck has written an extraordinary book on mental health called *The Road Less Traveled*. While reading the book, which chronicles many mental health problems (and their solutions), I was struck by the thought that Peck was not only describing mentally ill people, but government as well. One of Peck's premises is that life is difficult, and, in the words of Carl Jung, that, "Neurosis is always a substitute for *legitmate* suffering" (that should and eventually must be endured).

In the same sense, most pain and plunder government inflicts is a substitute for legitimate economic or political suffering. What is taxation, if not an attempt to avoid pain by reaping the rewards of someone else's labor? What is inflation (see INFLATION), if not an attempt to spend wealth that does not exist by embezzling wealth that does? What is the national debt (i.e., endless deficits), if not an attempt to spend wealth that has not been earned? What is government regulation, which permeates every facet of our lives, if not an attempt to play God (delusions of grandeur)? Take government to a panel of psychiatrists, and they will surely recommend that it be committed.

Peck says that a successful life with continuing personal growth can only come from legitimate suffering that must be experienced through four tools of discipline:

> What are these tools, these techniques of suffering, these means of experiencing the pain of problems constructively that I call discipline? There are four: delaying of gratification, acceptance of responsibility, dedication to truth, and balancing. As will be evident, these are not complex tools. . . . Yet presidents and kings will often forget to use them, to their own downfall. The problem lies not in the complexity of these tools but in the will to use them. For they are tools with which pain is confronted rather than avoided, and if one seeks to avoid legitimate suffering [as all governments do], then one will avoid the use of these tools.

Have you ever known government to delay gratification? Look at their budget deficits and waste (see WASTE). Have you ever known government to accept responsibility for the disasters they have caused? Look at inflation, which any dictionary will tell you is caused by government (see INFLATION), but which is treated by government as an act of nature, over which it has no control. Have you ever known government to be dedicated to truth, or to evidence even a nodding acquaintance with reality? Look at Social Security (see SOCIAL SECURITY), which has been bankrupt since its inception. Have you ever seen a time when government was capable of balancing anything other than the demands of special interest groups attempting to use the power of government for their own gains? While the Department of Health is using taxpayer wealth to mount a campaign against smoking, the Department of Agriculture is using it to subsidize tobacco farmers.

And what are the consequences of avoiding legitimate suffering? Are government, the economy, and society (see SOCIETY) exempt from the law of compensation? Peck writes:

> The substitute itself [such as taxation, regulation, inflation, and debt] ultimately becomes more painful than the legitimate suffering it was designed to avoid. The neurosis itself becomes the biggest problem. True to form, many [all politicians] will then attempt to avoid this pain and this problem in turn, building layer upon layer of neurosis [government]. . . . When we avoid the legitimate suffering that results from dealing with [economic] problems, we also avoid the [economic] growth [and prosperity and freedom] that problems demand from us. It is for this reason that in chronic mental illness [government growth] we [the economy] stop growing, we become stuck. And without healing, the human spirit [the economy] begins to shrivel.

It is impossible to deal with the subject of government (or insanity) without discussing evil. Peck offers some meaningful insight into this subject too:

> Truly evil people . . . actively rather than passively avoid extending themselves. They will take any action in their power to protect their own laziness [or public office], to preserve the integrity of their sick self [or the facade of their goodness]. Rather than nurturing others, they will even kill [as governments have done time and again], to escape the pain of their own spiritual growth. As the integrity [or power] of their sick self is threatened by the spiritual [or economic] health of those around them, they will seek by all manner of means to crush and demolish the spiritual [or economic] health that may exist near them. I define evil, then, as the exercise of political power—that is, the imposition of one's will upon others by overt or covert coercion— in order to avoid extending one's self for the purpose of nurturing spiritual [or economic] growth.

Robert Burns wrote the immortal words, "Man's inhumanity to man, Makes countless thousands mourn." Although this is undoubtedly true, man's inhumanity to man becomes insignificant when compared with government's inhumanity to man (which makes countless millions mourn). Was it man who started the two great wars of this century, or was it government? Was it man who slaughtered six million Jews, or was it the Nazi government? Was it man who exterminated twenty million defenseless Russian civilians and sent millions more to rot in *gulags* as slaves, or was it the communist government of Stalin? Was it man who instigated the devastation of Korea and Viet Nam, or was it government? Was it man who shot down an unarmed Korean airliner (which was so quickly and easily forgotten), or was it the Soviet government? Is it man who prevents millions of people from emigrating from communist countries, or is it government? Is it man who stockpiles nuclear weapons, or is it government? Is it man who legally "plunders" the property of other men (see LAW, THE), or is it government? Is it man who corrupts government, or is it government who corrupts man? The list of political crimes suffered by mankind is infinite and grows day by day, but suffice to say, government is largely evil and will become more so as it continues to grow (see GOVERNMENT GROWTH).

Commenting on the potential evil of the state, George Washington warned, "Government is not reason, it is not eloquence—it is force!" Government force is merely the application of state power. Without power, there can be no force. History has shown that government power adheres predictably to the following rules:

1. Government power always lusts for more power and continually usurps it from the people.
2. Government power corrupts, and absolute government power corrupts absolutely. The size of government and the amount of corruption are always directly proportional.
3. Government power is always abused by seizing and perverting the law. And with few exceptions, government always determines what is law.
4. Government power is overcome or held in check only by the application of a stronger power. Government power is never surrendered voluntarily.

Wendell Phillips delivered an excellent summary of the history of government and power:

Let History close the record. Let her show that "on the side of the oppressor [government] there was power"—power "to frame mischief by a law"; that on that side were all the forms of law, and behind these forms, most of the elements of control: wealth, greedy of increase and anxious for order at any sacrifice of principle—priests prophesying smooth things and arrogating to themselves the name of Christianity,—ambition, baptizing itself statesmanship,—and that unthinking patriotism [crowd mentality], child of habit and not of reason, which mistakes government for liberty, and law for justice.

GOVERNMENT, FORMS OF

All socialism involves slavery.

—HERBERT SPENCER

Communism possesses a language which every people can understand—its elements are hunger, envy, and death.

—HEINRICH HEINE

The Fascists cannot argue, so they kill.

—VICTOR MARGUERITTE

The great strength of the totalitarian state is that it forces those who fear it to imitate it.

—ADOLF HITLER

We are going to tax and tax, spend and spend, elect and elect.

—FRANKLIN D. ROOSEVELT

Only a country that is rich and safe can afford to be a democracy, for democracy is the most expensive and nefarious kind of government ever heard of on earth.

—H. L. MENCKEN

Capitalism and communism stand at opposite poles. Their essential difference is this: The communist, seeing the rich man and his fine home, says: "No man should have so much." The capitalist, seeing the same thing, says: "All men should have as much."

—PHELPS ADAMS

In the interest of explaining the way various forms of government function politically and economically, the following examples (based on an old European joke) are presented for your edification:

Socialism	You have two cows; there is an election. The new government takes one of your cows through taxes and gives it to your neighbor. The neighbor knows nothing about livestock so his new cow dies.
Communism	You have two cows; there is a revolution. The new government confiscates both your cows and gives you a small part of the milk they produce. Both cows soon die, but the government is able to get powdered milk on credit from a democratic government.
Fascism	You have two cows; there is a military coup. The new government confiscates both your cows and sells you part of the milk for ration coupons.
Nazism	You have two cows; there is an assassination. The new government confiscates both your cows and shoots you.
New Dealism	You have two cows; there is a depression caused by the government, and then an election. The new government buys your cows with currency it has just printed. It then shoots one cow, hires an unemployed person to milk the other cow, and throws the milk away in order to help raise milk prices.
Democracy	You have two cows; there is a surplus of milk and prices are low. You appeal to the government to subsidize your milk for the "good" of the country. The government enacts your program, raises taxes on its citizens, and buys your milk at inflated prices. It then stores the milk in rented warehouses until it spoils or they can find a communist government to buy it on credit (of course) and at a loss (naturally).
Capitalism	You have two cows. You sell one cow and buy a bull. There is freedom and prosperity.

GOVERNMENT GROWTH

(Or What Do You Get for the Government That Has (Taken) Everything?)

Government is not the doctor. It is the disease.

—H. S. FERNS
THE DISEASE OF GOVERNMENT

"Money is power." Money in your hands is power IN you. In the hands of the Government, it gives the Government power OVER you. Governments never use unlimited money for good. They quickly convert it to unlimited power. And unlimited power in any Government is oppression for all.

—T. COLEMAN ANDREWS

The lust of government is the greatest lust.

—JAMES HARRINGTON

All some folks want is their fair share—and yours.

—ARNOLD GLASOW

Any government big enough to give you anything you want is big enough to take everything you have.

—GERALD R. FORD

Further, political power has a ratchet action; it works only one way, to augment itself. A transfer occurs by which the power cannot be retracted, once it is bestowed.

—ISABEL PATERSON
THE GOD OF THE MACHINE

There is only one major crisis in the world today. It is not an energy crisis, a foreign debt crisis, a Middle East crisis, a deficit crisis, or a nuclear arms crisis. The crisis we face is government: its insanity and growth.

Thomas Jefferson once wrote, "The natural progress of things is for liberty to yield and government to gain ground." History has shown that over any significant period of time, government always grows (see PARKINSON'S LAW and SYSTEMS). The word *government* is only a polite euphemism for power and its growth. Government grows for primarily two reasons. The first is that governments are left to choose their own size since even democracies have no constitutional limit on the size of government. The second reason is given by Albert Einstein:

> The craving for power which characterizes the governing class in *every* nation [my emphasis] is hostile to any limitation of the national sovereignty.

The growth of government is the growth of evil and the death of freedom. It always means more plunder (taxation), oppression, inflation, regulation, corruption, and poverty. In economic terms, the more government, the less prosperity. Albert Jay Nock was well aware of these sad facts and correctly identified the source of state power when he wrote the following (painfully true) passage in *Our Enemy, The State*:

> It is unfortunately none too well understood that, just as the State has no money of its own, so it has no power of its own. All the power it has is what society gives it, plus what it confiscates [steals] from time to time on one pretext or another; there is no other source from which State power can be drawn. Therefore every assumption of State Power, whether by gift [stupidity and gullibility] or seizure, leaves society with so much less power: there is never, nor can be, any strengthening of State power without a corresponding and roughly equivalent depletion of social power [i.e., freedom].

From the following table, we can get some idea of what government growth costs its citizens and the world economy.

Government Growth Versus Growth of Real Per Capita Gross National Product (GNP)

COUNTRY	YEARS	AVERAGE ANNUAL GOVERNMENT GROWTH RATE AS PERCENTAGE OF GNP	AVERAGE ANNUAL REAL PER CAPITA GNP GROWTH
Brazil	1960–79	− 1.41	5.90
Japan	1960–79	− 0.45	5.59
Venezuela	1960–79	− 0.89	4.68
France	1960–78	− 0.50	4.13
West Germany	1960–80	0.57	3.78
Canada	1960–80	2.05	3.47
Australia	1960–80	1.39	2.83
Britain	1960–80	1.78	2.14
United States	1960–80	1.14	1.98
Argentina	1970–78	3.21	− 0.31

Unbelievably, there were some national governments—Brazil, Japan, Venezuela, and France—that actually shrank as a percentage of the gross national product (GNP) *for the periods shown*. Note the real per capita growth rates that were obtained by the countries that were able to shrink their government and thus move down the Laffer curve (see LAFFER CURVE).

It is interesting to ponder what would have happened if the U.S. government had chosen to follow the path of that well-known economic powerhouse Venezuela. In 1960, the government of Venezuela was consuming a hefty 24.7 percent of GNP, while the U.S. government was taking 18.3 percent. By 1980, however, the Venezuelan government's share of GNP had declined to 20.8 percent, but the U.S. government had increased its share to 22.9 percent. (Yet even with a declining share of GNP, the Venezuelan government's expenditures, after adjusting for inflation, were 370 percent higher in 1980 than they had been in 1960.) With its government shrinking *in relative terms* from 1960 to 1980, the Venezuelan economy was able to maintain compounded real per capita growth rate of 4.68 percent, while the United States economy, with its government consuming an ever greater share of GNP and moving up the Laffer curve, managed an anemic per capita growth rate of 1.98 percent over the same period.

Had U.S. government policies allowed the American economy to grow at even the same rate as that of Venezuela, the U.S. GNP would have been more than 68 percent higher in 1980: $4,433.9 billion instead of $2,626.1 billion. And with a GNP of $4,433.9 billion, the U.S. government could have taken only 20 percent (instead of 22.9 percent) of the GNP and have received $886.8 billion (which is $284.7 billion more than the $602.1 billion they actually spent in 1980). They could have delivered a budget with a $223.5 billion surplus, instead of a $61.2 billion deficit!

What do you think a $4.4 trillion GNP, with no budget deficit and federal spending at "only" 20 percent of GNP, would have done for your personal taxes and financial situation? And for inflation, interest rates, the capital markets, stock markets, and real estate markets? The people seeking work (not the "unemployed"; see UNEMPLOYMENT), and the poor? The world economy? Would the U.S. government have been able to spend an extra $284.7 billion? (According to my calculations: $4y$ waste $+ [3.7s$ incompetence $\times 8k$ corruption$/2.6b$ fraud$] - [0.000004234n$ efficiency $- 0.000000001p$ budget cuts$] + [25q$ government salary increases $\times 6.2a$ foreign aid$] + [28.55r$ pork barrel $\times 213.9w$ new foreign loans to communists $+ 987.22rp$ military assistance to Central America$] =$ YES!!)

Lest you think the fact that some countries were able to shrink their governments refutes the argument that government always grows, let's chronicle the present situation in each of the four countries that did shrink their governments. Brazil, which substituted foreign borrowing for taxation, is currently the world's largest foreign debtor. It has no way to repay the loans, except to adopt the traditional political solution to every problem: raise taxes. From 1970 to 1979, Japan's government (see JAPAN, A MODEL) *grew* at an annual rate that would rank it only below Argentina in the table. Venezuela, which also borrowed heavily, is behind on its payments and, thanks to U.S. oil price deregulation, has lost its free ride on the oil boom. And France elected a socialist government to free them from the burden of prosperity (and that requires no further comment).

Moving from the general to the specific, the following table traces the growth of the U.S. government, beginning in 1930:

U.S. Federal Expenditures as a Percentage of
Gross National Product (GNP)
(Dollar Amounts in Billions)

YEAR	GNP *(Dollars)*	FEDERAL EXPENDITURES *(Dollars)*	PERCENTAGE OF GNP
1930	90.7	2.8	3.0
1940	100.0	10.0	10.0
1950	286.5	40.8	14.3
1960	506.5	93.1	18.3
1970	992.7	204.3	20.6
1980	2,631.7	602.1	22.9
1981	2,957.8	689.2	23.3
1982	3,069.3	764.9	24.9
1983	3,304.8	819.7	24.8
1984	3,661.3	879.9	24.0

Note that the major impetus for the growth of the federal government sprang from the *government-induced* depression of the 1930s. During that decade, the U.S. government grew at a compounded yearly rate of 12.79 percent, (which is why the depression essentially lasted until the Second World War), in a futile effort to cure the economic disaster it had caused. Also note that no matter how fast the economy has grown, the government has nearly always been able to grow faster (although the Reagan "tax cuts" have temporarily helped to slow this growth). Even with the "cutting," "slashing," "budget balancing," conservative Ronald Reagan in Washington, the federal government has been growing at an estimated annual rate of 1.24 percent since he took office, as opposed to the rate of 1.06 percent that prevailed from 1970 to 1980. As you can see, it really makes no difference whether the country is being governed by Republicans or Democrats: government still grows (and we experience the "growing pains").

In *The Law and The Profits* C. Northcote Parkinson, the brilliant British historian, accurately traced the negative effects of government growth at all levels—federal, state and local—using his own country as a model.

So far it would seem that there are successive points at which evil results successively appear. With peacetime taxation amounting to over 10 per cent of national income, capital will begin to migrate. If its flight is prevented, whether by circumstances or by legislation, taxes can rise to 20 per cent but against a stiffening opposition which takes the form of tax avoidance and evasion carried to the utmost lengths of determination and skill. Above 20 per cent each tax increase will produce proportionately less. Above 30 per cent [the U.S. cracked this level in 1966, the same year as the real peak in the Dow Jones Industrial Average] the decline in national influence, observable long before to the expert, becomes obvious to the world at large. At 35 per cent there is a visible decline in freedom and stability. At 36 per cent there is disaster, complete and final although not always immediate. Taxation beyond that point, feasible and perhaps necessary in time of war, is lethal in time of peace. Of the taxation precipice, 36 per cent (for most countries) represents the brink.

For anyone who is not one of Eric Hoffer's "true believers" in terms of statism, but is still undecided as to whether government and its growth really are and have been disastrous for mankind, I will leave the following advice that applies to all forms of government:

1. Do not look to an entity that can grow only through greater immorality as a source of morality.
2. Do not look to an entity that can grow only through greater violence and plunder as a source of protection.
3. Do not look to an entity that can grow only by destroying liberty as a source of freedom.

HEALTH INSURANCE, NATIONAL

When a man dies, he does not just die of the disease that he has, he dies of his whole life.

—PÉGUY

The greatest mistake a man can make is to sacrifice health for any other advantage.

—ARTHUR SCHOPENHAUER

The doctor of the future will give no "drugs" but will interest his patients in the care of the human frame, in diet, and in the cause and prevention of human disease.

—THOMAS EDISON

To live by medicine is to live horribly.

—LINNAEUS

The proposed national health insurance program has been floating around Washington for quite some time, but it is so ludicrous that not even a majority of politicians will vote for it. Its support rests on the eternal political confusion between needs and rights (see NEEDS and RIGHTS). When reduced to its simplest form, it is merely another way of avoiding responsibility (see RESPONSIBILITY): People want doctors to take responsibility for making them well, and they want someone else to assume the responsibility for paying for it.

Medical statistics indicate that many people place a very low price on good health. They treat their bodies as something to be abused instead of maintained. The result is that about 70 percent of all health problems are self-induced. In a nation where 80 million people are overweight and 53 million are smokers, that is not too hard to imagine, but there are other contributing factors, such as poor nutrition, alcohol and drug abuse, and sedentary life-styles.

Daniel Rosenblatt gave a perfect description of the attitude that prevails among such people (predominantly poor but certainly spanning the entire spectrum of society) in his article "Barriers to Medical Care for the Urban Poor":

> The body can be seen as simply another class of objects to be worn out but not repaired. Thus teeth are left without dental care, later there is often small interest in dentures, whether free or not. In any event, false teeth may be little used. Corrective eye examinations, even for those people who wear glasses, are often neglected—regardless of clinic facilities. It is as though the middle class [more often] thinks of the body as a machine to be preserved and kept in perfect running... whereas the poor think of the body as having a limited span of utility: to be enjoyed in youth and then, with age and decrepitude, to be suffered and endured stoically.

The United States spent $280 billion on health care in 1981: more than was spent on housing, education, or national defense. Part of the explanation for this huge outlay lies in the fact that 90 percent of all hospital bills are paid by some form of insurance. Since patients don't pay these charges directly, they don't have any incentive to care about the exhorbitant expenses. This lack of incentive leads to a tremendous waste of medical resources. Yet 70 percent of this expense could have been eliminated by better health habits, which would have saved $196 billion in 1981 and produced an even larger benefit of a healthier, happier, and more productive population.

I do not question the right of people to abuse their health because the individual's ownership of his own body is the most basic property right (see PROPERTY RIGHTS) of each person. But the people who work to maintain good health have the right not to pay for the consequences of an involuntary health program that will do nothing but encourage bad health while ensuring lax medical treatment. (Government medical care, like all government services, is of very low quality and thus can be very hazardous to your health! Anyone who thinks differently is invited to visit any Veterans Administration hospital: in the good ones they let you die, and in the bad ones, they kill you.)

In this age of record government deficits and bankruptcy, a forced program of national health insurance has only a fair chance of becoming law, but the next time it comes up in Washington, think of the benefits of turning the responsibility for health care over to the same government that "delivers" the mail and has made Social Security (see SOCIAL SECURITY) what it is today: bankrupt. An ounce of prevention is still worth a pound of cure.

INCOME TAX

The income tax has made more liars out of the American people than golf has. Even when you make a tax form out on the level, you don't know when it's through if you are a crook or a martyr.

—WILL ROGERS

The hardest thing in the world to understand is the income tax.

—ALBERT EINSTEIN

You don't make the poor richer by making the rich poorer.

—WINSTON CHURCHILL

Bad laws are the worst sort of tyranny.

—EDMUND BURKE

The marvel of all history is the patience with which men and women submit to burdens unnecessarily laid upon them by their governments.

—WILLIAM E. BORAH

Our forefathers made one mistake. What they should have fought for was representation without taxation.

—FLETCHER KNEBEL

The income tax "law" (see LAW, THE) is the fountainhead of most government growth. Unless government can plunder the productive effort of its citizens directly, it is destined to remain small.

The method used to implement the income tax exemplifies the foot-in-the-door technique employed by all governments. The tax was first passed in 1861 (to pay for the Civil War) but was abolished in 1872.

It was passed again in 1892 but was declared unconstitutional by the Supreme Court the following year. In 1913 the government decided to rid itself of the burden of dealing with the Constitution by passing the Sixteenth Amendment (at Christmas, when most legislators had gone home), allowing that "The Congress shall have power to lay and collect taxes on incomes from whatever source derived..." and the proverbial foot was in the door.

When the law was first passed (under the theory of divide and conquer), it applied to less than 2 percent of the total population of America (a classic case of ignoring the rights of a small minority— initially taxing only "the rich"—that new income tax laws and inflation eventually converted to a majority). A family paid no tax on income of $4,000 or less. (This amount would equal more than $38,000 in 1982 purchasing power!) The maximum rate was 7 percent at $500,000. (This amount would equal more than $4,750,000 in 1982 purchasing power.)

By 1918, the surtax on four thousand dollars of income had risen from 0 to 6 percent, and the top rate (surprise, surprise) had sky-rocketed to 77 percent, supposedly to pay for World War I.

In 1925, taxes were cut because the war was then well over. The tax rate on four thousand dollars or less of income was cut back to 0 percent, but the top rate was only reduced to 25 percent. (Are you starting to pick up a pattern?) This tax cut did lead to one of the greatest periods of prosperity in United States history (probably *just* another coincidence). Then the government-induced depression bottomed in 1932, and to "help" recover from the worst economic crisis in our history, government raised taxes again. The surtax on a four thousand dollar income was set at 4 percent, while the top rate was increased to 63 percent (thus ensuring an almost permanent depression that required lots more government and government programs).

By 1954 (but accomplished mostly during the earlier leadership of the freedom-loving President Roosevelt), the surtax on a four thousand dollar to six thousand dollar income, now depreciated to *half* its 1940 value, had increased to 22 percent, and the maximum rate stood at 91 percent. (Welcome to Great (?) Britain!)

Since 1963, the maximum income tax rate has been cut twice (see TAX CUTS) to the current level of 50 percent, but government has continued to grow. In 1858 the British politician William Gladstone predicted the many disasters that would soon befall any country that adopted the income tax:

I believe that it does more than any other tax to demoralise and corrupt the people.... So long as you consent, without a special purpose, to levy the income tax as part of the ordinary and permanent revenue of the country, so long it will be vain to talk of economy and effective reduction of expenditure.

INDEXING

There is always an easy solution to every human problem—neat, plausible, and wrong.

—H. L. MENCKEN

To err is human and so is trying to avoid correcting it.

—R. REYCRAFT

Most of us would rather believe in the impossible than attempt the real.

—PAUL VON RINGELHEIM

Every year (as currency depreciation worsens) the cry for indexing grows louder. Economists eagerly point out that countries like Brazil have "solved" their currency problem by indexing virtually every economic statistic to adjust for rates of inflation in excess of 100 percent a year. I can't understand this praise of Brazil, which is currently "rescheduling" its debt (i.e., is bankrupt); nor can I understand the government's desire to emulate the distressing examples these countries have set in many other economic areas.

Indexing is a poor alternative for several reasons. First: every person and price is affected differently by inflation, technology (see TECH-NOLOGY), and market forces (see MARKETS [FREE]); there can be no correct adjustments, only approximations. If computer prices were adjusted only for inflation over the past twenty years, no one could afford them. Second: it would be a bureaucrat's dream and a businessman's nightmare (just what we need, more people figuring out what the correct price should be). Third: official government inflation figures are understated (see INFLATION, REAL), and currency depreciation adjustments can be made only after the fact, thus always keeping people one step behind inflation. Fourth: by indexing, we institutionalize *inflation* as an economic policy (instead of the politicians and bureaucrats who got us into this mess).

Indexing treats the symptom or effect (price increases) instead of the disease (inflation). It reminds me of a line from a Woody Allen movie: "I used to be a heroin addict, but now I'm a methadone addict" (Washington's idea of great progress). Besides, all the really important things, like bureaucrats' salaries and government pensions, are already indexed (these inflation adjustments should be stopped). We should not expect adjustments for currency depreciation in such trivial items as income taxes and government bonds.

Indexing merely admits that currency is now *officially* a depreciating asset, and most of us already know that. No system in existence that adjusts for inflation even comes close to the benefits derived from stopping it. The answer to inflation is to restore money (see MONEY) to our economic system—not to index currency.

INFLATION

The first panacea for a mismanaged nation is inflation of the currency; the second is war. Both bring a temporary [and false] prosperity; both bring a permanent ruin. But both are the refuge of political and economic opportunities.

—ERNEST HEMINGWAY

The way to crush the bourgeoisie is to grind them between the millstones of taxation and inflation.

—VLADIMIR LENIN

The stamping of paper is an operation so much easier than the laying of taxes, that a government, in the practice of paper emissions, would rarely fail, in any such emergency [such as an election], to indulge itself too far in the employment of that resource. . . .

—ALEXANDER HAMILTON

Inflation is repudiation.

—CALVIN COOLIDGE

Inflation is the one form of taxation which even the weakest government can enforce, when it can enforce nothing else.

—LEAGUE OF NATIONS
Report on European Inflations
of the 1920s

There is much confusion about what inflation is and is not. Predictably, all this confusion comes from economists and Washington. They would like you to think inflation is price increases that are tied to the unfathomable complexities of the economy and can only be understood and dealt with (through wage and price controls and other forms of coercion) by "experts." This is a classic example of confusing cause and effect. Here is the definition of inflation:

Inflation: undue expansion or increase of the currency of a country, especially by the issuing of paper notes or bank credits not redeemable in specie (gold or silver)

Now that we know what inflation is, we also know what it is not:

1. High prices: price increases are a symptom of inflation, not a cause. There was a large amount of inflation during the 1920s that did not cause a general price increase because it was offset by growing production and productivity (see INFLATION, REAL).
2. High interest rates (see INTEREST RATES).
3. OPEC price increases (see OIL AND GAS).
4. Union wage demands or increases (see WAGES).
5. Prices charged by large corporations.
6. Temporary shortages leading to temporary higher prices (this is just the law of supply and demand).
7. Low productivity of labor or capacity utilization of plant and equipment (see PRODUCTIVITY).

Remember: OPEC doesn't print our currency or determine the growth rate of the "money supply," unions don't set bank reserve requirements, and big business doesn't determine our deficit spending. These problems bear the same mark as most others: MADE IN WASHINGTON. As the definition clearly indicates, the entity in control of the currency and credit, the Federal Reserve Bank, determines how much inflation we shall have.

If you wish to track U.S. inflation accurately, I suggest you go directly to the source by watching the monthly increases in the "money supply." M2 is probably the best indicator. Whether prices go up, down, or sideways, the "money supply" is the measure of real inflation (see INFLATION, REAL). In spite of any and all economists' theories to the contrary, it really is that simple.

INFLATION, A HISTORY

All politicians have read history; but one might say that they read it only in order to learn from it how to repeat the same calamities all over again.

—PAUL VALÉRY

The worst thing about history is that every time it repeats itself, the price goes up.

—PILLAR

Human history becomes more and more a race between education and catastrophe.

—H. G. WELLS

The history of the great events of this world are scarcely more than the history of crimes.

—VOLTAIRE

Inflation, through the debasement of coinage or the printing of paper, has been with man since money (see MONEY) was invented and monopolized by governments. Although it is true that there have been long periods in which prices remained stable, these were merely a reflection of the fact that money (gold and silver), rather than unbacked paper currency, was being used as the medium of exchange.

The first recorded incidence of inflation involved the clipping of coins to reduce the weight of the gold and silver they contained. This theft was very obvious and the people quickly caught on to the process—until paper currency was invented. With this new medium of exchange, and the development of central banks, governments were in a position to secretly expropriate large amounts of wealth from their citizens. The blame for this loss could be placed on the productive segment of the economy, which "continually raised prices" to offset the loss from depreciating currency.

The government's fraud could have continued indefinitely, except for one problem: as the currency depreciates so does the society (see SOCIETY) that uses it. As Edgar Queeny wrote:

> The uprisings of 1789 cost Louis XVI some prerogatives, but four years later a valueless currency cost him his head. Germany's inflation of the 1920s laid the foundation upon which Hitler built. Indeed, a runaway inflation is the goal of revolutionists. The maxim of that apostle of revolution, Lenin, was "Debauch the currency!"

Queeny could have added that inflation cost Great Britain her position as the most powerful nation in the world, and it will do the same to America.

The most important thing to remember is that when currency has been substituted for money, inflation has generally been the *rule* and not the exception. By studying consumer prices, it is fairly easy to see whether money or currency was circulating in the United States from 1800 to 1981:

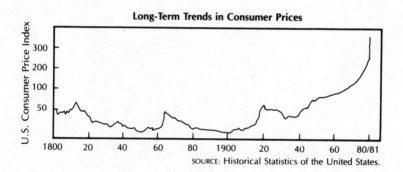

Long-Term Trends in Consumer Prices

SOURCE: Historical Statistics of the United States.

Until governments again issue money, inflation will be the rule, barring a deflationary accident, for the foreseeable future. Since 1939, the United States has had only two years in which our currency did not "officially" lose purchasing power.

Daniel Webster was well aware of the danger of inflation when he made the following statement:

> Our own history has recorded for our instruction enough, and more than enough of the demoralizing tendency, the injustice, and the in-

tolerable oppression on the virtuous and well disposed, of a degraded paper currency, authorized by law, or in any way countenanced by government [as it always is].

They were warned; the warning was ignored, and the people, not the politicians, have paid the price and will continue to do so.

INFLATION, REAL

We must always think about things, and we must think about
things as they are, not as they are said to be.

—GEORGE BERNARD SHAW

Fraud is the homage that force pays to reason.

—CHARLES P. CURTIS

Truth always lags behind, limping along on the arm of Time.

—BALTASAR GRACIAN

Tell the truth and run.

—ANONYMOUS

In a world where *money* (not currency; see MONEY) is used as
the medium of exchange, savings rates are high; interest rates and
taxes are low; thus capital investment and productivity are high. These
conditions lead to the inherent economies of large-scale production.
When this is coupled with the inventions and discoveries (see TECH-
NOLOGY) that spring from free economies, it can only lead to an
economy with continually falling prices. Let that thought sink into
your mind: continually falling prices.

Evidence to support this fact is everywhere you look, although it
is usually distorted by currency depreciation. For instance, transistor
radios have fallen in price from more than $100 when introduced, to
less than $10 today, for a vastly superior product. What was $1 million
worth of computer power in 1960 can now be had for less than $50.
A long-distance (Bell) phone call from New York to San Francisco
that cost $2.25 in 1960, cost $1.30 in 1979 (even though it was
supplied by a government-imposed monopoly that freely admitted that
high long-distance profits were used to subsidize local service). Other
long-distance companies were even cheaper. The list of similar examples is almost infinite.

But what is most amazing is that all these price declines came in spite of a dollar that, according to the government's own CPI figures, had lost almost two-thirds of its purchasing power from 1960 to 1980. That is the power of an economy that is even *semi*-free to deliver a higher standard of living.

With this in mind, we now know beyond a reasonable doubt that official government inflation figures are vastly understated for several reasons. First, they are understated because they do not reflect declines in quality and service. (Do you think that pumping your own gas at $1.20 per gallon now is the same as having someone do it for you and servicing your car for $.30 per gallon, as was the case many years ago?) Second, the official CPI does not even include the increase of taxes as a cost of living. From 1960 to 1980, taxes went up 637 percent while the CPI increased "only" 278 percent. But by far the major fallacy of government inflation figures is that they are based on the premise that prices should at best remain stable, not decline.

A far better inflation index can be constructed by taking the government inflation figures and adding productivity gains or subtracting productivity losses (see PRODUCTIVITY). The productivity rate seems to be a very close approximation of the amount that prices would have increased or fallen in an economy without currency depreciation, but also keep in mind the fact that government policies tremendously hamper increases in the nation's productivity. The following table shows the real rate of inflation:

Real Inflation
(Inflation Rate + Change In Productivity)

YEAR	INFLATION RATE (CPI) *(Percentage)*	CHANGE IN PRODUCTIVITY *(Percentage)*	REAL INFLATION *(Percentage)*
1960	1.6	1.6	3.2
1961	1.0	1.7	2.7
1962	1.1	5.5	6.6
1963	1.2	4.3	5.5
1964	1.3	6.0	7.3
1965	1.7	6.8	8.5
1966	2.9	5.5	8.4
1967	2.9	2.2	5.1
1968	4.2	5.1	9.3
1969	5.4	2.9	8.3

1970	5.9	− 0.8	5.1
1971	4.3	3.0	7.3
1972	3.3	6.6	9.9
1973	6.2	6.6	12.8
1974	11.0	− 1.9	9.1
1975	9.1	− 1.9	7.2
1976	5.8	6.3	12.1
1977	6.5	6.3	12.8
1978	7.7	4.7	12.4
1979	11.3	2.8	14.1
1980	13.5	− 0.8	12.7
1981	10.4	1.9	12.3

With this new index, the inflation rate takes on an even less friendly face. From 1960 thru 1981, the offical inflation rate (increase in the CPI) averaged 5.38 percent, while the real inflation rate averaged 8.76 percent, or 3.38 percent higher.

In looking for a confirming statistic that would back up my theory, I discovered that from 1960 to 1981, M2 (a broader measure of the supply of *currency and credit* than the narrow M1 figure) had increased at an average of 8.68 percent. This figure was 3.33 percent higher than the average rate of increase for M1, which is an even closer measure of the government's official inflation figures, as reflected in the misnamed consumer price index.

Now it should be easier to believe that inflation is an increase in the supply of currency and credit, and that the government has not only embezzled, at the very least, 85 percent of the value of the dollar since 1940 (as measured by their own CPI figures), but has also denied us the value, in the form of much *lower* prices, that capitalism would have bestowed through greater capital formation, technology, and productivity.

And before you get too excited or encouraged by the relatively new "low" rates of increase (i.e., rates of embezzlement) in the CPI, remember that although the increase in consumer prices was "only" 4.3 percent for 1984, the estimated gain in productivity was 8.8 percent, making the real rate of inflation 13.1 percent, and M2 grew at approximately 8.2 percent.

INTEREST RATES

Interest is the birth of money from money [not currency].

—ARISTOTLE

We have heard it said that five percent is the natural interest of money [not currency].

—THOMAS MACAULEY

It is always better policy to earn an interest than to make a thousand pounds.

—ROBERT L. STEVENSON

He shall alter his contract-tablet and he shall not pay the interest for that year.

—HAMMURABI

Real (see REAL [REALLY]) interest rates are the cost of renting money (see MONEY). They are also an excellent indication of the health of an economy and society (see SOCIETY). The higher the rates, the sicker and less stable the society. Low or negative real rates of interest indicate an economy that is consuming its savings because of the lack of incentives to save. Once savings are depleted and the economy becomes illiquid, the inevitable consequence is a high real rate of interest. In a healthy economy, real rates will, as in any market, ebb and flow with supply and demand pressures, but in the American economy the return on money (not currency) loaned to a prime credit risk has rarely exceeded 3 percent.

Currency loans in a sick economy are an entirely different matter for both lenders and borrowers. The lenders of currency must attempt to set a rate that will allow for the *inevitable decline* in value of the currency, and a risk premium for the uncertainties of a declining economy, plus a real rate of return. (We could call this the "interflation" rate.) With chronic inflation (there is no other kind), lenders rarely have a chance of getting a real return because rates are initially held down by the increasing supply of currency and credit (although this has the long-term effect of forcing both prices and interest rates to rise), and by government price controls on the interest that can be paid by financial institutions. But even when the free market begins to set rates, the biggest obstacle in obtaining a real rate of return on loans is the steeply progressive income taxes that must be paid with no consideration for the loss of purchasing power.

In the early stages of inflation, the lender is usually able to keep up with the low rates of currency depreciation, but once inflation reaches about 3 percent, the after-tax yields in the 50 percent bracket become negative. At this point most lenders are paying taxes for the "privilege" of losing purchasing power. When inflation surpasses 10 percent, real interest rates can temporarily produce negative yields, even before income taxes. The following table shows the "progress" of a man who continued to "invest" $1 million in ninety-day government Treasury Bills over a twenty-five year period, from 1960 to 1984:

Real Return on $1 Million Invested in Three-Month Treasury Bills 1960–1984
(Assuming Investor Is in the 50 Percent Tax Bracket)

YEAR	AVERAGE YIELD (Percentage)	INFLATION RATE (Percentage)	REAL YIELD (Percentage)	REAL AFTER-TAX YIELD (Percentage)	PURCHASING POWER OF $1 MILLION INVESTMENT (Dollar)
1960	2.928	1.6	1.328	−0.1360	998,640.00
1961	2.378	1.0	1.378	0.1890	1,000,527.40
1962	2.778	1.1	1.678	0.2890	1,003,419.00
1963	3.157	1.2	1.957	0.3785	1,007,216.90
1964	3.549	1.3	2.249	0.4745	1,011,996.10
1965	3.954	1.7	2.254	0.2770	1,014,799.40
1966	4.881	2.9	1.981	−0.4595	1,010,136.40
1967	4.321	2.9	1.421	−0.7395	1,002,666.40
1968	5.339	4.2	1.139	−1.5305	987,320.60
1969	6.677	5.4	1.277	−2.0615	966,966.98
1970	6.458	5.9	0.558	−2.6710	941,139.29
1971	4.348	4.3	0.048	−2.1260	921,130.67
1972	4.071	3.3	0.771	−1.2645	909,482.98
1973	7.041	6.2	0.841	−2.6795	885,113.38
1974	7.886	11.0	−3.114	−7.0570	822,650.93
1975	5.838	9.1	−3.262	−6.1810	771,802.87
1976	4.989	5.8	−0.811	−3.3055	746,290.93
1977	5.265	6.5	−1.235	−3.8675	717,428.13

1978	7.221	7.7	−0.479	−4.0895	688,088.91
1979	10.041	11.3	−1.259	−6.2795	644,880.38
1980	11.506	13.5	−1.994	−7.7470	594,921.48
1981	14.077	10.4	3.677	−3.3615	574,923.19
1982	10.686	6.1	4.586	−0.7570	570,571.02
1983	8.630	3.2	5.430	1.1150	576,932.88
1984	9.580	4.3	5.280	0.4900	579,759.85

Note that not only did the government not allow any return on his "investment," but it also confiscated almost half of his capital through "income" taxes and inflation (even according to their own understated inflation statistics). (Think his dream is coming due?)

Borrowers, however, can turn savers' losses into their gains, especially if they are in high tax brackets. In the early stages of inflation, the borrower is usually forced to pay a positive real rate of interest, even if he is in the 50 percent income tax bracket. But when currency depreciation reaches about 3 percent (assuming a 50 percent tax rate), the borrower begins to enjoy negative real interest rate costs (i.e., he is paid to borrow currency if he can place it in assets that keep pace with inflation). However, this incentive inevitably leads to low rates of saving (see SAVING), high debt, illiquidity (see LIQUIDITY), and eventually high *real* rates of interest. The following table shows that borrowers in the 50 percent or higher tax brackets reached the "free borrowed currency" stage in 1966, (and they stayed there every year through 1981):

Real Borrowing Costs for People in the 50% Tax Bracket

YEAR	PRIME RATE (*Percentage*)	INFLATION RATE (*Percentage*)	REAL PRIME RATE (*Percentage*)	AFTER-TAX REAL INTEREST COST (*Percentage*)
1960	4.82	1.6	3.22	0.81
1961	4.50	1.0	3.50	1.25
1962	4.50	1.1	3.40	1.20
1963	4.50	1.2	3.30	1.15
1964	4.50	1.3	3.20	1.10
1965	4.54	1.7	2.84	0.57
1966	5.63	2.9	2.73	−0.09
1967	5.61	2.9	2.71	−0.10
1968	6.30	4.2	2.10	−1.05
1969	7.96	5.4	2.56	−1.42

1970	7.91	5.9	2.01	− 1.95
1971	5.72	4.3	1.42	− 1.44
1972	5.25	3.3	1.95	− 0.68
1973	8.03	6.2	1.83	− 2.19
1974	10.81	11.0	− 0.19	− 5.60
1975	7.86	9.1	− 1.24	− 5.17
1976	6.84	5.8	1.04	− 2.38
1977	6.83	6.5	0.33	− 3.09
1978	9.06	7.7	1.36	− 3.17
1979	12.67	11.3	1.37	− 4.97
1980	15.27	13.5	1.77	− 5.86
1981	18.87	10.4	8.47	− 0.97
1982	14.86	6.1	8.76	1.33
1983	10.79	3.2	7.59	2.19
1984	12.04	4.3	7.74	1.72

The obvious beneficiaries of negative after-tax borrowing costs (other than the government) were those with highly leveraged investments, like real estate (see REAL ESTATE), which seemed to turn into wealth machines. The obvious losers were savers and, thus, the long-run health of the economy. But in 1979 two things began to happen:

1. The economy had become very illiquid because of the unlimited demand for free borrowed currency, and savers had gone on strike by refusing to lend for negative rates of return; instead, they began buying gold (real money), diamonds, or anything else the government couldn't print.
2. The market (see MARKETS [FREE]) found a way to circumvent government price controls on savings "investments," such as money market funds, (which you now know are really currency market funds), and soon interest rates again provided a real return, at least before income taxes.

These events brought an end, at least temporarily, to the era of "leveraged appreciation." The replacement became leveraged bankruptcy.

Any discussion of interest rates would be incomplete without considering the "high" interest rates of the late 1970s and early 1980s. "High" interest rates, whether "real" or merely a reflection of inflation, are nearly always an infallible indication of big government and, as previously mentioned, a signal of serious trouble for an economy. Politicians and bureaucrats are puzzled by high interest rates (though, for some reason, not by taxing and spending programs, deficits, or national debts). Anyone who understands markets or can comprehend the tables in this section must be puzzled only by why interest rates were not higher.

In short, currency interest rates are ruled by four factors:

1. *Supply and demand for loans* (i.e., liquidity of the economy): Since inflation encourages the flight from currency to more tangible assets and high debt, the economy becomes less and less liquid as the borrowing "needs" of government, business, and consumers become even greater. When government temporarily "fights" inflation by reducing the rate of growth of currency and credit, it forces interest rates higher until the economy can adjust to the new short-term policies through recession.

2. *The current rate of currency depreciation and future expectations:* Although inflation periodically recedes when the Federal Reserve "gets religion," financial markets have very good memories. From 1960 to 1980, every bounce upward from these periods of lower inflation has come from higher levels. The government will have to forgive savers for not rushing out to buy bonds after being defrauded for the past thirty-six years (see BONDS) as they watched bond prices collapse (even before allowing for currency depreciation), and "high yields" continue getting higher.

3. *Risk to the lender:* Government growth and inflation lead to a sickening economy. This increases uncertainty, volatility, and risk. When the "firmly tenative" economic policies of government shift to *temporarily* "fighting inflation," the rate of present and expected currency depreciation added by the lender is merely replaced by a "bankruptcy (risk) premium," as an illiquid economy and falling prices inflict huge losses on corporations, borrowers, businesses, and investors who bet on continuing inflation. Business failures in autos, housing, and energy, coupled with the realization that loans to socialist governments will have to be "rescheduled," add to everyone's borrowing cost.

4. *The tax rate on savings:* The government doesn't seem to understand that savers don't save for pretax returns. Every penny of loss taken by the investor (speculator?) with the $1 million in Treasury Bills, for example, went to the government in the form of income taxes or inflation gains. Taxes (both income and inflation) are the only overhead savers have. Lower both taxes

permanently (by shrinking the size of government) and saving rates will rise, bringing interest rates down.

Armed with these facts, we can return to the preceding tables of interest rates and make some interesting (forgive the pun) observations after adjusting for inflation. For instance, we see that the highest *real* Treasury Bill rate between 1960 and 1980 was not the 11.506 percent of 1980, but the 3.954 percent rate of 1965! We also see that the highest *real* prime rate between 1960 and 1980 was not the 15.27 percent of 1980, but the 4.5 percent of 1961! True, 1981 set new records for both rates, but for anyone in the 50 percent tax bracket after-tax yields and borrowing costs *were still negative* even then.

Here are some questions for anyone who thinks interest rates have been too high:

1. Are they too high before or after tax? (See the table showing the Treasury Bill "investment.")
2. Did you cry out in righteous indignation against rates being *too low* when real Treasury Bill rates went to negative after-tax yields in 1966 or negative pretax yields in the years 1974 through 1980?
3. How negative should yields be to encourage saving? (You can only borrow what has been saved.)

If our economy is ever to reliquify and our capital stock to resume a healthy growth, *real* rates of interest are going to have to stay high to encourage people to save depreciating currency under our existing tax law. And since inflation is not going to be stopped voluntarily by government, the basic trend of currency interest rates will probably continue to remain up, as it has for the past forty years.

The dream of encouraging saving with negative yields and free borrowed currency through continual inflation has come due.

INVESTMENT

We are all dependent upon the investment of capital.

—WILLIAM H. TAFT

We will never have real safety and security for the wage earners unless we provide for safety and security for the wage payers and wage savers [investors]. . . .

—WILLIAM J. H. BOETCKER

A broker is a man who runs your fortune into a shoestring.

—ALEXANDER WOOLLCOTT

Investment is the outlay of *money* for income or appreciation. Increasing long-term investment is the *only* road to a higher standard of living because, as economies advance and become more complex, more capital must be allocated for projects with longer time horizons.

Since government has substituted unbacked currency (i.e., guaranteed inflation) for money (see MONEY), investment has, in reality, ceased to exist. There is no way to "invest" currency for a return because, although all currency loses its value, no one can predict the amount of depreciation that a currency will experience, i.e., the amount of purchasing power that will be plundered by government. Therefore, one cannot know whether the fixed return of debt instruments (such as mortgages; see REAL ESTATE), or the projected return of equity ventures, will provide a real (see REAL) return on capital. Because the uncertainty of value lost by currency increases over time, time horizons for capital commitment (both debt and equity) must shorten drastically. Thus, as money is replaced by currency, saving (see SAVING) and long-term investment are replaced by consumption and short-term speculation (see SPECULATION), with dire long-term consequences for the economy (see MOMENTUM). The dream of "investment" without money will eventually come due.

JAPAN, A MODEL

Prosperity destroys fools and endangers the wise.

—GEORGE HERBERT

We [governments] are corrupted by prosperity.

—TACITUS

We call Japanese soldiers fanatics when they die rather than surrender, whereas American soldiers who do the same thing are heroes.

—ROBERT MAYNARD HUTCHINS

The quest to discover Japan's formula for economic growth is a popular endeavor today. Surprisingly, it is not a deep secret of the Orient, nor is it a mystery (to anyone other than a politician, bureaucrat, or Keynesian economist). Japan does not represent an *economic* challenge to America, but rather a *political* challenge.

From 1960 to 1980, Japan's real compounded growth in GNP per capita was 5.59 percent. The United States', by contrast, was 1.98 percent. The following table reveals the main reason for this growth:

Growth of Government and Gross National Product

COUNTRY	GOVERNMENT SPENDING AS PERCENTAGE OF GNP		COMPOUND GOVERNMENT GROWTH RATE AS PERCENTAGE OF GNP, 1969–1979	REAL COMPOUND GROWTH PER CAPITA GNP, 1960–1980
	1960	1979		
JAPAN	15.24	13.99	−0.45	5.59
U.S.	18.20	21.06	0.77	1.98

Japan's federal government took 15.24 percent of her GNP in 1960, but in 1979 took only 13.99 percent or 8 percent less. These figures show that the Japanese government's share of GNP for that period was *shrinking* at an annual rate of 0.45 percent, thus moving the economy down the Laffer curve (see LAFFER CURVE) because of meaningful tax reductions that were being made each and every year.

Meanwhile, in our corner of the world, the federal government took 18.20 percent of GNP in 1960, and in 1979, mainly because of inflation, took 21.06 percent, or 15 percent more. This means that the U.S. government's share of GNP was growing at an annual rate of 0.77 percent. And in 1981 the Fed's share was 23 percent. (Weren't those Reagan spending cuts something?)

Had the U.S. government consumed the same share of GNP as Japan's did in 1979, we could have had a $142 billion (with a *b*) tax cut *and* a balanced budget. Consider the effect of a balanced federal budget and $142 billion left in the private sector of the economy, and tell me Japan is an economic challenge.

With a smaller government (i.e., lower taxes), a policy of constant tax cuts for the past twenty years, and virtually no taxes on dividends or interest, Japan has the highest savings rate in the industrialized world. With this huge pool of savings, their capital formation per capita is twice that of the United States.

Unfortunately, though, Japan also has a dream coming due. Its democracy has reached a point of prosperity where the malignancy of envy, and thus government growth, is now starting to show. From 1960 to 1970, the Japanese government's share of GNP *declined* at an annual rate of 2.82 percent and the real per capita GNP was growing at an astounding 9.32 percent per year, but from 1970 to 1979, the government's share of GNP *grew* at an annual rate of 2.26 percent, and the yearly growth of real per capita GNP fell to 3.56 percent per year. (From 1970 to 1979, the U.S. government's share of GNP was growing at less than 0.4 percent a year.) If Japan's government holds that rate of growth, it will match the U.S. government's current share of GNP by the end of this century. Using history as a guide, I expect the Japanese government's share of GNP soon to be growing in excess of 3 percent a year, as the U.S. government's did from 1951 to 1960.

It is astonishing that in the convoluted world of governments, Japan is using the United States as a model, instead of the other way around. But as Seneca said, and the Japanese are currently proving, "We become wiser by adversity; prosperity destroys our appreciation of the right." The government of Japan and other democracies would do much better if they followed the advice of Confucius: "When prosperity comes, do not use [steal] all of it."

LAFFER CURVE

If you tax too high, the revenue will yield nothing.

—RALPH WALDO EMERSON

It requires a very unusual mind to make an analysis of the obvious.

—A. N. WHITEHEAD

New opinions are always suspected and usually opposed, for no other reason than because they are not already common.

—JOHN LOCKE

Facts are stubborn things.

—ALAN RENÉ LE SAGE

Practical politics consists in ignoring the facts.

—HENRY ADAMS

The more precarious the state of a nation's economy at election time, the stronger the temptations for politicians to make "redistribution" their main plank, even when they know how little margin is left for redistributive measures and, worse still, how likely they are to retard economic growth.

—HELMUT SHOECK
ENVY: A THEORY OF SOCIAL BEHAVIOR

What a prosperous place the world would be if politicians could understand and live with this truth: There are always two tax rates—

one high and one low—that will yield the same government revenue. The Laffer curve was first drawn in 1974 by economist Arthur Laffer, but even after several years few people have heard of it and even fewer understand it.

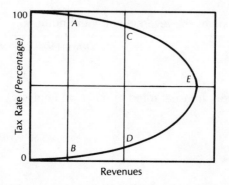

The basic idea of this drawing is irrefutable: if the tax rate is zero, government revenues will be zero. If the tax rate is 100 percent, government revenues will still be zero, because no one will work if everything he earns is confiscated. Since it is obvious that revenues will increase as the tax rate leaves zero and moves to point E (the bottom side of the curve), it should also be obvious that from point E to a 100 percent tax rate (the top side of the curve), revenue must decline as tax rates become prohibitive, and destroy incentives to be productive and take risks. (It is interesting to see this theory at work in federal tax receipts for 1962, when the maximum tax rate was still a modest 91 percent. Tax rates in excess of 50 percent brought in only 1.9 percent of total revenues; rates over 65 percent supplied only 0.6 percent; while rates above 75 percent yielded a whopping *0.2 percent.*)

One can quickly see which side of the curve a country is on. If it is on the top of the curve, a *real* tax cut (as opposed to the government's recent tax increase disguised as a tax cut; see TAX CUTS) will ultimately bring in more revenue; if it is on the bottom side of the curve, a tax cut will temporarily decrease the government's revenue but will stimulate economic growth and eventually bring in more revenue, as well as an increased standard of living for the people. (When the maximum tax rate on long-term capital gains was cut from about 49 percent to 28 percent in the late 1970s, federal treasury "experts" estimated that it would "cost" the Treasury at least $2 billion in the fiscal year following the cut. Instead, it *added* almost $2 billion to government revenues, greatly enriching the economy at the same time.)

Guess which side of the curve the United States (and most other countries in the world) is on (no prompting, Tip). (It's so hard to steal intelligently.)

LAW, THE

The state calls its own violence law, but that of the individual crime.

—MAX STIRNER
THE EGO AND HIS OWN

Modern demagogues carry favor with the people by confiscating large amounts of property through the medium of the law courts.

—ARISTOTLE

It is a besetting vice of democracies to substitute public opinion for law. This is the usual form in which masses of men exhibit their tyranny.

—JAMES FENIMORE COOPER

We may define "right" (i.e., law) as the might of a community. Yet, it, too, is nothing else than violence . . . it is the communal, not individual, violence that has its way.

—SIGMUND FREUD

It is legal because I wish it.

—LOUIS XIV

In 1850 Frederic Bastiat wrote the most complete and concise book ever published on the laws of mankind. *The Law* contains all the knowledge men ever need to know to establish just laws; it is a very short book. And naturally, it has been totally ignored by every government in the world.

Note Bastiat's introduction and remember he wrote it more than one hundred years ago:

The law perverted! And the police powers of the state along with it! The law, I say, not only turned from its proper purpose but made to follow an entirely contrary purpose! The law become the weapon of every greed! Instead of checking crime, the law itself guilty of the evils it is supposed to punish!

According to Bastiat there are two types of plunder: illegal (criminal) and "legal" (government). Any time wealth is tranferred from the person who owns it—without his free choice or consent and without compensation—to any other entity, then an act of plunder has been committed.

Many problems of democracies today stem from the confusion between "laws" and justice, but Bastiat clarifies such confusion.

There is in all of us a strong disposition to believe that anything lawful is also legitimate. This belief is so widespread that many persons have erroneously held that things are "just" because law makes them so. Thus, in order to make plunder appear just and sacred to many consciences, it is only necessary for the law to decree and sanction it. Slavery, restrictions, and monopoly find defenders not only among those who profit from them but also among those who suffer from them.

And how do you separate just law from legal plunder? Again, we have only to look to Bastiat:

But how is legal plunder to be identified? Quite simply. See if the law takes from some persons what belongs to them, and gives it to other persons to whom it does not belong. See if the law benefits one citizen at the expense of another by doing what the citizen himself cannot do without committing a crime.

Bastiat warns that the sole purpose of the law is to protect property rights (see PROPERTY RIGHTS) by preventing injustice. Do not ask the law to produce what it does not contain: wealth, science, religion, education, charity, or fraternity. And Bastiat closes with a final warning that became an unfortunate prophecy:

The mission of the law is not to oppress persons and plunder them of their property, even though the law may be acting in a philanthrope spirit. Its mission is to protect persons and property. . . . If you exceed this proper limit—if you attempt to make the law religious, fraternal, equalizing, philanthropic, industrial, literary, or artistic—you will then be lost in an uncharted territory, in vagueness and uncertainty, in a forced utopia, or, even worse, in a multitude of utopias, each striving to seize the law and impose it upon you. This is true because fraternity and philanthropy, unlike justice, do not have precise limits. Once started, where will you stop? And where will the law stop itself?

The answer to Bastiat's last question is that the "law" (government) will never stop itself. Freud once observed that "The State has never shown any disposition to suppress crime, but only to safeguard its own monopoly of crime." True to this form, governments debate each day about which new type of plunder will be passed as "law" (see LEG-ISLATION). We have arrived at the point where people believe that voting creates just laws, and any law can be changed at the whim of the next legislature. Herbert Spencer faced the same problem in the last century when he had the following conversation with a member of the British Parliament:

I asked one of their members of Parliament whether a majority of the House could legitimize murder. He said, No. I asked him whether it could sanctify robbery. He thought not. But I could not make him see that if murder and robbery are intrinsically wrong, and not to be made right by decisions of statesmen, that similarly all actions must be either right or wrong, apart from the authority of the law; and that if the right and wrong of the law are not in harmony with this intrinsic right and wrong, the law itself is criminal.

And what examples do we have of illegal laws and the whims of legislatures changing from one day to the next? They are infinite. Today liquor is illegal, but tomorrow it is legal. Today it is illegal to own gold (money), but tomorrow it is legal. In this industry "price fixing" is legal, but in that industry it is an antitrust violation. Today gold and silver are money, but tomorrow paper notes and copper slugs are "legal tender." Today the maximum legal income tax rate is 94 percent, but tomorrow the maximum legal tax rate is "only" 50 percent. Today the "legal price" for oil is eight dollars per barrel, but tomorrow the "legal price" is thirty-four dollars per barrel. Today there are still over twenty legal prices for the same amount of natural gas, but tomorrow, who knows? As Tacitus said, "When the state is corrupt then the laws are most multiplied."

It is said the ancient Greeks used a simple method to stop the multiplication of "laws." Perhaps we should try it on our Congress.

Anyone wishing to propose a new law had to do so while standing on a public platform with a rope around his neck. If the law was passed, the rope was removed. If the law was voted down, the platform was removed.

LEGISLATION

No law [legislation] can give power to private persons; every law transfers power from private persons to government.

—ISABEL PATERSON
THE GOD OF THE MACHINE

There is not, never has been, and never will be any substitute for productive work. No amount of legislation, no amount of money, borrowed or coined, no economic prestidigitation, governmental or otherwise, can, as such, increase by one iota the wealth of a nation or the standard of living of a people. Existing wealth or property can be and is being redistributed by law, but new wealth can be created only by men and by man-made machines they guide.

—PHILIP D. REED

Nothing can be proposed so wild or so absurd as not to find a party, and often a very large party, to espouse it.

—CECIL

Good laws lead to the making of better ones; bad ones bring about worse.

—JEAN JACQUES ROUSSEAU

The good Lord set definite limits on man's wisdom, but set no limits on his stupidity—and that's just not fair!

—KONRAD ADENAUER

What is done to-day may be undone tomorrow.

—MAHATMA GANDHI

Laws [legislation] ... are the product of selfishness, deception, and party prejudice. True justice is not in them, and cannot be in them.

—LEO TOLSTOY

Nevertheless, in the inexplicable universal votings and debatings of these Ages, an idea or rather a dumb presumption to the contrary has gone idly abroad; and at this day, over extensive tracts of the world, poor human beings are to be found, whose practical belief it is that if we "vote" this or that, so this or that will thenceforth be.... Practically, men have come to imagine that the Laws of this Universe, like the laws of constitutional countries, are decided by voting.... It is an idle fancy. The Laws of this Universe, of which if the Laws of England are not an exact transcript, they should passionately study to become such, are fixed by the everlasting congruity of things, and are not fixable or changeable by voting!

—ANONYMOUS

An unknown author wrote this more than one hundred years ago, yet nothing has changed. Government still thinks it can change any natural law by voting. Since legislation is subject only to the whims of politicians and is passed and repealed at the drop of a Gallup Poll (like the recent "law" on withholding taxes from interest and dividends), it usually works entirely against individual freedom, and creates a tremendous degree of uncertainty and waste in the economy (e.g., shortened capital commitments, increasing volatility, and misallocation of capital).

One of my favorite examples of the disasters that result from government's stupidity and arrogance is the Employment Act of 1946. This act shows clearly what happens when Congress, an entity that produces nothing except disasters, attempts to legislate control of economic factors that are directed by markets (which produce everything).

The Employment Act of 1946: "It is the continuing policy and responsibility of the Federal government to use all practical [i.e., impractical] means ... to promote employment,

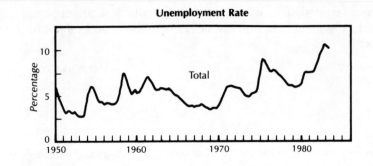

Unemployment Rate

production,

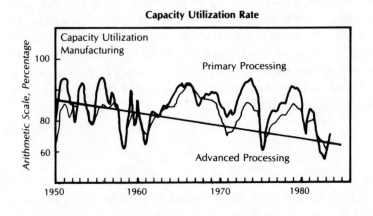

Capacity Utilization Rate

and purchasing power."

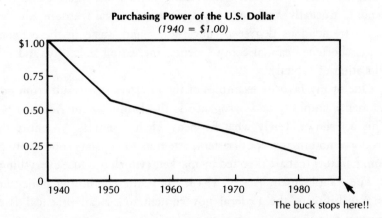

Purchasing Power of the U.S. Dollar
(1940 = $1.00)

The buck stops here!!

Note the "success" of each part of this Act. As can be seen in the charts, the results of government interference are always predictably consistent: abject failure with severe consequences for the people the legislation was supposed to protect. As Will Rogers once remarked, "When I make a joke, nobody's injured; when Congress makes a joke, it's a law."

Apparently, markets don't realize the potential consequences of ignoring legislation, and Congress still does not (and will probably never) realize the futility of voting jokes into "law." They might as well try to suspend the law of gravity. If only they could grasp the truth of this statement by Herbert Spencer:

> And yet the mischiefs wrought by uninstructed lawmaking, enormous in their amount as compared with those caused by uninstructed medical treatment, are conspicuous to all who do but glance over its history. ... Thus, while every day chronicles a failure, there every day reappears the belief that it needs but an Act of Parliament and a staff of officers to effect any end desired. Nowhere is the perennial faith of mankind better seen. Ever since society existed Disappointment has been preaching, "Put not your trust in legislation"; and yet the trust in legislation seems scarcely diminished.

Spencer traced the normal life cycle of most (if not all) legislation in the following:

> The history of one scheme is the history of all. First comes enactment, then probation, then failure; next an amendment and, after many alternate tinkerings and abortive trials, arrives at length repeal, followed by the substitution of some fresh plan, doomed to run the same course and share a like fate.

Frederic Bastiat was aware of the futility of trying to provide "political solutions" for economic problems when he wrote *The Law*.

> All of these proposals are the high road to communism; legislation will then be—in fact, already is—the battlefield for the fantasies [dreams] and greed of everyone.

Congress has proved this to be.

LIBERTARIANISM

We no longer believe that it is just for one man to govern two men, but we have yet to outgrow the absurd belief that it is just for two men to govern one man.

—CHARLES T. SPRADING
LIBERTY AND THE GREAT LIBERTARIANS

Any man more right than his neighbors constitutes a majority of one.

—HENRY DAVID THOREAU

All we ask is to be let alone.

—JEFFERSON DAVIS

Government of man by man in every form is oppression.

—PIERRE JOSEPH

Our wretched species is so made that those who walk on the well-trodden path always throw stones at those who are showing a new road.

—VOLTAIRE

There are a thousand hacking at the branches of evil to one who is striking at the root.

—HENRY DAVID THOREAU

He who has conquered weakness, and has put away all selfish thoughts, belongs neither to oppressor nor oppressed. He is free.

—JAMES ALLEN

There is only one political philosophy that truly embraces freedom, individual rights, and thus capitalism—Libertarianism. It is the simplest possible system (see SYSTEMS), and that is why it would work so well, although no proponent claims it would be the utopia that the communists have established in *their* countries. Libertarianism is based on the reality of human nature (not the dreams of social planners who keep trying to recreate society and man in their image) and the natural liberty to which every human is born, but which is quickly usurped to a greater or lesser degree by every form of government on earth. It totally rejects the political demands of envy, whether directed against ability, property, or any religion's concept of personal "morality." It seeks only to protect the individual against the use of force or fraud. Murray N. Rothbard gave an excellent summation of this philosophy in his book *For a New Liberty*:

> The Libertarian creed rests upon one central axiom: that no man or group of men may aggress against the person or property of anyone else. This may be called the "nonaggression axiom." "Aggression" is defined as the initiation of the use or threat of physical violence against the person or property of anyone else. Aggression is therefore synonymous with invasion.
>
> If no man may aggress against another; if, in short, everyone has the absolute right to be "free" from aggression, then this at once implies that the libertarian stands foursquare for what are generally known as "civil liberties": the freedom to speak, publish, assemble, and to engage in such "victimless crimes" as pornography, sexual deviation, and prostitution (which the Libertarian does not regard as "crimes" at all, since he defines a "crime" as violent invasion of someone else's person or property). Furthermore, he regards conscription as slavery on a massive scale. And since war, especially modern war, entails the mass slaughter of civilians, the libertarian regards such conflicts as mass murder and therefore totally illegitimate.

Because of government's irrefutable history of exploitation, oppression, corruption, and futility, and its failure to protect its citizens from force and fraud, Libertarians reject all government. They realize that the only basis for government is authority or power, not freedom. As Charles T. Sprading explains in *Liberty and the Great Libertarians*:

> Governments cannot accept liberty as their fundamental basis for justice, because governments rest upon authority and not upon liberty. To accept liberty as the fundamental basis is to discard authority; that is, to discard government itself; as this would mean the dethronement of the leaders

of government, we can expect only those who have no economic compromise to make to accept equal liberty as the basis of justice.

Noah Webster once issued this warning about government: "Power is always right, weakness always wrong. Power is always insolent and despotic." With political dreams coming due at an accelerating pace, mankind is just now beginning to realize the truth of that warning. While the rest of mankind has insisted on trying to "reform" government, or seize it for their own purpose, libertarians have always realized the total destructive nature of power inherent in any form of government. George Herron captured the essence and results of this power:

> The possession of power over others is inherently destructive both to the possessor of the power and to those over whom it is exercised. And the great man of the future, in distinction from the great man of the past, is he who will seek to create power in people, and not gain power over them. The great man of the future is he who will refuse to be great at all, in the historic sense; he is the man who will literally lose himself, who will altogether diffuse himself in the life of humanity.

These are the types of men and women who will have to come forward for the Libertarians' dream to come true. At best, this dream lies somewhere in the future, if at all. How far ahead we cannot know, but mankind has (for the most part) evolved past the belief in human sacrifice, false gods, the divine right of kings, witches and trust in politicians. It is just beginning to realize that government is not only an instrument of plunder and oppression but also totally unnecessary. The following quotation from Bertrand Russell's essay "The Harm That Good Men Do" should give hope to all who love freedom (and thus hate government and its insanity):

> Reason may be a small force, but it is constant, and works always in one direction, while the forces of unreason destroy one another in futile strife. Therefore every orgy of unreason [such as the world is currently experiencing] in the end strengthens the friends of reason, and shows afresh that they are the only true friends of humanity.

Let those who profess to love and defend freedom accept and support the ultimate simplicity and wisdom of this final quotation from Sprading:

The Libertarians say: Let those who believe in religion have religion; let those who believe in government have government; but let those who believe in liberty, have liberty and do not compel them to accept a religion or a government they do not want.

LIQUIDITY

A man with a surplus can control circumstances, but a man without a surplus is controlled by them, and often he has no opportunity to exercise judgement.

—HARVEY S. FIRESTONE

Lots of folks confuse bad management with destiny.

—ELBERT HUBBARD

Things refuse to be mismanaged long.

—RALPH WALDO EMERSON

By the late 1970s the American government, "led" by Jimmy Carter, had finally convinced *everyone* (people and corporations) that under its astute economic leadership (i.e., record spending and taxes) and "balanced budgets" (i.e., four more years of deficits), the dollar, as all currencies eventually do, would reach par value with toilet paper as the result of inflation.

During an inflation, as we have seen, it is usually impossible for an individual to obtain a real rate of return on savings (see SAVING), even before income taxes. This makes currency one of the least intelligent assets you can have. Therefore, savings rates always drop to very low levels, and personal debt skyrockets, as everyone learns to play the inflation game by speculating (see SPECULATION). People will borrow and spend currency on anything even remotely resembling an inflation hedge (i.e., anything the government can't print). Corporations follow the same pattern. Corporate cash and equivalents are allowed to decline to dangerously low levels, and debt climbs past any semblance of responsible (or repayable) behavior.

As can be seen in the following charts from Martin Weiss's *The Great Money Panic*, the United States as a nation, U.S. consumers, U.S. banks and thrift institutions, and most U.S. corporations currently have the lowest liquidity and the highest debt of the twentieth century:

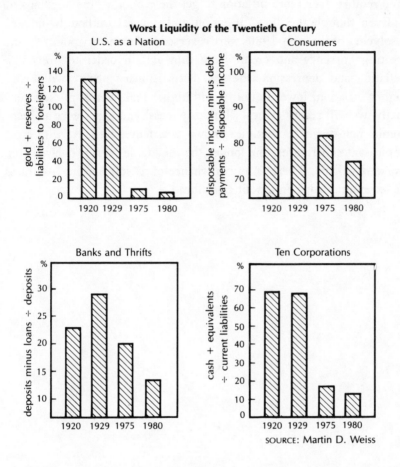

Worst Liquidity of the Twentieth Century

SOURCE: Martin D. Weiss

Massive debt and illiquidity are nothing more than the market's reaction to inflation, and they simply represent *irreversible* bets that it will continue in the future. This would be a simple formula for wealth accumulation if inflation followed a predictable course. But it doesn't! The ultimate consequences of inflation are always low rates of saving, high debt, low liquidity, and high real interest rates (i.e., tight currency) that will eventually throw some market, or the entire economy, into a panic. The bankruptcies, market crashes, and recessions that we experienced in 1966, 1970, 1974, 1980, and 1982, and that we will continue to experience at an increasing rate in the future, were merely part of the constantly recurring temporary adjustments of an economic system that has come to expect increasing inflation; a government under pressure to stop creating currency and credit (inflation); and an economy suffering the decay and malinvestment generated by inflation. These adjustments are always more painful each time they occur, and they require ever more inflation to get the economy "moving" again.

Even though the "low" inflation and general (although hidden) insolvency of the early 1980s were reversed by "monetary policy" (i.e., creating currency and credit from thin air) in order to prevent a deflation and depression, the *next* "expansionary phase" will bring higher inflation, lower liquidity, and higher real interest rates. Eventually, we will reach "critical illiquidity mass" and experience an "economic melt-down" (sometimes known as a depression). As with most unpleasant experiences, the longer the inevitable pain is delayed, the worse it will be. There is no real chance of a "soft landing"—unless the economy drops on a politician's head.

LITIGATION

(Paying America's Bar Bill)

Litigious terms, fat contentions, and flowing fees.

—JOHN MILTON

They have no lawyers among them, for they consider them as a sort of people whose profession it is to disguise matters.

—SIR THOMAS MORE

... a technical system [the judicial system] invented for the creation of costs.

—SIR JOHN ROMILLY

Avoid law suits beyond all things; they influence your conscience, impair your health, and dissipate your property.

—JEAN DE LA BRUYÈRE

As government policies have continued to multiply our laws, and changed them from means of protecting property rights (see PROPERTY RIGHTS) to means of plunder, society's morality has fallen accordingly, and the struggle to amass (not produce) wealth (and unjustly transfer responsibility and risk) has moved from the marketplace to the courtroom.

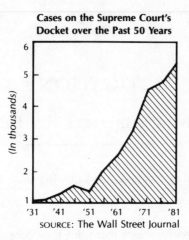

Cases on the Supreme Court's Docket over the Past 50 Years

(In thousands)

6
5
4
3
2
1

'31 '41 '51 '61 '71 '81

SOURCE: The Wall Street Journal

Today, as you may already suspect, the United States is the most litigious society in the world, currently spending $30 billion a year on legal fees. Since 1940, the amount of litigation has grown seven times faster than our population. In 1984 there was one civil lawsuit filed for every fifteen Americans.

To supply this "need" (and to cash in on the contingent fees), the number of practicing lawyers—some people pronounce it "liars"—increased more than 80 percent from 1971 to 1981, and there are currently forty thousand new law graduates each year. We now have, within our borders, two-thirds of all the world's lawyers: five times as many lawyers per capita as Germany, and twenty times as many as Japan. Jeremy Bentham's eighteenth-century description of his legal colleagues seems even more appropriate today:

> ...a passive and enervate race, ready to swallow anything, and to acquiesce in anything; with intellects incapable of distinguishing right from wrong, and with affections alike indifferent to either; insensible, short-sighted, obstinate; lethargic, yet liable to be driven in convulsions by false terrors; deaf to the voice of reason and public utility; obsequious only to the whisper of interest, and to the beck of power.

It isn't too hard to understand our current legal predicament when you realize that lawyers dominate most state legislatures and have a virtual lock on the federal legislature. (Lawyers take to politics as governments take to spending programs.) The government employs hoards of lawyers to regulate and enforce the laws written in the legislatures. Last, but certainly not least (judging from their fees) is the lawyer in private practice whom we're forced to retain to interpret the unintelligible laws written by legislative lawyers and to defend us against the bureaucratic lawyers who try to enforce them. It's a perfect circle with the lawyers on the outside and us in the middle, paying the bills through either outrageous fees, outrageous taxes, or both. Welcome to the land of the free and the home of the brave.

The laws and regulations (see REGULATION) written by these lawyers and passed by Congress are the worst and most expensive form of pollution (possibly Congressional or legal pollution?) suffered by our country. Legal technicalities and court interpretations have become more important than freedom, and right or wrong. Our "system of justice" (see SYSTEMS) has been perverted to the point where most people will accept grievous loss or injustice, rather than "risk" a lawsuit (the average product liability award in 1984 was over $1 million). Herbert Spencer presented an eloquent summary of our current situation in his essay "Over-Legislation":

> This institution [the judicial system] which should succor the man who has fallen among thieves, turns him over to solicitors, barristers, and a legion of law-officers; drains his purse for writs, briefs, affidavits, subpoenas, fees of all kinds and expenses innumerable; involves him in the intracacies of common courts, chancery-courts, suits, counter-suits, and appeals; and often ruins where it should aid.

As the old saying goes, "I have been broke twice in my life, once when I lost a lawsuit and once when I won one."

We will leave this section with a quote from *The New York Times*:

> The story is told that when Congress passed legislation on automobile emission control some years ago, the first thing auto makers did in Japan was to hire 2,000 more engineers. In Detroit, they hired 2,000 more lawyers.

MARKETS (FREE)

Politicians think that by stopping up the chimney they can stop its smoking. They try the experiment, they drive the smoke back, and there is more smoke than ever; but they do not see that their want of common sense has increased the evil they would have prevented.

—BORNE

The more restrictions and prohibitions are in the Empire, the poorer grow the people.

—LAO-TZU

If you destroy a free market you create a black market.

—WINSTON CHURCHILL

Free markets reflect truth and reality. Not surprisingly, neither is in demand in Washington, or any other center of government. Governments and politicians hate free markets because they cannot be controlled and shine like a spotlight to expose their seemingly endless supply of legislative and regulatory mistakes (i.e., dreams). Governments have never understood markets, or anything economic or moral, and try to prevent them from performing their most important function—relaying *freely* negotiated price information (sometimes unpleasant, but usually pleasant, unless government is "helping"; see OIL AND GAS) to producers and consumers, and, thus, rationing scarce resources.

Throughout history, governments and individuals have mistakenly thought (or dreamed) it possible to control markets for their own benefit. The usual pattern is very temporary success, followed by abject and disastrous failure when the law of supply and demand (reality) finally and always wins. Sooner or later, it is the markets that dictate to the politicians, not the politicians who dictate to the markets.

One of the most recent lessons in free market economics has been taught to OPEC. OPEC was absolutely sure the law of supply and demand did not apply to them, and that they, not the market, set the price of oil. Then the United States deregulated the price of its oil, and spot market prices fell from more than forty dollars a barrel to less than twenty-eight dollars. (After adjusting for inflation, this was a decrease of more than fifty percent and, depending on the stability of the Middle East and the strength of the dollar, prices are probably headed significantly lower.) Even with this steep price decline, OPEC's share of world oil output has fallen from a high of 53 percent (32 million barrels per day) to less than 30 percent (16 million barrels per day).

Before OPEC, the Hunts thought they could put the price of silver anywhere they wanted by cornering the market, but that dream came due with the price falling from fifty dollars an ounce to less than five dollars. Prior to the Hunts, the United States government (a consummate price manipulator and speculator) thought the correct price for gold was thirty-five dollars per ounce. The market decided it was too low by a factor of at least 10 (sounds like a typically accurate government estimate).

The list of entities imagining themselves bigger than the market goes back to the beginning of history; but the laws of markets are like the laws of physics: they can be delayed or distorted by government (and are every day, to the detriment of mankind), but not suspended. The best price, the most efficient price, and the fairest price is always the free market price that is set by voluntary exchange between the buyer and the seller. *There cannot be free men without free markets.*

MOMENTUM

Our country is now taking so steady a course as to show by what road it will pass to destruction, to wit: by consolidation [of power] first, and then corruption, its necessary consequence.

—THOMAS JEFFERSON

It takes time to ruin a world [country], but time is all it takes.

—BERNARD DEFOUTENELLE

States, like men, have their growth, their manhood, their decrepitude and their decay.

—WALTER SAVAGE LANDOR

I have watched this famous island [Britain] descending incontinently, fecklessly, the stairway which leads to a dark gulf. It is a fine broad stairway at the beginning, but after a bit the carpet ends. A little farther on there are only flagstones, and a little farther on still these break beneath your feet.

—WINSTON CHURCHILL

■ The growth of government, and the negative compounding it always entails, eventually eliminates any chance of economic growth and forces a country to begin to consume the capital (i.e., savings) that was accumulated when government was small. Once a country begins to pay bills with savings instead of earnings (which initially seems so painless), it starts on the road to oblivion. (Great [?] Britain is almost there.) C. Northcote Parkinson gave an excellent description of this decline in his book *The Law and the Profits*:

> In one respect the simile of the precipice is misleading, for the fall of
> a nation is less dramatic than the fall of a single vehicle or man. It can
> live for a time on borrowings and capital. There will be a dwindling
> but still valuable stock of integrity, enterprise, energy and hope. Older
> people will go on working from habit even after the younger folk have

seen that it is pointless. People will go on saving from habit even after they have seen past savings shrivel to nothing. People will retain a professional pride for years after they have ceased to retain more than a fraction of their professional fee. The machine goes on for a while even after the power has been switched off. For a time the slowing down is not even perceptible. Then the whine of the engine becomes a throb, the throb becomes a slow pulsation and that becomes in turn a measured and lessening groan and hiss. The blurred flywheel becomes visible, its spokes marking a slower rhythm, and so the engine wheezes and grunts its way to a final grinding, clanging halt. It is the end of the journey and, in this instance, the end of the train.

Parkinson continues by describing the various stages of decline in the life of a country:

The danger signs appear in this order: First, it becomes apparent that government is absorbing too great a share of the available talent and energy; there is a decline, therefore, in individual initiative and the spirit of inertia takes its place. Second, there is a decline in the sense of property, and the spirit of envy takes its place. Third, there is a decline of freedom, and the spirit of dependence takes its place. Fourth, there is a decline in the sense of purpose and the spirit of rebellion takes its place. All this adds up to a decline in the sense of individual responsibility, and so to a decline of individuality itself. And while the technical trend of the age goes to make the individual matter more, politically the trend is to make him matter less.

Parkinson wrote this in 1960, yet he has exactly described the recent decline of the United States. It is fairly obvious that America has been living on momentum (i.e., capital consumption and debt accumulation) for the past twenty years. Our fate was sealed by Lyndon Johnson's Great Society and his Viet Nam adventure. Now that our reserves have been nearly depleted, most government action brings virtually immediate negative consequences. It has itself painted into a corner. Every time government pushes down the bumps in the carpet (inflation, interest rates, or unemployment, to name just a few), they just pop up somewhere else (recession, inflation, or larger deficits). This explains the increasing volatility in all areas of the economy during the past decade. Like a spinning top, which makes its most violent oscillations right before it crashes, an economy becomes most volatile just before it crashes. Interest rates swing up and down ten points in two years, the stock market crashes and then explodes in a rally, gold moves from $100 to $875 and back to $300, but the government (the source of most of our problems) is now out of "answers" (except to raise taxes and spending, print more currency, and supply more credit). The dreams are now coming due before our eyes. The bills, as always, will be paid.

For those who marvel at our ability to stagger from crisis to crisis without experiencing a disaster (such as a depression) and think we can continue indefinitely to overload our economic and social system with laws of plunder and legislative nonsense, I will remind you that the man who is guillotined is breathing right up to the moment the blade hits his neck.

MONEY

Money is not an invention of the state. It is not the product of a legislative act. The sanction of political authority is not necessary for its existence.

—CARL MENGER

Money is indispensable to a long-circuit heavy load energy system [a free, highly productive economy]. . . . Money represents a storage battery when idle, and a generalized mode of the conversion of energy when it is in motion. . . .

—ISABEL PATERSON
THE GOD OF THE MACHINE

Money is the sign of liberty. To curse money is to curse liberty— to curse life, which is nothing, if it be not free.

—DE GOURMONT

. . . and in societies of low civilization, there is no money.

—HERBERT SPENCER

Money for me has only one sound: liberty.

—GABRIELLE CHANEL

Money: a medium of exchange and a store of value.

The greatest fraud and confusion perpetrated by governments has been the substitution of unbacked currency for money. People now believe that currency is money. Nothing could be further from the truth.

There can be no compromise to the definition of money. Many things can have one of the traits of money. Currency is a medium of exchange and land can be a store of value, but neither one is money, especially currency, because *no* currency in history (not one) has ever retained its value. There is no currency in the world today (including the Swiss franc) that is not losing purchasing power (i.e., being inflated) every year.

Once this concept is grasped, many current concepts must be altered. The government does not print money; it prints currency. The government controls the currency supply (C1?), not the money supply (M1, M2, etc.). You *do not* earn money; you earn currency.

Money cannot lose its value (i.e., be inflated or printed), but currency always does. Currency is paper notes that can be increased in value by merely adding zeros or made worthless by the fall of a government. Money has historically been gold or silver. As we have already seen, money continually buys more, and currency continually buys less. If money talks, currency barely whispers.

A remark by George Bernard Shaw sums up the world's situation: "Lack of money is the root of all evil."

MONOPOLY

Nature hates monopolies and exceptions.

—RALPH WALDO EMERSON

There is far more danger in public than in private monopoly, for when Government goes into business it can always shift its losses to the taxpayers. Government never makes ends meet—and that is the first requisite of business.

—THOMAS EDISON

As freak legislation, the antitrust laws stand alone. *Nobody knows what it is they forbid.*

—ISABEL PATERSON
THE GOD OF THE MACHINE

A big corporation is more or less blamed for being big. It is only because it gives service. If it doesn't give service, it gets small faster than it grew.

—WILLIAM S. KNUDSEN

If bigness alone is bad, maybe we should begin dismantling the government.

—THOMAS MURPHY
Former Chairman, General Motors

Monopoly: an exclusive privilege to carry on a traffic or service, granted by a sovereign state, etc.

As you can see from the definition, a monopoly in a free market is impossible. On rare occasions a company may have 100 percent of a market for a time (such as Alcoa Aluminum in the first half of the twentieth century), but such a case is a market monopoly to which customers freely choose to give their business, and it is always subject to new competition if profits are high. A *true* monopoly can only be sustained with government sanctions because government (with its monopoly on "legitimate" force) is itself the ultimate coercive monopoly.

The two most "popular" government-instituted coercive monopolies that come to mind are the postal service (see POSTAL SERVICE) and the new regional phone companies resulting from the breakup of AT&T, all "serving" us exclusively thanks to "laws" against competition. In other words, according to government "logic," monopolies (which can only exist at the government's pleasure) are always bad unless the government says they are good: then, of course, they are "good." Isabel Paterson gave a clear and concise explanation of this irrational government competition "policy" in her book *The God of the Machine*:

> Government cannot "restore competition" or "ensure" it. Government is monopoly; and all it can do is to impose restrictions which may issue in monopoly, when they go so far as to require permission for the individual to engage in production. This is the essence of the Society-of-Status. The reversion to status law in the antitrust legislation went unnoticed . . . the politicians . . . had secured a law under which it was impossible for the citizen to know beforehand what constituted a crime, and which therefore made all productive effort liable to prosecution if not to certain conviction.

Since nearly all governments, and a large majority of the world's population, are dominated by envy, they cannot stand to see great success in any private endeavor. Most people, and all bureaucrats, think any large *profitable* company is, by definition, a monopoly. General Motors was widely regarded as a monopoly in the 1960s, but the Japanese auto makers have convincingly laid that illusion to rest. There is no "fair" amount of market share or "correct" number of competitors for a given industry. GM commanded a large market share because it *was* building cars the public wanted to buy. Since the auto industry is extremely capital-intensive, a company must be very large and sell nationally to participate. This condition naturally limits the number of competitors.

The latest monopoly candidates were the oil companies and OPEC (see OIL AND GAS) during the 1970s. (Funny how they lost their "monopoly" without any lawsuits from the Department of Justice.) But there will forever be new private "monopolies" coming to the public's attention, and the government always has the guilty-until-proved-innocent antitrust laws handy if any of their attorneys become bored or need publicity. (They can always take another run at their perennial whipping-boy: IBM.)

For corporations that do not have twenty years and $20 million to fight an antitrust action, here are some guidelines for product pricing:

1. High prices are considered to be monopolistic price gouging that exploit the public (who voluntarily choose to pay the prices).
2. Low prices (which benefit consumers) are considered to be cutthroat and predatory because they attempt to destroy your competition.
3. Prices that are the same as those of other competitors (because production costs are basically the same) are obviously collusive and indicative of a ploy to fix prices.

Good Luck!

NEEDS

Necessity [need] is the plea for every infringement of human freedom. It is the argument of tyrants; it is the creed of slaves.

—WILLIAM PITT

The trouble with most people is that they think with their hopes or fears or wishes rather than with their minds.

—WILL DURANT

That's when I found out about need. It goes much better with hate than with love.

—LOIS GOULD

don't hold the sprout against the seed
don't hold this need against me....

—MELANIE
"Gather on a Hill of Wildflowers"

It is nothing short of amusing to watch the outrage and moaning precipitated by the minuscule cuts *attempted* in the *rate of increase* of government spending. (Reagan's 1982 budget was $100 billion more than Carter's estimate and took one of the largest shares of GNP in our history, and since then, spending and deficits have gone completely out of control.) In this theater of the absurd, witnesses parade before the congressional committees, crying about the good work they do and about the "needs" of the people (i.e., their special interest groups). No one asks, "Can we afford it?" (No!) "Who will pay?" (Blankout.) "What about the needs and, more important, the property rights (see PROPERTY RIGHTS) of the people who are being forced to pay by 'legal' plunder?" (Blankout.) These questions are ignored, for only the "needs" and the attempted satisfaction of envy are of any political concern. As Emerson said in his essay *Politics*:

This is the history of governments—one man does something which is to bind another. A man who cannot be acquainted with me, taxes me; looking from afar at me ordains that a part of my labor shall go to this or that whimsical end—not as I, but as he happens to fancy. Behold the consequence. Of all debts men are least willing to pay the taxes.

In his book *The Crowd* Gustave Le Bon issued the following warning about the ultimate outcome of satisfying envy-motivated demands (disguised as "needs") of crowds.

> To-day the claims of the masses are becoming more and more sharply defined, and amount to nothing less than a determination to utterly destroy society as it now exists, with a view to making it hark back to that primitive communism which was the normal condition of all human groups before the dawn of civilisation. Limitations of the hours of labour, the nationalisation of mines, railways, factories, and the soil, the equal distribution of all products, the elimination of all the upper classes for the benefit of the popular classes, &c., such are these claims.
>
> Little adapted to reasoning crowds, on the contrary, are quick to act. As the result of their present organisation their strength has become immense. The dogmas whose birth we are witnessing will soon have the force of the old dogmas; that is to say, the tyrannical and sovereign force of being above discussion.

At least 75 percent of Washington's "needs" are actually desires or envy in disguise (see WASTE), but by the twisted reasoning of socialism, "needs" have become "rights" to someone else's property. In a just society, needs cannot place the "law" above the rights of property.

Edmund Burke correctly refuted the dream of government providing for the needs of the people:

> To provide for us in our necessities is not in the power of Government. It would be a vain presumption in statesmen to think they can do it. The people maintain them, and not they the people. It is in the power of Government to prevent much evil; it can do very little positive good in this or perhaps in anything else.

We are fast approaching critical mass in the world today, as the irresistible force of *infinite* demands for unearned (expropriated) benefits ("needs") generated by envy and greed meet the immovable object of *finite* resources and increasingly limited incentives to produce. Once that point is reached, only an "omnipotent" government can redistribute the wealth of a stagnating economy.

OIL AND GAS

We've always had a finite amount of energy.... We had finite supplies of wood in the early pioneer days. How did we make the transition from using wood to using coal, from using coal to using oil, from using oil to using natural gas? How in God's name did we make the transition without a Federal Energy Agency?

—MILTON FRIEDMAN

Wildcattin'? All it takes is guts and acreage. It seems to help some, too, if you're smart and lucky....

—COLUMBUS MARION (DAD) JOINER,
Discoverer of Giant East Texas Oil Field

The guy that drills the most has the chance of coming up with the most.

—H. L. HUNT

Dig a well before you are thirsty [or cold, hungry, and without energy].

—CHINESE PROVERB

The dream of unlimited, continually cheaper oil and gas has died just in time to save us from becoming a client state of Saudi Arabia. As with most of our problems, the latest "energy crisis" was started and continually assisted by United States government decisions. It began in the 1950s (not 1973), when the Supreme Court ruled that the government, instead of the buyers and sellers, had the "right" (or was it the need?) to set interstate natural gas prices (which were scheduled to be deregulated in 1985). Well footage drilled in the United States went into an immediate seventeen-year decline (as shown in the following chart), and imports of foreign oil went into an immediate seventeen-year increase (probably just a coincidence).

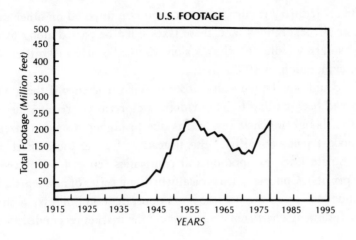

U.S. FOOTAGE

YEARS

(Total Footage (Million feet) vs. Years, 1915–1995)

The next step in the government's unpublicized foreign aid program for the Arabs was to slash the 35 percent depletion allowance on oil and gas production in 1969. This cut was advertised as a way to hurt the rich, but the 35 percent depletion allowance was basically an energy subsidy that stimulated exploration and production, thus helping keep prices low for the consumer. As revenue was taxed away from producers, not only did drilling fall off, but maintenance on our existing production was allowed to decline. With lower incentives and rising costs, oil explorers were forced to search for the larger and cheaper (but politically less stable) reserves in the Middle East. We continued to produce domestically, but we did not replace our depleting reserves. We were consuming our energy capital and substituting more and more foreign oil. By 1972 we were producing our oil wells at 100 percent of "allowable" production, and in 1973 the Arabs, who were becoming increasingly impatient with fixed oil prices set by the Texas Railroad Commission and denominated in a steadily depreciating currency, realized they were now in the driver's seat.

Once the Arabs took the wheel, the government could have deregulated U.S. oil and gas prices to stimulate domestic production and voluntary conservation, but with public envy running wild against the oil and gas industry, it was much easier to waste taxpayers' dollars on a Department of Energy (whose initial budget was about four dollars for each barrel of oil produced in the United States that year) and blame the oil companies and their "obscene profits" ("profits" that were merely inflation adjustments on oil inventory; not real profits [see REAL], although still conveniently taxable). Federal and state taxation of the oil industry is currently twice the rate imposed on other major industrial corporations, and these taxes must be passed along to consumers. The windfall profits tax alone drained nearly $10 billion away from exploration in 1982.

We could now be ten years closer to self-sufficiency if the government had been willing to let our domestic producers receive the same price (although much lower profits due to higher costs and taxes) as our good friends at OPEC. But instead of freeing the market price to stimulate U.S. exploration (oil companies reinvest 80 percent of their profits), Congress, in a typically brilliant series of new legislation, continued to force us to become more dependent on imports, as shown in the following chart (note how quickly the market responded to each new law):

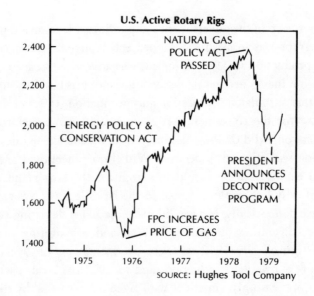

U.S. Active Rotary Rigs

SOURCE: Hughes Tool Company

(Government handled the "energy crisis" so adeptly that in February 1976, three years *after* the Arab embargo, U.S. oil imports exceeded domestic production for the first time in history. Two years later, a poll showed that half of the American public was still not aware that we imported *any* oil.)

We needlessly suffered ten years of massive disruptions to our economy—and dreams which are still coming due, such as the horrendous losses suffered by the domestic auto industry, the total bankruptcy of the LDCs that were forced to borrow billions to finance needlessly higher oil prices, and the wholesale failure of large segments of our domestic oil and gas economy and U.S. banks, like Continental Illinois, which dumped loans into a totally artificial "energy boom"—waiting in gasoline lines, until even the government could no longer ignore market forces: ten long years of Middle East maniacs dictating policy to the largest economy in the world.

The laws of economics have prevailed as they always do, and with free market prices for oil, OPEC is now virtually finished as a cohesive market force. The gallon of gasoline that could be bought for around twenty cents in the 1850s can now be bought for even less money (not currency). At current prices two silver dimes will buy a gallon of gasoline and return some change, and that is even after silver has fallen from fifty dollars an ounce to less than ten dollars. In 1970 one ounce of gold would buy about twelve barrels of oil, and in 1985 the same ounce of gold would still buy twelve barrels.

These low money prices for energy are exactly what you would expect from an industry that has become increasingly productive through better exploration technology and the economies of scale possible from larger, more efficient transportation and refining facilities. Think about that the next time someone complains about the high cost of energy. In spite of massive government interference stifling every facet of energy production (including the latest five-cent gasoline tax and the current congressional mania to block oil mergers), these precious resources, that are being depleted every day, have actually slightly decreased in price in terms of money. The *supposed* higher price of oil and gas is basically only the lower value of America's currency turned upside down.

PARKINSON'S LAW

The suppression of unnecessary offices, of useless establishments
and expenses, enabled us to discontinue our internal taxes. These
covering our land with officers and opening our doors to their
intrusions, had already begun that process of domiciliary
vexation which once entered is scarcely to be restrained from
reaching, successively, every article of property and produce.

—THOMAS JEFFERSON

Democracy does not contain any force which will check the
constant tendency to put more and more on the public payroll.
The state is like a hive of bees in which the drones display,
multiply and starve the workers so the idlers will consume the
food and the workers will perish.

—PLATO

My reading of history convinces me that most bad government
results from too much government.

—THOMAS JEFFERSON

To understand the government and its bureaucracy (or any bureaucracy, for that matter), one must be acquainted with some aspects
of C. Northcote Parkinson's classic, *Parkinson's Law*. Though his book
is amusing and highly entertaining, his conclusions are painfully true.
Here is the theory, quoted in capsule form:

The fact is that the number of the officials and the quantity of the work
are not related at all. The rise in the total of those employed is governed
by Parkinson's Law and would be much the same whether the volume
of work were to increase, diminish, or even disappear.

The basis of Parkinson's law rests on two axiomatic statements:

1. "An official wants to multiply subordinates, not rivals."
2. "Officials make work for each other."

According to Parkinson's formula (which has been proved in the real world time after time), any government bureaucracy will grow at "between 5.17 percent and 6.56 percent, irrespective of any variation in the amount of work (if any) to be done." As proof of this statement, Parkinson offers the following evidence:

> Here are some typical figures. The strength of the Navy in 1914 could be shown as 146,000 officers and men, 3249 dockyard officials and clerks, and 57,000 dockyard workmen. By 1928 there were only 100,000 officers and men and only 62,439 workmen, but the dockyard officials and clerks by then numbered 4558. As for warships, the strength in 1928 was a mere fraction of what it had been in 1914—fewer than 20 capital ships in commission as compared with 62. Over the same period the Admiralty officials had increased in number from 2000 to 3569, providing (as was remarked) "a magnificent navy on land."

Lest you think that Parkinson is presenting an isolated, historical example, the U.S. military, whose present strength is about 2 million men, currently has more three-star military officers than it had at the peak of its war strength in 1945, when 12 million Americans were in the armed services.

Perhaps now it is easier to understand why and how governments *always* grow and impoverish their people, and to a greater or lesser extent the entire world.

POPULATION

Population, when unchecked, increases in a geometrical ratio.

—THOMAS ROBERT MALTHUS

... and it is futile to expect a hungry and squalid population to be anything but violent and gross.

—THOMAS HUXLEY

One of the most immediate and critical world problems is the four billion (plus) inhabitants of this fragile planet. In the less developed (read: less free) countries, more than 60 percent of the population is undernourished; yet this is where population continues to explode. A United Nations estimate places probable population at over six billion souls by the year 2000. (I believe the earth may rebel long before this number is reached.)

The governments of the world have been waging a three-point attack on the problem:

1. Throwing currency at it through family planning clinics and "free" contraceptives.
2. Sending "free food" (at the expense of U. S. taxpayers) to starving areas of the world (so they can be maintained at subsistence levels and produce even more population).
3. Organizing "humanitarian" political actions like those of the late Prime Minister Gandhi of India, who, with her son, unleashed sterilization squads to kidnap and sterilize their population's young men. (She obviously stole this idea from another great humanitarian, Adolf Hitler!)

As usual, governments have mistaken an *economic problem* (which they have caused) for a social one. Children in poor countries are a form of capital investment. They are cheap labor while they are growing up, and a form of social security, should their parents be lucky enough to have an old age. There is a direct correlation between income (levels of prosperity) and fertility rates as shown in the following graph:

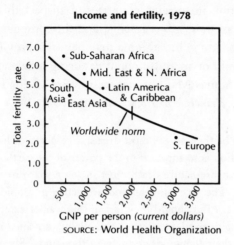

Income and fertility, 1978

GNP per person *(current dollars)*
SOURCE: World Health Organization

As income rises, birth rates drop, but income can rise only as capital formation and investment increase, and this can only happen in relatively free countries. (In fact, population growth is probably a very good inverse indicator of the freedom and economic growth potential of a country.)

Envy-dominated governments in less developed countries ensure their continuing poverty by taxing away and wasting income (and foreign aid) that would become capital, or by blocking trade and foreign and domestic investment with insane regulations (and they usually manage to do both at the same time). Professor T. S. Ashton stated the consequence of these actions in his book *The Industrial Revolution, 1760–1830*:

> There are today on the plains of India and China [and every country where there is no freedom] men and women, plague-ridden and hungry, living lives little better, to outward appearance, than those of the cattle that toil with them by day and share their places of sleep at night. Such Asiatic standards, and such unmechanized horrors, are the lot of those who increase their numbers without passing through an industrial revolution.

If the governments of the less developed world would adopt capitalism, their people would be able to form and retain financial and physical capital. This would automatically lower the amount of human capital created and increase the standard of living by a geometric factor.

The only alternative to capitalism is for nature to provide the control of human population in socialist countries. I suspect this alternative will be the choice of these governments, and the consequences will be unimaginable (the famine in Ethiopia may be just a preview). Nature has never been timid or merciful about restoring a balance to uncontrolled growth. Thomas Malthus was well aware of this fact when he wrote *Essay on the Principle of Population* in 1798:

> Famine seems to be the last, the most dreadful resource of nature. The power of population is so superior to the power of the earth to provide subsistence . . . that premature death must in some shape or other visit the human race. The vices of mankind are active and able ministers of depopulation. . . . But should they fail in this war of extermination, sickly seasons, epidemical pestilence, and plague advance in terrible array, sweep off their thousands and tens of thousands. Should success still be incomplete, gigantic inevitable famine stalks in the rear, and with one mighty blow, levels the population with the food of the world.

The dream of government "population control" will soon become a nightmare that won't fade with the light of dawn. Governments may shirk their responsibility to control population by refusing to grant freedom to the people, but nature will not.

POSTAL SERVICE

(Delivering Less For More!)

If there's anything a public servant hates to do it's something for the public.

—K. HUBBARD

Your true dull minds are generally preferred for public employ. . . .

—WASHINGTON IRVING

The inefficient offer their inefficiency to the highest bidder. . . .

—HENRY DAVID THOREAU

A governmental monopoly need not worry that customers may go elsewhere or that inefficiency [i.e., endless losses] may mean its demise.

—MURRAY N. ROTHBARD
POWER AND MARKET

Here in the Postal Service is government "enterprise" at its best: a coercive monopoly in *every* sense of the word, but under the control of a fair and benevolent government that will not allow it to exploit the people it allegedly serves. But the major problem of the Post Office is the same one shared by most politicians: it can't stand on its record.

In 1950, the Postal System (see SYSTEMS) operated 41,464 post offices, but in its relentless drive for ever-elusive efficiency and greater service, it cut back to 30,449 by 1979 (currently, 12,000 post offices serve towns of fewer than 100 people). The price of a stamp, however, "edged up" from $0.02 in 1960 to $0.15 in 1979 (and is currently "holding" at $0.22,) even though delivery time efficiency peaked in the 1960s (along with the Dow Jones Average and corporate profits).

The Post Office was moving in perfect harmony with Congress in terms of revenue and expenditures by running a deficit for roughly twenty-eight of the thirty years from 1950 to 1980. (Isn't it grand to see other agencies chipping in to spend their fair share?) As yet, the Post Office hasn't been able to increase its deficits as Congress has, but then it *is* limited to only one area of waste and inefficiency, whereas Congress is able to exercise its versatile financial incompetence over every part of the budget.

By any measurement you find the Post Office doesn't deliver. From 1970 to 1979 revenues increased 177 percent from about $6.5 billion to $18 billion, but the average deficit for those ten years was $374.1 million a year. The number of pieces of mail increased only 18 percent from 1970 to 1979, and the weight of mail delivered *decreased* 7.3 percent. You would think the high cost of fuel increased expenses, but transportation cost didn't even double, going from $572 million in 1970 to $955 million in 1979, up 67 percent. How about labor? (Now we're getting warm.) Thanks to the "free marketeers" in the postal union and our weak-kneed politicians, labor costs outpaced revenue gains by increasing 192 percent from $3.072 billion in 1970 to $8.961 billion in 1979, while the number of employees was *declining* 10.5 percent, from 741,000 to 663,000. (Current labor costs are about twenty dollars an hour and increasing at twice the rate of revenues.) The champion gainer was overhead, up from $399 million in 1970 to $1.803 billion in 1979, a modest 352 percent increase, while the number of post offices *decreased* by 4.8 percent.

With all these increases in prices and costs, the Post Office services were declining to a point where other government agencies were using United Parcel Service (an exceptionally efficient private company that delivers service and profits) for their package delivery. (Strange how bureaucrats invariably don't use their own "services" such as Social Security, Amtrak, and the Post Office.) Currently, each day 10 percent (i.e., ten thousand envelopes) of the Postal Service's (pony?) Express Mail misses its overnight delivery deadline by margins of up to ten days because the package gets lost! (Federal Express delivers more than 99 percent of its business on time and makes excellent profits.)

The dream that government can do something (or anything) even as simple as delivering the mail has obviously come due. This annual multibillion-dollar consumer rip-off should be stopped. Sadly, we can't count on outside help: Japan doesn't manufacture post offices, and even if they did, Congress would place a tariff on them. However, the problem is very simple to cure: deregulate first-class mail service. Free enterprise will take care of the post office ... *and deliver*!

PRODUCERS

To build [produce] is to be robbed.

—SAMUEL JOHNSON

We have no rights [of property] which anyone [government] need respect.

—ANONYMOUS

The reward of energy, enterprise and thrift is taxes.

—WILLIAM FEATHER

A government is free in proportion to the rights it guarantees to the minority.

—ALFRED M. LANDON

Don't expect to build up the weak by pulling down the strong.

—CALVIN COOLIDGE

Whoever makes two ears of corn or two blades of grass to grow where only one grew before, deserves better of mankind, and does more essential services to his country, than the whole race of politicians put together.

—JONATHAN SWIFT

Producers and men of extraordinary ability are nearly always the prime targets of envy. Everyone (but most especially government) wishes to help redistribute their "ill-gotten gains" to the people they have "exploited." Show me one person who was exploited by the Wright brothers, by the inventor of polio vaccine, the inventor of the radio, the inventor of the telephone, the inventor of television, or the inventor of the Xerox machine. This book is being composed on a two thousand dollar personal computer that twenty-five years ago could not have been purchased for $2 million. Even though I can now buy a newer model with four times the power for the same two thousand dollars, I still marvel at the capabilities of my "antiquated" machine.

The personal rewards for the producers of these achievements, no matter how large, have been an *infinitesimal* amount of the wealth and benefits they created for mankind. As Isabel Paterson so stunningly stated in *The God of the Machine:*

> If the full roll of *sincere* philanthropists were called, from the beginning of time, it would be found that all of them together by their strictly philanthropic activities have never conferred upon humanity one-tenth of the benefit derived from the normally self-interested efforts of Thomas Alva Edison, to say nothing of the greater minds who worked out the scientific principles which Edison applied. Innumerable speculative thinkers, inventors, and organizers, have contributed to the comfort, health, and happiness of their fellow men—because that was not their objective....
>
> The philanthropist, the politician, and the pimp are inevitably found in alliance because they have the same motives, they seek the same ends, to exist for, through, and by others, [i.e., producers]. And the good people cannot be exonerated for supporting them. Neither can it be believed that the good people are wholly unaware of what actually happens. But when the good people do know, as they certainly do, that three million persons (at the least estimate) were starved to death [or taxed to insolvency] in one year by the methods they approve, why do they still fraternize with the murderers [or plunderers] and support the measures? Because they have been told that the lingering death [or lingering plunder] of the three millions might ultimately benefit a greater number. *The argument applies equally well to cannibalism.*

And what is the ultimate source of wealth and the great leap forward made by mankind in the past two centuries? Capital? Management? Labor? No, it resides in the mind of the producers (see TECHNOLOGY) and the freedom to produce. These sources of wealth were given the best environment in history with the founding of the United States. Paterson brings this truth into sharp focus in another passage from *The God of the Machine:*

> What happened was that the dynamo of the energy used in human association was located. It is in the individual. And it was withdrawn [temporarily] from political interference by a formal reservation, along with the means and material by which it can organize the great world circuit of energy. The dynamo [of production] is the mind [of the producers], the creative intelligence, which our Bill of Rights and the treason clause [a clause in the Constitution protecting private property] assert to be free of political control.

For the benefit of all "government worshippers," Paterson further clarified the point that government does not and cannot produce *anything*. The "production" or "service" for which they receive credit is simply a very *small* return of the wealth extorted from the private sector that produces everything:

> The post office is usually pointed out as the prize example of government undertaking; but postal service depends entirely on the means of conveyance invented and operated by private enterprise. It is the simplest form of business imaginable, pure routine; yet, even as a government monopoly, it always runs at a deficit. . . . Good roads exist only by reason of private enterprise progress in materials and machinery. City water supplies were first provided by private enterprise, and expropriated by government. For centuries government fostered disease, discomfort, and gloom by window taxes, hearth taxes, salt taxes. Private enterprise dug the Suez Canal and provided the machinery, knowledge, and skill [and money] to dig the Panama Canal. Always and everywhere, progress has been made solely by private invention, enterprise, labor, and savings, and in inverse ratio to the extent of government.

To the producers who either cannot or refuse to go on strike (and many have by withholding their capital and ability from new ventures) or cannot find their way to the underground economy (see UNDERGROUND ECONOMY): *you* will be the "sacrificial animals" left to support the past and future dreams of men who produce nothing (i.e., government). Government growth has now reached the point where the producers must not only ask permission to produce, but are also told what portion of their wealth they will be allowed to keep, just as Paterson predicted:

> By the opposite approach, when the acquisition, possession or use of every material object is made permissive, then every productive action of which a man is capable can be performed only by permission. As such actions constitute a man's mode of being, the primary assumption is implicit. . . . Men are presumed to exist only by permission. At long last, the persistent purpose of the nonproducers has been attained, with no reservations, no limitations; and most extraordinarily, with no other claim than that of their own incompetence. They have got a stranglehold on the producers. . . . If the various taxes recently imposed in previously [more] free economies, under the pretext of helping the indigent, are examined, their nature becomes evident. They are paid even though the producer goes bankrupt.

PRODUCTIVITY

It is worth remembering that output per man in this country has increased on the average about two per cent a year during this century. Mere continuation of this trend will mean a future full of better things for more people.

—HENRY FORD II

Productive power [productivity] is the foundation of a country's economic strength.

—STAFFORD CRIPPS

Unless each man produces more than he receives, increases his output, there will be less for him and all the others.

—BERNARD M. BARUCH

Long-term improvement in productivity is the result of a continually increasing capital base and advancing technology (see TECH-NOLOGY). Increasing productivity is the key to *lower prices*, higher wages, and thus, a higher standard of living.

In the twenty-two years prior to 1970, the United States experienced only three years in which productivity declined. In the twelve years from 1970 to 1981, productivity fell in four different years, and in 1974 and 1975, recorded the only back-to-back declines for the entire period since 1947.

The average productivity increase following the three declines prior to 1970 was 8.1 percent, but the average increase following the declines since 1970 has averaged a very weak 3.73 percent. Our economy is rapidly approaching the productivity rates of politicians and bureaucrats (i.e., south of 0).

We do not have to look far for one source of this problem. The following table shows a steady decline in capital formation since the period from 1965 to 1969, and decreasing real growth in GNP since 1965:

Growth Rates of Real GNP, Capital Formation, and Total Factor Productivity

PERIOD	REAL GNP (Percentage)	CAPITAL FORMATION (Percentage)	TOTAL FACTOR PRODUCTIVITY (Percentage)
1959–1965	4.3	3.8	2.5
1965–1969	4.0	4.1	1.9
1969–1973	3.6	3.5	2.3
1973–1979	2.8	2.5	1.2

Is it any wonder why Japan, with the highest rate of saving (see SAVING) in the developed world, was able to outpace the United States so decisively in productivity gains and economic growth during the past decade?

A second component of our declining productivity is that many talented people are being drawn into financially rewarding but non-productive occupations (such as civil service) that have been created by exploding government regulation, spending, and taxes. Between 1972 and 1980, employment increased by about 20 percent, but the number of social scientists increased by 97 percent, health administrators by 78 percent, lawyers by 72 percent, and accountants by 46 percent. (In the long run, a nation's prosperity is *inversely* proportional to its number of tax accountants and lawyers, as we shall soon see.) During the same period, the number of scientists increased by 23 percent, and engineers by 22 percent.

Combine these career figures with inflation-bloated, marginal tax rates on persons and corporations (there is an inverse relation between the size of government and the growth of productivity: the more government, the less the growth of productivity), needless regulations in every area of the economy, and moronic government fiscal and monetary policies, and you see why economically, we are leaping toward the nineteenth century.

Governments tax saving, work, and capital formation at confiscatory rates, and they subsidize "unemployment" to the point where people have to take a "pay cut" if they find a job. Yet they are surprised by rising unemployment, low saving rates, anemic capital formation, and declining rates of productivity gains.

Are you surprised?

PROFITS, CORPORATE

The law of harvest is to reap more than you sow.

—G. D. BOARDMAN

Nothing contributes so much to the prosperity and happiness of a country as high profits.

—DAVID RICARDO

The worst crime against working people is a company which fails to operate at a profit.

—SAMUEL GOMPERS

Society can progress only if men's labors show a profit—if they yield more than is put in. To produce at a loss must leave less for all to share.

—BERNARD M. BARUCH

It is a socialist idea that making profits is a vice. I consider the real vice is making losses.

—WINSTON CHURCHILL

The successful producer of an article sells it for more than it cost him to make, and that's his profit. But the customer buys it only because it is worth more to him than he pays for it, and that's his profit. No one can long make a profit producing anything unless the customer makes a profit using it.

—SAMUEL B. PETTENGILL

Profits, at best, are the prerequisite for staying in business. If there are no profits, there can be no capital formation and a business must eventually fail. At the worst (during inflation), currency-denominated profits become an illusion due to fictitious inventory gains, depreciation schedules that are understated because they are based on acquisition costs rather than on inflated replacement costs, and long-term debt capital acquired at low, fixed rates (when inflation was much lower) that must eventually be replaced at much higher rates of interest. The following table shows corporate profits adjusted for currency depreciation:

After-Tax Corporate Profits Adjusted for Inflation
(1940 Dollars)

YEAR	AFTER-TAX CORPORATE PROFITS CURRENT DOLLARS (Billions)	REAL CORPORATE PROFITS (Billions)
1950	16.0	9.32
1955	23.4	12.24
1960	24.9	11.79
1965	49.1	21.84
1966	51.4	22.21
1967	49.9	20.95
1968	50.0	20.15
1969	45.6	18.44
1970	37.2	13.43
1971	45.7	15.83
1972	55.0	18.44
1973	59.3	18.72
1974	43.3	12.32
1975	59.9	15.59
1976	74.3	18.30
1977	94.6	21.89
1978	109.1	23.45
1979	107.2	20.71
1980	90.6	15.42
1981	109.5	16.88
1982	105.6	15.34
1983	149.4	21.02

As you can see, real corporate profits (prior to 1978) made their all-time high in 1966 (probably only coincidentally along with the Dow Jones Industrial Average) at $22.21 billion. And, in 1983, even with the Reagan administration's significant corporate tax relief that reversed a disastrous four-year slide, real corporate profits were 5 percent lower than 1966, at $21.02 billion. Real corporate earnings in 1983 were actually below the level achieved in 1965. Also, even during the record real-profit year of 1978, the real Dow Jones Industrial Average was much lower than in 1966. The stock market rightly capitalized these profits at a much lower rate because of the subsequent growth of every facet of government and the worsening economic outlook this growth entailed.

The best kept secret about corporate profits is how small they really are in relation to other measures of national income and expenditure. The following table shows that corporate profits as a percentage of gross national product had declined from a modest 5.58 percent in 1950 to an alarming 4.52 percent in 1983:

After-Tax Corporate Profits as a Percentage of Gross National Product (GNP)
(Billions of Dollars)

YEAR	AFTER-TAX CORPORATE PROFITS (Dollars)	GNP (Dollars)	CORPORATE PROFITS AS A PERCENTAGE OF GNP
1950	16.0	286.5	5.58
1955	23.4	400.0	5.85
1960	24.9	506.5	4.92
1965	49.1	691.1	7.10
1970	37.2	992.7	3.75
1975	59.9	1,549.2	3.87
1980	90.6	2,631.7	3.44
1983	149.4	3,304.8	4.52

The next table compares corporate profits with compensation of employees (this is the table no labor union wants to be reminded of):

After-Tax Corporate Profits as a Percentage of Compensation of Employees
(Billions of Dollars)

YEAR	AFTER-TAX CORPORATE PROFITS (Dollars)	COMPENSATION OF EMPLOYEES (Dollars)	CORPORATE PROFITS AS PERCENTAGE OF COMPENSATION OF EMPLOYEES
1950	16.0	154.8	10.33
1955	23.4	224.9	10.40
1960	24.9	294.9	8.44
1965	49.1	396.5	12.38
1970	37.2	612.0	6.08
1975	59.9	931.4	6.43
1980	90.6	1,599.6	5.67
1983	149.4	1,984.9	7.53

Again, the same long-term, downward trend is evident. Take special note of the fact that while corporate profits measured in currency were declining 24 percent from 1965 to 1970, employee compensation was increasing more than 54 percent during the same period.

One of the most interesting measures of corporate profits is in comparison with federal government spending:

After-Tax Corporate Profits as a Percentage of Federal Spending
(Billions of Dollars)

YEAR	AFTER-TAX CORPORATE PROFITS (Dollars)	FEDERAL SPENDING (Dollars)	CORPORATE PROFITS AS A PERCENTAGE OF FEDERAL SPENDING
1950	16.0	40.8	39.22
1955	23.4	68.1	34.36
1960	24.9	93.1	26.75
1965	49.1	123.8	39.66
1970	37.2	204.3	18.21
1975	59.9	356.6	16.80
1980	90.6	602.1	15.05
1983	149.4	819.7	18.23

Even in 1950, corporate profits represented only 39.22 percent of federal expenditures, but by 1983, instead of growing as it had in Japan, this percentage had fallen by more than 53 percent to 18.23 percent. (Is that still too obscene, Jimmy?) Even if corporate income taxes had been eliminated in 1983 (and if government really wants new jobs, prosperity, and economic growth, they should be totally eliminated), gross corporate income would have equaled only 27.5 percent of federal spending.

Politicians and bureaucrats don't seem to understand that a substantial amount of their salaries and the wealth they feel compelled to waste comes from corporate operations. (Corporate income taxes alone were more than $75 billion in 1983, and the income taxes and Social Security taxes corporate employees paid was many times higher.) According to their reasoning, large profits are evil, but when some companies (like Chrysler) attempt to remedy this travesty of economic justice by generating losses, that is bad because jobs are lost when companies fail. It reminds me of a quote by Cullen Hightower: "We all like to see everybody make a little profit . . . a very little." This wish has been granted.

In any country, economic growth, national wealth, and the standard of living are *always* a function of profits: the higher the profits the greater the prosperity for the entire nation. The dream of "prosperity without profits" will come due. I just hope our government isn't too disappointed that Poland beat us to this goal.

PROPERTY RIGHTS

The crucial test of private property is the attitude of government toward money. Devaluation [inflation] of currency is outright expropriation.

—ISABEL PATERSON
THE GOD OF THE MACHINE

Let the people have property and they will have power—a power that will forever be exerted to prevent the restriction of the press, the abolition of trial by jury, or the abridgement of any other privilege.

—NOAH WEBSTER

The last point for consideration is the supposed disposition of the people to interfere with the rights of property. So essential does it appear to me, to the cause of good government, that the rights of property should be held sacred, that I would agree to deprive those of the elective franchise against whom it could justly be alleged that they considered it their interest to invade them.

—DAVID RICARDO

Private property was the original source of freedom. It still is its main bulwark.

—WALTER LIPPMANN

When you begin to live by others' property, there is no end to it. . . .

—MACHIAVELLI

Modern civilization was made possible by private property.

—F. A. HAYEK

Important principles may and must be inflexible.

—ABRAHAM LINCOLN

Property rights are, in reality, the only natural rights that human beings can have or, indeed, need to have, but they are constantly decimated by *unrestricted* government "legal" plunder. The following observation by Herbert Spencer shows that it has never been any different:

> Though, by current maxims and usages, the English Government recognize the right of property as sacred—though the infraction of it is considered by them one of the gravest crimes—though the laws profess to be so jealous of it as to punish even the stealing of a turnip; yet their legislators suspend it at will. They take the money of citizens for any project which they choose to undertake; though such project was not in the least contemplated by those who gave them authority— nay, though the greater part of the citizens from whom the money is taken had no share in giving them such authority. Each citizen can hold property only so long as the 654 deputies do not want it. It seemed to me that an exploded doctrine once current among them of "the divine right of kings," had simply been changed into the divine right of Parliaments [government].

Property rights are not a creation of law (although plunder can, has, and does come from that source). They existed long before written laws. In enlightened societies that know the true meaning of freedom and human rights, property rights have always been justly placed out of reach of envy and "legal" plunder by keeping them above the law (i.e., no legislation can be passed that violates property rights). The only legitimate function of the law is to protect property from plunder. The first written laws were instituted for this purpose, but like all systems (see SYSTEMS) the law eventually came to oppose its own proper function. "Laws" (of envy) and political power have become the basis of property instead of labor.

But how could this happen? What is the key assumption that allows the law to become an instrument of plunder and thus allows government to grow? Again we look to Herbert Spencer for the answer:

> For what is the tacit assumption on which such Acts [legislation] proceed? It is the assumption that no man has any claim to his property, not even to that which he has earned by the sweat of his brow, save by permission of the community [i.e., the majority]; and that the community may cancel the claim to any extent it thinks fit. No defence can be made for this appropriation of A's possessions for the benefit of B,

save one which sets out with the postulate that society as a whole has an absolute right over the possessions of each member. And now this doctrine, which has been tacitly assumed, is being openly proclaimed.

Once the law is perverted by envy to a point where it is placed above property rights, there is no limit to the size of government or the amount of "legal" plunder that can be voted into "law." "Property rights" become subject *only* to the whims of a growing government and the "needs" of special interests that are able to seize the law for their own purpose. Since "needs" are unlimited, the "necessary" amount of "legal" plunder and government continually grows. This is the fatal flaw (which no constitution can ever address) that allows democracy to mutate into socialism.

According to statists, all our problems stem from the "inequality" that comes from what is left of private property rights. Once these rights are removed, envy will be placated and all our problems will be solved. As usual they have everything exactly backward. The reality is that most of our problems stem from a lack of private property rights. The air, rivers, lakes, and oceans are not polluted because they belong to someone; they are polluted because they belong to everyone (no one). The buffalo and whales were slaughtered because they belonged to no one (everyone). The federal budget is a cesspool of waste because the wealth (once stolen from taxpayers) belongs to everyone (no one).

Owners of private property, such as farmers, are interested in maximizing the utility and returns on their property. They very seldom abuse or pollute their property or wastefully slaughter their livestock (although it is certainly their right to do so). In private property we nearly always see conservation and efficient utilization but in public property we see only corruption, waste (see WASTE), and inefficiency. It is the existence of more private property and less public property that should be the goal of any government devoted to freedom (obviously there is no such government).

Governments are so worried about attempting to satisfy envy, by passing new laws and seizing more power, that they have forgotten the most important one: "Thou shalt not steal." As we saw in the Dictionary of Government Euphemisms, theft disguised by any other name, whether you call it legislation, law, justice, taxes, welfare, insurance, subsidy, fairness, equity, equality, common good, conservation, tariffs, or majority rule, is still only theft.

John C. Calhoun had the following warning for governments of majority rule (democracies) that refuse to protect the rights of property (as they all do):

> No government based on the naked principle that the majority ought to govern, however true the maxim in its proper sense, and under proper restrictions, can preserve its liberty even for a single generation. The history of all has been the same—violence, injustice, and anarchy, succeeded by the government of one, or a few, under which the people seek refuge from the more oppressive despotism of the many.

PROPHECY

Men who are not surprised when the future comes live very close to the truth.

—ANONYMOUS

People and governments have never learned anything from history or acted upon principles deducible from it.

—GEORGE WILHELM

Ancient Rome declined because it had a Senate; now what's going to happen to us with both a Senate and a House?

—WILL ROGERS

Let us not dream that reason can ever be popular. Passions, emotions, may be made popular, but reason remains ever the property of the few.

—JOHANN WOLFGANG VON GOETHE

Time will reveal everything. It is a babbler, and speaks even when not asked.

—EURIPIDES

No one in the world knows, or can predict, exactly what is going to happen to the United States economy, but there is some handwriting on the wall. Many past grandiose dreams are currently coming due faster than our politicians can make new promises or retire.

The safest prediction I can make is that no matter what happens ultimately (as dreams come due), you are not going to like it! In addition, I think we can safely expect the following general predictions to hold true:

1. No politician will be elected who has the courage to tell the country what must be done (cut the size of government and pay

its debts) or the ability to do it, so government (i.e., plunder and debt) will continue to grow with increasingly disastrous consequences for the economy and (what is left of) our freedom.

2. The U.S. government will eventually be forced to try to make our currency worthless in order to save debtors, and they may succeed if they don't miscalculate and cause a deflationary crash with their stop-and-go economic policies.

3. We will have less and less stability in our society and economy as we stagger from one crisis to another while the Federal Reserve walks a thinning tightrope, trying to balance inflation and recession, and Congress agonizes over whether to tax or spend, spend and then tax, or just spend.

4. The official economy will not grow as much, as more and more economic activity moves to the less efficient, but government-free, underground economy.

5. Capitalism (which does not exist anywhere in the world) will continue to take the blame for socialism's failure, precipitating even greater government control over what's left of the "above-ground" economy. This will cause a stagnating economy and a lower standard of living for the American people and the world. Our society will continue to become less stable as morals, ethics, and competence fall to government levels, and "laws" of envy and plunder run out of control.

REAL (REALLY)

For the great majority of mankind are satisfied with appearances, as though they were realities, and are often more influenced by the things that seem than by those that are.

—MACHIAVELLI

The world is governed more by appearances than by realities, so that it is fully as necessary to seem to know something as to know it.

—DANIEL WEBSTER

Human kind [government] cannot bear very much reality.

—T. S. ELIOT

One of the criteria of emotional maturity is having the ability to deal constructively with reality.

—WILLIAM C. MENNINGER

The word *real* has become a necessary adjective for just about every financial figure published by the United States government. (It is always necessary when an economy is measured in currency, instead of money.) If the latest gross national product is X, the *real* gross national product (i.e., adjusted for inflation) is $0.5X$.

It's too bad the press can't be as accurate when they give us the latest Dow Jones Averages, or when they scream hysterically about "obscene" corporate profits. It would also be nice if the IRS could understand that $100,000 of income in 1984 equals about $14,000 in 1940 purchasing power, and tax us accordingly.

The fact that it is necessary to precede currency numbers with a word like *real* is indicative that the original number (much like government itself) is unreal and meaningless. People are slowly beginning to grasp the reality of this situation (or the unreality of unbacked currency), but it is still more fun to count depreciating pieces of paper than to compute real purchasing power.

If we are to be aware of government fraud and encroachments on our freedom, we must dedicate ourselves to reality. We would do well to follow the advice of Jean Jacques Rousseau:

The world of reality has limits; the world of imagination is boundless. Not being able to enlarge the one, let us contract the other; for it is from their difference that the evils arise which render us unhappy.

REAL ESTATE

About 78 percent of the earth is covered with water. The rest is covered with mortgages.

—MOTIVATIONAL ENTERPRISES
THE DOTTED LINE..........

Where profit is, loss is hidden nearby.

—JAPANESE PROVERB

Great profits, great risks.

—CHINESE PROVERB

Fish see the bait, but not the hook; men see the profit, but not the peril.

—CHINESE PROVERB

Neither trees nor bull markets grow to the sky.

—OLD WALL STREET ADAGE

In the dreams of real estate owners and investors, theirs is the only market that cannot go down. This dream has been shared by investors in other markets. Every one knew that diamonds could not go down: DeBeers, the diamond monopoly, would not allow it. Everyone knew that gold could not go down: inflation would not allow it. Everyone knew that silver could not go down: the Hunts would not allow it. Everyone knew that oil could not go down: OPEC would not allow it. These dreams of one-way markets have all come due. Real estate will have its turn someday (maybe soon).

The following chart clearly shows there is no historical immunity to price declines in the real estate market:

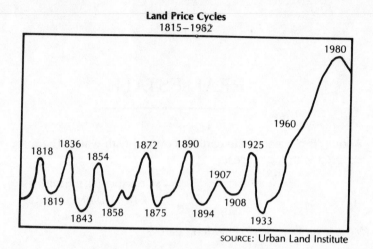

SOURCE: Urban Land Institute

The only extraordinary fact shown in this chart is that we have gone almost fifty years without a price decline of any significance. I get the same feeling looking at this chart today as I do looking at 1929 stock charts.

Speculative markets are nearly always the result of government manipulation of the supply of currency and credit, or interference in the free market. The normal progression is from conservatism and thrift to a rising market (prosperity), followed by easy credit and excessive debt, to the misallocation of resources leading to unsustainable prices, finally resulting in distress liquidation (panic) and depression. For a recent example of this type of politically induced disaster, we have only to look at the oil and gas industry.

The long upward trend in real estate, which started at the bottom of the depression in 1933, has primarily been the result of two factors:

1. Real estate has been used as a substitute for the store-of-value function of money that the government has removed from circulation.
2. Real estate has been used to shelter income from confiscatory progressive taxation, by means of interest and depreciation deductions, and by currency appreciation (real or imagined) at more favorable capital gain rates.

Housing has been the the chief beneficiary of the real estate boom, outpacing the stock market, gold, and the CPI (DDI) since 1930. I suspect that the only reason it had superior performance was that it had the advantages of long-term financing at fixed rates (largely sub-sidized by the government) and tremendous leverage (10 percent down, just like the stock market in 1929) and could offer two types of shelter (tax and housing). The other markets could not.

Using 1932 as a base year, we find that the average currency price of a home changed from about $2,800 to $72,000 in 1982, or a compounded increase of 6.7 percent per year. The real increase after adjusting for currency depreciation has been only 2.7 percent per year, not exactly the quick road to riches.

The worst result of the government-induced housing boom has been a tremendous misallocation of capital. More capital flows into mort-gages than into any other investment, and 75 percent of all mortgages are for housing. We are the most "overhoused" country in the world, relative to our wealth. In 1950, housing debt as a percentage of GNP was 19.3 percent, but by 1980, it had grown to 42.7 percent. Housing debt, which was 26.8 percent of disposable income in 1950, grew to 61.5 percent of disposable income by 1980. Also remember that the 1980 figures are understated because it costs much more to finance debt now than it did in 1950. (At 16 percent interest, you pay for a house five times.) Mortgage payments that took 19 percent of dis-posable income as recently as 1971 took more than 30 percent in 1980.

Japan builds factories and we build houses, but it takes factories (production) to pay for houses. If government would stop punishing areas of productive capital commitment (such as savings; see SAVING) through inflation and taxation, a healthier balance could be restored between housing (which, contrary to what real estate brokers say, is consumption, not an "investment") and capital formation (factors of production).

Huge fortunes have been made in all areas of real estate, but the greater part of these fortunes were merely inflation transfers of wealth from mortgage lenders, savers who watched the rate of inflation exceed their mortgage yields, to mortgage borrowers, speculators who cor-rectly bet that real estate would appreciate at rates higher than inflation. With relatively new, free market interest rates and variable-rate mort-gages (that move up with inflation), *these transfers are over*! Investors today are getting long-term fixed-rate mortgages with the same en-thusiasm they have for long-term bonds. A look at the following table shows why:

Real Mortgage Rates

YEAR	NEW HOME MORTGAGE RATES (Percentage)	INFLATION RATE (Percentage)	REAL MORTGAGE RATE (Percentage)	YEAR MORTGAGE RATE WAS EXCEEDED BY CPI
1963	5.89	1.2	4.69	1970
1964	5.83	1.3	4.53	1970
1965	5.81	1.7	4.11	1970
1966	6.25	2.9	3.35	1974
1967	5.46	2.9	2.56	1970
1968	6.97	4.2	2.77	1974
1969	7.81	5.4	2.41	1974
1970	8.45	5.9	2.55	1974
1971	7.74	4.3	3.44	1974
1972	7.60	3.3	4.30	1974
1973	7.96	6.2	1.76	1974
1974	8.92	11.0	−2.08	1974
1975	9.00	9.1	−0.10	1975
1976	9.00	5.8	3.20	1979
1977	9.02	6.5	2.52	1979
1978	9.56	7.7	1.86	1979
1979	10.78	11.3	−0.52	1979
1980	12.66	13.5	−0.84	1980
1981	14.70	10.4	4.30	?
1982	15.14	6.1	9.04	?
1983	12.57	3.2	9.37	?
1984	12.38	4.3	8.08	?

We see the same pattern in mortgages as we do in other interest rates. From 1963 to 1981, the record real mortgage rate is not the 14.7 percent (real mortgage rate, 4.30 percent) of 1981, but the 5.89 percent (real mortgage rate, 4.69 percent) of 1963.

However, in 1982, we entered a new era that should signal the end of the extraordinary bull market in real estate. Note that the real mortgage rate for 1982 was 9.04 percent, almost double the 4.69 percent real rate of 1963. The real mortgage rate for 1983 was even higher at 9.38 percent, and 1984 was still more than 8 percent. There is really no way for the real estate dream to continue by out-appreciating the new, crushing real mortgage rates. (Remember, as previously stated, that housing prices showed a real yearly appreciation of only 2.7 percent from 1932 to 1982, hardly a rate that can stand up against current real mortgage rates in excess of 8 percent.)

As you can see, the uncertainty caused by inflation is destroying our long-term capital markets (as it always does), and it is hard (if not impossible) to envision a real estate market without a mortgage market. This is why it is such a mistake to assume that real estate appreciation must inevitably continue with more inflation. Mexico, like most Latin American countries, is currently experiencing greater than 100 percent yearly inflation, but property is going down because the economy (which must support property values) is dying from government growth. In England, real estate dropped almost 30 percent in the early 1970s in spite of high inflation, for essentially the same reasons.

Government attacks on any form of property rights will increase as government grows and the economy declines, and will, eventually, negatively affect the value of all forms of property to a greater or lesser degree. Real estate is a highly visible form of property with easily traceable ownership, and it is becoming an increasingly popular target for government plunder because it cannot hide or be transported to safer areas (i.e., run away). This increasing taxation will reduce its advantages as an "investment" as well as its value. New York (where else?) recently voted a 10 percent tax on real estate gains over $1 million (sounds like the same method they used to start the income tax: start with the rich and work down), and Connecticut voted a 0.5 percent "conveyance" tax on all real estate transactions. Virtually all state and local governments are beginning to rely more and more on property taxes.

The U.S. real estate market may hold on for quite a while longer, although I doubt it, on seller financing, before the next cycle of decline, but sooner or later, the pool of sellers with enough equity to provide purchase mortgages, which have helped mask price declines because of their below-market interest rates, will be used up. Any further decline in prices will merely speed up the process. If inflation accelerates, real price declines may be masked by currency price increases, but if we experience deflation instead, *prices will crash*. No matter which way things go, the easy money in real estate is now history.

Since the last real estate decline was largely the result of deflation, it should be interesting and educational to look back at that part of history. For those who need further proof that real estate can go down, perhaps the following passages from Gerald Loeb's book *The Battle for Stock Market Profits* will be of interest:

> I lived in New York City in 1929. Hotels of all kinds were then going up on every side. They were in deep financial trouble almost overnight. I paid $12,000 a year rental for my two-bedroom-and-living room suite in the Savoy Plaza. A year later I paid $4,000 a year, and this rate prevailed for about ten years. . . .
>
> Cash was king. If you had cash you could buy tremendous bargains. There were equities in co-op luxury apartments that sold for six figures in 1929 going for just one dollar in the 1930s. The owners could not pay their taxes, mortgage interest, and maintenance. (Like everything else, co-op apartments are inflated again.). . . . Prices of homes declined sharply.

An example of the bargains Loeb alluded to is taken from a biography of Joe Kennedy called *The Founding Father* by Richard J. Whalen:

> Though spectacular, his transactions in Manhattan shrank beside his biggest acquisition—Chicago's Merchandise Mart. Real estate men still marvel over the deal that made Kennedy owner of the world's largest commercial building.
>
> Opened by Marshall Field in 1930, the twenty-four-story Mart boasted ninety-three acres of rentable space. It had been built at a cost of some $30,000,000, and in 1945 was valued on the books of Marshall Field and Company at more than $21,000,000. . . .
>
> Not since his days in Hollywood had Kennedy come upon such a situation. In a boldly conceived and executed deal, he bought the Mart for $12,956,516. . . .

In other words, twenty years after the 1925 peak in real estate (and twelve years after the 1933 bottom), Kennedy was able to buy the Mart for less than 45 percent of its original cost and less than 65 percent of its depreciated book value. Also note that even at that price, Whalen still describes the purchase as "boldly conceived."

Even real estate dreams can, and have, come due. This cycle is no different. The law of markets has not been suspended for real estate. There is no market that just goes up. There have been several periods in history when real estate depreciated and currency did not.

REGULATION

Government always has exercised the liberty of universal
interference, and nobody ever questioned its right to do so.

—HERBERT SPENCER

Nothing is so galling to a people, not broken in from the birth, as
a paternal or, in other words, a meddling government, a
government which tells them what to read and say and eat and
drink and wear.

—THOMAS MACAULAY

Anything that interferes with individual progress ultimately will
retard group progress.

—GEORGE H. HOUSTON

As soon as government management begins it upsets the natural
equilibrium of industrial relations, and each interference only
requires further bureaucratic control until the end is the tyranny
of the totalitarian state.

—ADAM SMITH

If you have ten thousand regulations you destroy all respect for
the law.

—WINSTON CHURCHILL

The U. S. government (like all governments) possesses a versatile
incompetence. Although it cannot even provide its citizens protection
from force and fraud, it presumes to regulate every facet of our lives.
Nowhere is what is seen and what is not seen better demonstrated than
in the area of regulation.

Regulation is merely a partially hidden form of taxation and waste
and thus represents one of the more insidious aspects of government
growth. It currently costs the private sector more than $160 billion a

year to comply with government regulation. In addition to the waste of this staggering expense, our national productivity is decreased by well over 1 percent each year because the private sector is forced to disguise government employees on their payrolls—people they *must* hire to comply with government regulations—from the people who pay their salaries in the form of higher prices.

Gustave Le Bon described the consequences of "unregulated" regulation (which is even more prevalent in socialist and totalitarian states) in his book *The Crowd*:

> This incessant creation of restrictive laws and regulations, surrounding the pettiest actions of existence with the most complicated formalities, inevitably has for its result the confining within narrower and narrower limits of the sphere in which the citizen may move freely. Victims of the delusion that equality and liberty are the better assured by the multiplication of laws, nations daily consent to put up with trammels increasingly burdensome. They do not accept this legislation with impunity. Accustomed to put up with every yoke, they soon end by desiring servitude, and lose all spontaneousness and energy. They are then no more than vain shadows, passive, unresisting and powerless automata.

In *The Man Versus the State* Herbert Spencer had the following comment on the inevitable outcome of government regulation and the various systems (see SYSTEMS) it must entail:

> If, as we have seen in a large class of cases, government measures do not remedy the evils they aim at; if, in another large class, they make these evils worse instead of remedying them; and if, in a third large class, while curing some evils they entail others, and often greater ones; if, as we lately saw, public action is continually outdone in efficiency by private action; and if, as just shown, private action is obliged to make up for the shortcomings of public action [as it always is], even in fulfilling the vital functions of the State; what reason is there for wishing more public administrations? The advocates of such may claim credit for philanthropy [vicarious generosity], but not for wisdom; unless wisdom is shown by disregarding experience [a prime qualification for serving in any government].

So why does the state continue to regulate in spite of the costs and its glaring failures? Is it really that irrational and dedicated to insanity? Not at all. Max Stirner provides the answer in his book *The Ego and His Own*:

The state seeks to hinder every free activity by its censorship, its supervision, its police, and holds this hindering to be its duty, because it is in truth a duty of self-preservation. The State wants to make something out of a man, therefore there live in it only made men; everyone who wants to be his own self is its opponent.

Whenever I see a once successful business fail (such as the wholesale bankruptcy of the oil and gas industry), a massive private project blocked, a great producer silently go on strike, or one of the endless stream of government officials on trial for corruption, all because of some form of needless regulation, I am reminded of a passage from *Our Enemy, The State* by Albert J. Nock:

> It is a curious anomaly. State power has an unbroken record of inability to do anything efficiently, economically, disinterestedly or honestly; yet when the slightest dissatisfaction arises over any exercise of social [i.e., private] power, the aid of the agent least qualified to give aid is immediately called for. Does social power mismanage banking-practice in this-or-that special instance—then let the State, which never has shown itself able to keep its own finances from sinking promptly into the slough of misfeasance, wastefulness and corruption, intervene to "supervise" or "regulate" the whole body of banking-practice, or even take it over entirely. Does social power, in this-or-that case, bungle the business of railway-management—then let the State, which has bungled every business it has ever undertaken, intervene and put its hand to the business of "regulating" railway-operation [or the oil and gas industry].

If we measure the world's current situation in general, and America's current situation in particular, by Nock's criteria, then it is painfully obvious that regulation is a dream that is fast coming due.

RESPONSIBILITY

Liberty means responsibility. That is why most men dread it.

—GEORGE BERNARD SHAW

The real freedom of any individual can always be measured by the amount of responsibility which he must assume for his own welfare and security.

—ROBERT WELCH

No man was ever endowed with a right without being at the same time saddled with a responsibility.

—GERALD W. JOHNSON

Any doctrine that...weakens personal responsibility for judgment and for action...helps create the attitudes that welcome and support the totalitarian state.

—JOHN DEWEY

People do not lack strength, they lack will.

—VICTOR HUGO

You cannot help men permanently by doing for them what they could and should do for themselves.

—ABRAHAM LINCOLN

One of the foremost problems in the world today is a growing unwillingness of individuals, business, and government to accept responsibility for their actions on any level. Responsibility always brings the risk (see RISK) of decisions and the potential pain or reward of the consequences. Strangely enough, no one seeks to transfer the rewards of responsibility, but only the pains. Ralph Waldo Emerson's admonition in "Compensation" relates to the inseparability of reward and pain:

We can no more halve things and get the sensual good, by itself, than we can get an inside that shall have no outside, or a light without a shadow.

Any time we seek to avoid the painful parts of responsibility by shifting them to someone else, we automatically surrender, by default, our freedom and thus any chance for rewards.

Congress will not accept responsibility for the budget, so in thirty-six of the last forty-two years, we've had a federal deficit. Socialist governments will not accept responsibility for their inherently weak economies and pathetic "investments," so the credit markets of the West get endless demands for loans that will never be repaid. Bankers will not accept responsibility for loans to socialist governments, so they issue demands for government guarantees (i.e., taxpayer guarantees) of these loans to "save" the banking system (by compounding the losses). Business will not accept responsibility for management decisions, so we get Lockheed and Chrysler showing up in Washington (but not for a handout—just for a hand). Labor will not accept responsibility for its decisions that impose higher costs on business, so we hear cries for tariffs (see TARIFFS) and other forms of import restrictions to save "disloyal" consumers from better and cheaper foreign products (or the most current demand for a government reindustrialization policy and re-regulation of the airlines). A growing number of people will not accept responsibility for their lives, so we get a government bureaucracy that devours 42 percent of our gross national product to deliver "services" ranging from making intermittent mail delivery to giving massive handouts to foreign governments that hate us and are totally hostile to human freedom.

The long-term effect of government control and its growth is the destruction of industry's ability to compete and people's ability to make decisions and assume responsibility. Note the following observation of Herbert Spencer in his essay "The Proper Sphere of Government":

Nature provides nothing in vain. Instincts and organs are only preserved so long as they are required. Place a tribe of animals in a situation where one of their attributes is unnecessary—take away its natural exercise—diminish its activity, and you will gradually destroy its power. Successive generations will see the faculty, or instinct, or whatever it may be, become gradually weaker, and an ultimate degeneracy of the race will inevitably ensue. All this is true of man. He, in like manner, has wants, many and varied—he is provided with moral and intellectual faculties, commensurate with the complexity of his relation to the external world—his happiness essentially depends upon the activity of those faculties; and with him, as with all the rest of creation, that activity is chiefly influenced by the requirements of his condition. The demands made upon his mental powers by his every day want—by the endeavour to overcome difficulties or avoid dangers, and by desire to secure a comfortable provision for the decline of life, are so many natural and salutary incentives to the exercise of those powers. Imperious necessity is the grand stimulus to man's physical and mental endowments, and without it he would sink into a state of hopeless torpidity.

In America today, the individuals are disappearing and the "crowds" are forming. Sixteen million people "depend" on government for their jobs, 22 million receive food stamps, and 36 million are required to believe Social Security is solvent (i.e., reject reality) because they draw checks on it every month. In *The True Believer* Eric Hoffer clearly described the main characteristics of people who surrender the responsibilities of personal independence to a paternalistic government and join the "crowd."

People whose lives are barren and insecure seem to show a greater willingness to obey than people who are self-sufficient and self-confident. To the frustrated, freedom from responsibility is more attractive than freedom from restraint.

Time is running very short for us to realize that personal freedom and personal responsibility have always been, and will always be, inseparable.

REVOLUTION

Every revolution, and even every war, creates illusions and is conducted in the name of unrealizable ideals.

—MILOVAN DJILAS

Is it really surprising that whenever you get striving for equality and fraternity, the guillotine appears on the scene?

—VLADIMIR BUKOVSKY

Every revolutionary ends by becoming either an oppressor or a heretic.

—ALBERT CAMUS

Most revolutionaries are potential Tories [dictators], because they imagine that everything can be put to rights by altering the shape of society.

—GEORGE ORWELL

Revolutions have never lightened the burden of tyranny: they have only shifted it to another shoulder.

—GEORGE BERNARD SHAW

Revolutions, as long and bitter experience reveals, are apt to take their color from the regime they overthrow.

—RICHARD H. TAWNEY

When a monarch, despot or right-wing government finally usurps enough power from its people to achieve utter economic incompetence, and the corresponding disasters that it ensures, the stage is set for a revolution (usually from the Left) led by some humanistic messiah (such as Lenin or "Chairman" Mao). Things will always be "much better" after the next slaughter (or next election when the budget will be "balanced," inflation will be "whipped," and government will be taken off our very weary backs). The new revolutionary government (or elected officials) will create a utopia. There will be "freedom," "equality," "brotherhood," and "wealth" for all—maybe even an election, and maybe with more than one candidate, once the revolution is "secure." But as Bertrand Russell noted in the *Saturday Review*, the revolution never quite becomes secure:

> Those who have seized power, even for the noblest of motives, soon persuade themselves that there are good reasons for not relinquishing it. This is particularly likely to happen if they believe themselves to represent some immensely important cause [as they always do]. They will feel that their opponents are ignorant and perverse; before long they will come to hate them. . . . The important thing is to keep their power, not to use it as a means to an eventual paradise. And so what were means become ends, and the original ends are forgotten except on Sundays.

In keeping with Russell's remarks, the lesson of history is that the government that springs from a revolution will invariably be worse than the one it replaced. Revolutions cannot and will not ever alter human nature. They are fueled to a large extent by envy, and thus, always use the prior administration as a role model for the new government. The only significant changes are new scapegoats (i.e., America, the rich, or some defenseless minority), more plunder, repression, and terror. (The class system remains completely intact, but the "higher classes" are populated by a new more vicious set of looters and thugs.)

The examples of the perverse nature of violent revolutions are well documented by history, as Ayn Rand has noted. The cry of the French Revolution was "Liberty, Equality, and Fraternity!" They got Robespierre and the guillotine. The Russian peasants wanted to be rid of the evil Czar. They got the communists and mass starvation. The Germans were convinced they needed "Room to live!" They got the Nazis, "Room to die," and lost half of their country to the Soviet Union. The Cubans wanted "Freedom," but got Castro; the Iranians wanted to rid themselves of the cruel Shah and his terror and corruption. They did, and now have the benevolent Khomeini shattering all the Shah's records for repression, death, and carnage; and most recently, the impoverished people of Nicaragua wanted to rid themselves of the dictator Somoza and have "Democracy," and instead they got the Sandinistas (i.e., communists) and even greater repression and poverty.

Many people would claim that the American Revolution was the one great exception to the rule, but it was not. That revolution was slowly dying from the first days of the new government (when Washington solved the Whiskey Rebellion by unleashing the army on American farmers who were rebelling against a government tax on their tea—I mean, corn whiskey) and finally perished once and for all in the 1930s with the government's depression, which culminated in an orgy of regulation and government growth that would have literally astounded the framers of the Constitution. (The first American revolutionaries were, in fact, rebelling against a level of taxation and regulation that would seem nonexistent in our current environment.)

H. L. Mencken echoed these sad facts in the following passage from his essay "On Government":

> Politics, as hopeful men practise it in the world, consists mainly of the delusion that a change in form is a change in substance. The American colonists, when they got rid of the Potsdam tyrant, believed fondly that they were getting rid of oppressive taxes forever and setting up complete liberty. They found almost instantly that taxes were higher than ever, and before many years they were writhing under the Alien and Sedition Acts.

There is only one revolution that has a chance of restoring freedom to mankind, and that will have to be a continuing and prolonged revolution to reduce the size of government. All other revolutions that substitute one form of government (i.e., force and plunder) for another will remain dreams that quickly come due.

RIGHTS

Man has a primary property right to his person and his labor.

—LOUIS THIERS

The reigning error of mankind is that we are not content with the conditions on which the goods of life are granted.

—SAMUEL JOHNSON

Give to every other human being every right that you claim for yourself—that is my doctrine.

—THOMAS PAINE

Let us first ask what are the natural rights of men, and endeavor to secure them, before we propose either to beg or to pillage.

—HENRY GEORGE

Ludwig von Mises addressed the current misconception of rights in his book *The Anti-Capitalistic Mentality*:

The worst of all these delusions is the idea that nature has bestowed upon every man certain rights. According to this doctrine nature is openhanded toward every child born. There is plenty of everything for everybody. Consequently, everyone has a fair inalienable claim against all his fellow men and against society that he should get the full portion which nature has allotted to him. The eternal laws of natural and divine justice require that nobody should appropriate to himself what by rights belongs to other people. The poor are needy only because unjust people have deprived them of their birthright. It is the task of the church and the secular authorities to prevent such spoliation and to make all people prosperous. *Every word of this doctrine is false* [my emphasis]. Nature is not bountiful but stingy. It has restricted the supply of all things indispensable for the preservation of human life. It has populated the world with animals and plants to whom the impulse to destroy human life and welfare is inwrought. It displays powers and elements whose operation is damaging to human life and to human endeavors to preserve it. Man's survival and well-being are an achievement of the skill with which nature has equipped him—reason. Men, cooperating under the system of the division of labor, have created all the wealth which the daydreamers consider as a free gift of nature. With regard to the "distribution" of this wealth, it is nonsensical to refer to an allegedly divine or natural principle of justice. What matters is not the allocation of portions out of a fund presented to man by nature. The problem is rather to further those social institutions which enable people to continue and to enlarge the production of all those things which they need.

Rights is probably the favorite word of politicians and special interest groups, who have almost completely obscured the meaning of the word. The *only* natural rights humans have are the rights to their persons and property, but government has continually usurped these rights by placing its "law" above them. As these legitimate natural rights have been sacrificed to the forces of vicarious generosity, envy, and greed, they have been replaced by "needs" that have gradually become "rights" acquired either by or from the government and its plunder.

Louis Thiers gave an excellent description of true rights when he said:

Either rights exist, or they do not exist. If they exist, they involve absolute consequences. . . . Furthermore, if a right exists, it exists at every moment. It is absolute today, yesterday, tomorrow, the day after tomorrow, in summer as in winter, not when it pleases you [government] to declare it in force. . . .

Using these criteria, we can see that there is no such thing as a right to decent housing, a right to a good education, a right to a job or any other privilege acquired by plunder, except in the dreams of politicians. The natural rights of the people are stolen by government everyday, but that does not change the legal owner of these rights. The task before us is to reclaim them.

RISK

Contrary to the commonly accepted belief, it is the risk element in our capitalistic system which produces an economy of security. Risk brings out the ingenuity and resourcefulness which ensure the success of enough ventures to keep the economy growing and secure.

—ROBERT RAWLS

All men's gains are the fruit of venturing.

—HERODOTUS

Uncertainty and expectation are the joys of life. Security is an insipid thing, though the overtaking and possessing of a wish discovers the folly of the chase.

—WILLIAM CONGREVE

It's an old adage that the way to be safe is never to be secure. . . . Each one of us requires the spur of insecurity to force us to do our best.

—DR. HAROLD W. DODDS

We all covet wealth, but not its perils.

—JEAN DE LA BRUYÈRE

Who dares nothing, need hope for nothing.

—JOHANN SHILLER

RISK IS THE PRICE FOR OPPORTUNITY.

Nothing in our material world has been won without risk. Nothing will be won in the future without risk, but a person must have the incentive to risk time from his life or wealth that has been won by his time. There cannot be rewards without risk, and there will be no risks taken without rewards.

Risk has two facets:

1. The ability and resources to accept a risk
2. The willingness or desire to assume a risk

Every dollar taxed away from the successful risk taker lowers his ability and incentive (and therefore his desire) to take a further risk.

Today, there is a massive effort by various entities who have made disastrous mistakes, or want to be insulated from the free market decisions, to transfer their risk (or losses) to the federal government (i.e., the people of the United States). This has led to some of the following consequences:

1. The U.S. government's (i.e., the taxpayers) bailing out domestic banks that lent (gave) money to socialist governments
2. The U.S. government's (i.e., the taxpayers) bailing out failed corporations like Chrysler, Penn Central, and Lockheed
3. The U.S. government's supporting socialist or right-wing foreign governments, such as those of Viet Nam, Nicaragua, the Philippines, and Mexico, and their justly failing economies, with outright *gifts* of American citizens' wealth
4. The U.S. government's buying billions of dollars' worth of farm commodities at inflated prices to insulate farmers from the free market
5. Ad infinitum

All the efforts to shift the risks to defenseless taxpayers without any compensation have resulted in a trickling down of these risks to three repositories: producers, property owners, and holders of American currency. (Did you think the government could make these risks disappear? Where did you think they would go?)

Risk has always rightly implied a possibility of success and *failure*. Failure is just as important as success to the equation because, as Ben Franklin said, "Things that hurt instruct." Mankind (but no governments) has, unfortunately, always learned more from failure than from success. I am once again reminded of an idea from Emerson:

Our strength grows out of our weakness. The indignation which arms itself with secret forces does not awaken until we are pricked and stung and sorely assailed. . . . When he [man] is pushed, tormented, defeated, he has a chance to learn something; he has been put on his wits, on his manhood; he has gained facts; learns his ignorance; is cured of the insanity of conceit; has got moderation and real skill.

SAVING

You cannot bring prosperity by discouraging thrift.

—ABRAHAM LINCOLN

To save something each month develops self-control. This power frees one from fear and gives abiding courage.

—SAMUEL REYBURN

It took thrift and savings, together with tremendous character and vision, to make our nation what it is today. And it will take thrift and savings, together with constant ingenuity and stamina, to conserve our remaining resources to enable us to continue to be a great nation.

—JOHN W. SNYDER

A man with surplus can control circumstances, but a man without a surplus is controlled by them, and often he has no opportunity to exercise judgment.

—HARVEY S. FIRESTONE

He will always be a slave who does not know how to live upon a little.

—HORACE

The habit of saving is itself an education; it fosters every virtue, teaches self-denial, cultivates the sense of order, trains to forethought, and so broadens the mind.

—T. T. MUNGER

Saving is the one and only source of new capital. Producing more than you consume is the only road to increasing wealth and a higher standard of living. People who achieve wealth through their own efforts do not save because they are rich; they are rich because they save. The foresight and planning of savers sets the upper-income classes apart from the lower. But, as we have seen, inflation is a tax on saving, and thus, on capital formation too, so it attacks the primary source of society's existing wealth (see WEALTH).

What amount of inflation taxes have producers and savers been forced to pay? The American Institute of Economic Research has compiled the following table of estimates, using the CPI (which we know is understated). The losses just through 1981 are staggering:

Inflation Losses of U.S. Savers' Wealth 1939–1981 by Type of Asset
(In Billions of 1981 Dollars)

TYPE OF ASSET	LOSS (Dollars)
Savings and time deposits	1,320
Reserves for life insurance, private pensions, and annuities	720
Government trust funds	256
Government debt securities	696
State and local government debt securities	149
Corporate debt securities	147
Money-market funds shares	5
Currency and demand deposits	794
Other fixed-dollars assets (mortgages)	395
Total loss (embezzlement)	4,480

Although "investors" *thought* they had saved $7.9 trillion (1981 dollars) during those forty-three years, as you can see from the table, government inflation had embezzled a minimum of $4.48 trillion, or more than 50 percent of those savings.

But are America's savers really the upper-income classes, and therefore the chief victims of this fraud? A recent survey by William J. Fitzgerald, Inc., came up with the following statistics:

Savings by Family Income
(In Millions of Dollars, Total U.S. Population)

MONTH	LESS THAN $15,000	$15,000 to $25,000	$25,000 AND OVER	TOTAL
March 1980	−264.9	38.2	653.8	501.2
June 1980	−222.6	188.4	747.9	713.7
July 1980	−504.4	19.8	227.5	−257.1
October 1980	−264.9	38.2	653.8	427.1

Note that for every period shown in the table, the highest income group was responsible for more than the total amount saved because lower income groups are essentially nonsavers. Naturally the highest income group is constantly hit for the greatest amount of income taxes, while being endlessly inflated into higher brackets. (This is the government's idea of encouraging saving.) The United States hits savings with some of the highest taxes in the world but can't understand why interest rates are so high and saving rates are so low. (Japan allows a certain amount of individual saving with no tax on the income, and thus enjoys the highest saving rate in the world.)

Since government taxation, regulation, and inflation are the enemies of saving, you would expect the rate of saving to decline as government grows and inflation accelerates. The following table shows that to be exactly the case:

Average Annual Government Consumption, Inflation, and Savings Rates, 1951–1980
(Percentage of Net National Product [NNP])

PERIOD	TOTAL GOVERNMENT CONSUMPTION AS PERCENTAGE OF NNP	AVERAGE RATE OF INFLATION (CPI)	NET NATIONAL SAVINGS AS PERCENTAGE OF NNP
1951–1960	14.1	2.12	16.4
1961–1970	16.7	2.76	15.2
1971–1980	18.9	7.87	11.7

Note the uniform growth in government consumption and inflation, and the corresponding decline in the rate of saving. (As the security of property rights declines, so does the rate of saving.)

Since there cannot be capital formation without savings, you would expect the declining rate of U.S. savings to show up in lower rates of expenditure for plant and equipment. It does. In the latter half of the 1970s, 2.5 percent of GNP went for new factors of production, down more than 38 percent from the same period in the 1960s. This decline was one of the major factors in our low productivity and income growth and contributed significantly to higher "unemployment" (see UNEMPLOYMENT).

The dream of greater "investment," employment, and productivity through decreased saving is about to come due.

SECURITY

Those who give up essential liberty to obtain a little temporary
safety [security] deserve neither liberty nor safety [and will have
neither].

—BENJAMIN FRANKLIN

Too many people are thinking of security instead of opportunity.
They seem more afraid of life than death.

—JAMES F. BYRNES

Security is mostly a superstition.

—HELEN KELLER

Security is when everything is settled, when nothing can happen
to you; security is the denial of life.

—GERMAINE GREER

Although total security is the driving force behind most human
action and is a worthy objective for which to strive, it does not exist
in this life. The world is an extremely insecure and dangerous place.
It always has been and probably always will be.

Material security can only come from production and saving, and
all savings must first be earned. Government growth, which is man-
ifested by the loss of property rights through increasing taxation,
regulation, and inflation, is the main threat to mankind's security
because it destroys the ability and incentive to produce and save.
Governments try to offset the economic damage they do by attempting
to "legislate" material security into existence. It cannot be done.

In "Compensation," Emerson captured the fallacy and result of this
"something-for-nothing" thinking in the following comment on the
perfect compensation of the universe:

the doctrine that every thing [including security] has its price—and if that price is not paid, not that thing but something else is obtained, and that it is impossible to get anything without its price—is not less sublime in the columns of a ledger than in the budgets of states. . . .

Politicians think that they can ignore the law of compensation and create security out of air (like currency and credit) by the "legal" plunder of the productive elements of society, but there can never be security from plunder: only poverty and revolt. By trying to provide something that has not first been earned and does not therefore exist, politicians create exactly the opposite effect (see SYSTEMS). Social Security (see SOCIAL SECURITY) has already brought this country to the brink of bankruptcy. The "benefits" that have been "promised" (i.e., legislated) do not exist now and will not in the future. The people drawing checks on this system are the most insecure, frightened people in our population (next to the ones being *forced* to support it) because they sense this dream is about to come due.

The only legitimate security that government is responsible for is security from force or fraud. Material security, like health, is a personal responsibility. People can never hope for and should not expect absolute security under the best of conditions, but there can be no hope for any security as long as inflation and government growth are allowed to continue. No one can have any chance of knowing how much earning or saving will be enough because of the continually declining value of our (and everyone else's) currency, and government's insatiable desire for a greater share of its citizens' wealth.

Money (not currency), which cannot lose its value, the *freedom* to produce wealth, and strong property rights (i.e., low levels of taxation and regulation) are still mankind's best hope for increasing its wealth, and thus its security. The rule is and has always been, the more government, the less security. There is simply no way to trade freedom for security.

SOCIAL SECURITY

(Ponzi, Where Are You?)

The certainties of one age are the problems of the next.

—RICHARD H. TAWNEY

He that diggeth a pit shall fall into it.

—ECCLESIASTES

If you allow a political catchword to go on and grow, you will awaken some day to find it standing over you, arbiter of your destiny, against which you are powerless.

—WILLIAM GRAHAM SUMNER

There's a sucker [taxpayer] born every minute.

—P. T. BARNUM

There is no dependence that can be sure but dependence upon one's self.

—JOHN GAY

A beautiful theory, killed by a nasty, ugly little fact.

—THOMAS H. HUXLEY

Social Security is another example of the foot-in-the-door technique employed by governments. When this pyramid scheme first became law, the rate was 1 percent of the first $3,000 in wages, or $30. In 1985, the rate was 7.05 percent of the first $39,600 or $2,970. When measured in currency, this represents an increase of more than 9900 percent in forty-four years. After adjusting for inflation, the increase is still more than 1100 percent.

Now for the bad news: Without massive increases in this tax and significant cuts in benefits, the system will go broke before the end of this century. This dream is fast coming due.

The problem, as usual, stems from government's ability to give away benefits faster than the people who have to pay can earn them. Since 1960, Congress has raised the benefits at almost twice the rate it has raised the "contributions." As with most government programs, the system (see SYSTEMS) was never placed on a sound actuarial basis from its inception, and it has never been changed to reflect the new demographics. Full benefits were paid after only five years of contributions even though it took more than thirty-five years of contributions to earn them. Very few people have paid into the system for a length of time, or at high enough rates, to earn the current payments they claim to be entitled to, so a large portion of their monthly check is really disguised welfare. Even with the unbelievable increases in "contributions" over the past decade, current Social Security *unfunded* liabilities total more than 5 trillion (with a *t*) dollars.

One of the chief architects of the Social Security Administration, Bob Myers, describes the current dilemma as follows:

Social Security got into trouble because the system's commitments expanded faster than its resources. [Sounds like a typical government program to me.] From its beginning in 1935, as a relatively austere [that's the way most government programs start] retirement insurance system closely tied to the amount of payroll taxes that his employer contributed, Social Security just grew and grew. [Oh, really?]

Commenting on the future *certain* bankruptcy of the system Myers continues:

Doomsday is so bad that politically, it will never be allowed to happen. Congress will always [try to] do something to postpone the day.

Myers doesn't explain *how* Congress is going to be able to legislate more than $5 trillion into existence, merely to avoid "unpleasant consequences." (But if you think it is somehow possible, I have a good buy on a bridge in Brooklyn that I'd like to show you.)

Now every bankrupt idea has a champion, and Social Security is no exception. One of the reigning Kings of Dreams Come Due has got to be Congressman Claude Pepper (who once described Stalin as "a man Americans can trust"). Pepper has the distinction of being one of the only supporters of the original Social Security legislation, who was still around when the bills started coming due. Never one to shirk responsibility, Pepper came up with an "answer" to Social Security's inevitable, continual insolvency. Can you guess? Pepper's plan was to borrow the shortfall in Social Security from general budget revenues. In other words, borrow from the "revenue" of a budget that's more than $100 billion in deficit. A brilliant and original idea! As Pepper has said, and personally proved over and over again, "One has a right to be wrong in a democracy." Since we know the ultimate answer to Social Security's problem will be more taxes and more borrowing, note the hypocrisy in my other "favorite" idea from Pepper: "If more politicians in this country were thinking about the next generation instead of the next election, it might be better for the United States and the world." Amen, Claude.

To demonstrate what a pathetic investment Social Security is for anyone, take a look at this example: assume you are thirty years of age and want to be able to retire at age sixty-five. By that time, you and your employer (making maximum payments) will have paid about $220,000 into the system under the 1982 law. If the same contributions had been put into an Individual Retirement Account (IRA) at an 8 percent compounded rate of return, it would total more than $1.2 million by the time you reached age sixty-five, which, at an 8 percent yield would allow you a monthly income of $8,000, without touching the principal. Also keep in mind that the IRA income would be available to you even if you chose to keep working for the rest of your life. With Social Security, you effectively forfeit nearly all benefits if you continue working after age sixty-five and earn more than the princely sum of $7,000 per year. (Currently, some older workers can actually end up in the equivalent of a 96 percent tax bracket.) But, let's be generous (and gullible), and assume that Social Security payments *could* match the monthly income of the private plan. We still find one big difference: In the IRA program, the principal of $1.2 million is still part of *your estate*, to dispose of any way you please. In the Social Security plan, you have no principal. The tax receipts are spent faster than they come in.

Some estimates indicate that by early next century, one-half of all wages will be needed to maintain social Security payments. Younger workers will rebel long before that point is reached. The system will not *officially* go broke (even though it already is), but even with higher taxes, it will be forced to "reschedule its payments" by means of depreciating currency or benefit cuts, much to the sorrow of the people who believe in, or will depend on this program. Anyone who can add and subtract knows this is true. The only way to keep a pyramid scheme going is with a new crop of suckers; there is no way it can be "saved." In spite of P. T. Barnum's theory, any demographic survey will tell you that we are running very short of new suckers. Either admit that a bankrupt system is bankrupt, or bankrupt the country, pretending it is not. Keep your currency rolling in and stay tuned.

SOCIETY

Society exists for the benefit of its members, not the members for the benefit of society.

—HERBERT SPENCER

The pillars of truth and the pillars of freedom—they are the pillars of society.

—HENRIK IBSEN

France fell because there was corruption without indignation.

—ROMAIN ROLLAND

Society and government are different in themselves, and have different origins. Society is produced by our wants, and government by our wickedness. Society is in every state a blessing; government even in its best state but a necessary evil.

—WILLIAM GODWIN

The most severe costs imposed by government plunder and disruption of an economy are borne by the society that must suffer them. Government always brings envy, plunder, and corruption in direct proportion to its size. It first corrupts itself, then the law, next the currency, soon thereafter the economy, and finally the people. This progression of corruption causes society to begin a breakdown, as was foreseen by Frederic Bastiat in *The Law*:

No society can exist if respect for the law does not to some extent prevail; but the surest way to have the laws respected is to make them respectable. When law and morality are in contradiction, the citizen finds himself in the cruel dilemma of either losing his moral sense or of losing respect for the law, two evils of which one is as great as the other, and between which it is difficult to choose.

Since all relationships within a civilization must be based on a trust that can be destroyed by corruption, society must rightfully lose faith in government as it continues to grow. This betrayal eventually undermines trust in all of society's institutions.

As the people are increasingly plundered by corruption and "laws" arising from envy, they are forced to work harder and harder (while consuming savings and assuming more debt) to maintain a stagnant or declining standard of living (and a growing government). They finally begin to suspect that some of their neighbors are profiting at their expense (which is usually not true, unless they live next door to a politician or bureaucrat). Suspicion breeds increasing envy, fear, and hate and decreases the humanity in humans. The growth of these emotions drives a divisive wedge through a country and leads to increasing class warfare. The less affluent (crowds), who can no longer advance in a disintegrating economy, and are most easily influenced by intellectuals and economists preaching redistribution and more government, become consumed by envy and drift to the left (socialism), while the owners of capital or established political power become consumed by fear and drift to the right (authoritarianism). (El Salvador is a perfect example of this split.) No one can see that it is government that is living well while sabotaging the economy (and the society) through taxation, inflation, regulation, and debt.

Government growth and the subsequent distortions and destruction of the economy always have very uneven results that favor speculation (see SPECULATION) over production and investment. Seemingly overnight, riches ebb and flow to various segments of what is left of the private sector, as "policies" and "laws" change from legislature to legislature. Business blames labor, and labor blames business, while "oppressed minorities" demand "justice," and government passes new "laws" and establishes new bureaucracies to seize wealth from the producers and redistribute it on the basis of "need."

It is impossible for society to control its envy and remain moral when its government (dominated by envy) is immoral, and becomes more so day by day. As laws of plunder continue to grow, the morality of society will continue to decline. As Bastiat once wrote, "To use force is not to produce, but to destroy." People will not remain moral or voluntarily obey laws when it causes their own destruction.

Albert J. Nock's observation from his book *Our Enemy, The State* may prove to be very prophetic:

The historical method, moreover, establishes the important fact that, as in the case of tabetic or parasitic diseases, the depletion of social power [i.e., society's power] by the State cannot be checked after a certain point of progress is passed. History does not show an instance where, once beyond this point, this depletion has not ended in complete and permanent collapse. . . . Of two things, however, we may be certain: the first is, that the rate of America's approach to that point is being prodigiously accelerated; and the second is, that there is no evidence of any disposition to retard it, or any intelligent apprehension of the danger which that acceleration betokens.

As Helmut Schoeck correctly perceived in *Envy: A Theory of Social Behavior* (and as Lebanon is currently proving):

There is one state that no society can live in for any length of time, accepting it as official doctrine, and that is mutual envy.

SPECULATION

Deliberate, planned speculation is, in my opinion, the best and safest method to improve one's chances of preserving the purchasing power of capital or maintaining its constant convertability into cash without loss.

—GERALD M. LOEB
THE BATTLE FOR INVESTMENT SURVIVAL

Probabilities are not always dependable.

—H. L. HUNT

There are two times in a man's life when he should not speculate: when he can't afford it and when he can.

—MARK TWAIN

It is the business of the future to be dangerous.

—ALFRED NORTH WHITEHEAD

John Maynard Keynes once said, "Nothing is more suicidal than a rational investment strategy in an irrational (or speculative) world." One of the greatest tragedies of the world's current economic state of rampant government growth, inflation, and irrationality is that it forces *all* people to speculate, instead of to work, save, and invest, as they flee from various depreciating currencies, "legal" plunder (taxes and regulation), and empty government promises of reform, trying to protect whatever is left of their wealth. It does not matter that they are not equipped to speculate, or do not wish to speculate; governmental policies give them no choice.

Many people and corporations, through no fault or ability of their own, become wealthy from speculation during the early stages of inflation, but it is not at the expense of the poor or the working class. It is just a fact that inflation favors leveraged speculators (i.e., borrowers), or owners of tangible wealth, and the poor and working classes have little borrowing power or tangible wealth. The uneven (few) "benefits" and (infinite) hardships (such as the "oil price explosion") bestowed by government growth and inflation tend to breed runaway envy, and fragment society into various warring factions, as each class imagines that these "benefits" occur to their detriment, and try to restore "equality," "equity," and "fairness" by seizing the law for their own gain.

The faster government grows and currency depreciates, the faster speculation increases. This increase draws entrepreneurial talent and capital away from productive endeavors, destroys the moral fiber of society, and hastens the decline of the economy. The forces that breed speculation are the same that destroy incentives to produce, and, thus, doom the economy and, ultimately, the speculative markets themselves.

As with all dreams, speculators' dreams of increasing wealth through government growth, declining currencies, crushing debt, and illiquidity eventually come due (farmers, real estate developers, and the oil and gas industry are some of the latest examples) and government distortions upset the economy and stimulate corrective market forces, sometimes known as recessions and depressions. Even the few (and I mean very few) successful speculators whose ability and foresight allows them to acquire and hold wealth will find that wealth to be of much smaller benefit in an increasingly socialist world.

It would be better for everyone (rich and poor) if we returned to a world where saving, investment, and production are rewarded, and speculation is voluntary (instead of a means of survival, as it is in many countries in the world). The only way to do this is to substitute money (gold) for unbacked currency. As long as gold prices are quoted hourly on the radio (in terms of depreciating currency), and political developments ("legal" plunder, legislation, and regulation) are more important than business decisions, what is left of the world economy will belong to the speculators and financial gurus who have figured a surefire way for the passengers of the *Titanic* to have a safe and profitable voyage.

SYSTEMS

Government Systems, acting in accordance with the Laws of
Growth, Tend to Expand and Encroach. In encroaching upon
their own citizens, they produce Tyranny, and encroaching on
other Government Systems, they engage in Warfare.

—JOHN GALL
SYSTEMANTICS

Having by long struggles emancipated itself from the hard
discipline of the ancient regime, and having discovered that the
new regime into which it has grown, though relatively easy, is
not without stresses and pains, [mankind's] impatience with these
prompts the wish to try another system: which other system is, in
principle if not in appearance, the same as that which during
past generations was escaped from with much rejoicing.

—HERBERT SPENCER

A large share of government's failure in most of its endeavors
can be attributed to its lack of knowledge about everything, in general,
and systems, in particular. In the 19th century, Herbert Spencer made
the following observation about the vicissitudes of systems:

When the early Christian missionaries, having humble externals and
passing self-denying lives, spread over pagan Europe, preaching for-
giveness of injuries and the returning of good for evil, no one dreamt
that in course of time their representatives would form a vast hierarchy,
possessing everywhere a large part of the land, distinguished by the
haughtiness of its members grade above grade, ruled by the military
bishops who led their retainers to battle, and headed by a pope exercising
supreme power over kings. . . .

Thus in social arrangements, as in all other things change is inevitable. It is foolish to suppose that new institutions [systems] set up,
will long retain the character given them by those who set them up.
Rapidly or slowly they will be transformed into institutions unlike those
intended—so unlike as even to be recognizable by their devisers.

Based on similar observations by others, and the work of C. North-cote Parkinson, John Gall developed a definitive theory on systems, which he presented in his highly entertaining book *Systemantics*. His findings are as profound as they are certain. The following is a list of some of the laws of systems that Gall has discovered; they are most relevant to public systems because they do not need to produce any results to continue to receive taxpayer funding indefinitely: They spend; therefore they are.

1. SYSTEMS [governments and bureaucracy] IN GENERAL WORK POORLY OR NOT AT ALL.
2. Large systems [such as welfare] usually operate in failure mode. [The larger the system, the greater the failure.]
3. The system tends to oppose its own proper function. [HUD produces slums instead of eliminating them.]
4. The system itself tends to grow at 5 to 6 percent per annum [confirming Parkinson's estimate of the growth of bureaucracy].
5. To those within a system, the outside reality tends to pale and disappear.
6. The system takes the credit (for what would probably have happened anyway). [I think Gall is right on this rule as far as it goes, but he fails to mention that the system *never* takes the blame for any unpleasant results. That fault always lies outside the system and can be cured with *only a few* billion more dollars, or some new legislation.]
7. In complex systems, malfunction, and even total nonfunction, may not be detectable for long periods, if ever. [Exhibit A: Congress.]
8. The system has a will to live [and to grow just like cancer]. [This is why government cannot stop doing anything, no matter how stupid, wasteful, or insane.]
9. Systems [governments] can do many things; but one thing they emphatically cannot do is to solve problems. [Look at any government agency.]

H. L. Mencken was one of the early pioneers in writing on the futility of trying to use government systems as solutions to insolvable "problems" (such as drugs, alcohol, gambling, and prostitution). The following passages from his essay "The Cult of Hope" are even more humorous and relevant to the paternalistic dreamers, social planners, and wishful thinkers of today:

And the plan [or system] of reform, in politics, sociology or what not, is simply beyond the pale of reason; no change in it or improvement of it will ever make it achieve the downright impossible. Here, precisely, is what is the matter with most of the notions that go floating about the country, particularly in the field of governmental reform. The trouble with them is not only that they won't and don't work; the trouble with them, more importantly, is that the thing they propose to accomplish is intrinsically, or at all events most probably, beyond accomplishment. That is to say, the problem they are ostensibly designed to solve is a problem that is insoluble. To tackle them with a proof of that insolubility, or even with a colorable argument of it, is sound criticism; to tackle them with another solution [i.e., system] that is quite as bad, or even worse, is to pick the pocket of one knocked down by an automobile. [One] remedy, in brief is to abandon all attempts at a solution, to let the whole thing go, to cork up all the reformers and try to forget it.... The disease is bad, but ... the medicine [i.e., the system to "cure" the problem] is infinitely worse, and so ... [go] back to the plain disease, and ... [bear] it with philosophy, as we bear colds in the head, marriage, the noises of the city, bad cooking and the certainty of death.

Since government is the largest man-made system in the world, and almost totally staffed by complete incompetents, is it really any wonder that it and the systems it spawns cannot be made to work? We will leave this topic with one final quotation from Gall:

What is the track record of large systems designed for the express purpose of solving a major problem? A decent respect for our predecessors prevents us from dwelling upon the efforts of governmental administrations to eradicate poverty, reduce crime, or even get the mail delivered on time.

TARIFFS

A self-contained nation is a backward nation, with large numbers of people either permanently out of work, or very poorly paid in purchasing power. A nation which trades freely with all the world, selling to others those commodities which it can best produce, and buying from others those commodities which others can best produce, is by far the best conditioned nation for all practical purposes.

—WALTER PARKER

For cutting off our Trade with all parts of the world...

—DECLARATION OF INDEPENDENCE

Free trade, one of the greatest blessings which a government can confer on a people, is in almost every country unpopular.

—THOMAS MACAULAY

A protective tariff is a typical conspiracy in restraint of trade.

—THORSTEIN VEBLEN

What protection teaches us is to do to ourselves in time of peace what enemies do to us in time of war.

—HENRY GEORGE

Free-trade, they [governments] concede, is very well as a principle, but it is never quite time for its adoption.

—RALPH WALDO EMERSON

We all now know pretty well, probably, that the primary reason for a tariff is that it enables the exploitation of the domestic consumer by a process indistinguishable from sheer robbery.

—ALBERT JAY NOCK

When the growth of government and its primary fraud, the substitution of currency for money, reach a certain point, all domestic economies must begin to decline for reasons previously stated. International trade is severely disrupted by weak economies and wildly fluctuating exchange rates, as currencies race to their intrinsic value, and various governments race to out-inflate (out-devalue) one another. Governments must find a scapegoat to take the responsibility for the economic disasters they have induced, and obsolete businesses and monopolistic unions must be shielded from efficient competition, so they use envy to shift the blame to foreign countries who are "dumping" their goods on domestic markets, or practicing "unfair" competition.

There are three "political (vote-getting) cures" for this problem of foreign competition: competitive devaluations (more inflation), "voluntary" import quotas, or tariffs. No matter which "solution" is chosen, international trade begins to breakdown, and with it, the world economy.

Tariffs are the most politically expedient solution and win the greatest number of points from special interest groups, so they are usually chosen. They are nothing more than a form of government welfare for unions and corporations, and, as with all welfare, come at the expense of the consumer. They form part of a massive system of coercion in which the government uses the economy to serve its own purpose (instead of the consumers'), by limiting competition and subsidizing inefficiency. And like most systems, they have the long-term effect of destroying what they are trying to "protect."

As is typical of most government programs, trade restrictions have been given a euphemistic name to rally support—"protectionism." Herbert Spencer exploded the myth of protection long ago (while giving an accurate description of tariffs):

> While the one party has habitually ignored, the other party has habitually failed to emphasize, the truth that this so-called protection always involves aggression; and that the name aggressionist ought to be substituted for the name protectionist. For nothing can be more certain than that if, to maintain A's profit, B is forbidden to buy of C, or is fined to the extent of the duty if he buys of C, then B is aggressed upon that A may be "protected". Nay, "aggressionists" is a title doubly more applicable to the anti-free-trader than is the euphemistic title "protectionists"; since, that one producer may gain, ten consumers are fleeced. . . .
>
> That system only is beneficial to the world at large, and to each

nation individually, under which every commodity is obtained with the least expenditure of time and labour. Were it otherwise, we might as well grow sugar and cotton in English hot-houses, and then flatter ourselves that we were deriving advantage from the encouragement of home-grown instead of foreign produce.

Spencer's last observation proved to be a remarkable prophecy on the debilitating effects of tariffs on a nation's economy, as shown by Peter Drucker in *The Age of Discontinuity*, in 1968 when comparing the industry of Japan with Great Britain:

> The difference is best seen in the costumes that the two economies don when they show themselves abroad. At any world's fair or trade exhibition of the last twenty years, the British have featured their good old stand-bys—whiskey, woolens, china—all of exceptional quality and all yesterday. The Japanese have featured the new—e.g., the electron microscope ... modern assembly-line shipbuilding methods; synthetic fibers; and of course cameras, tape recorders, and transistor radios.

Drucker gives further damning evidence against "protection," while showing *one small example* of what is seen and *what is not seen* (who is "helped" and who is hurt) in *Managing in Turbulent Times* when he describes the various consequences of placing tariffs on foreign-made shoes:

> To take the American shoe industry again, the beneficiaries of production sharing [free trade] in the industry outnumber the workers threatened by at least ten to one [even if no one considers the long-suffering consumer]. There are more than 500,000 livestock growers and their families in the country whose profit is the hides and who depend on their being tanned and converted into leather at a price at which they can compete in the whole market. There are at least another 500,000 employees of shoe wholesalers and shoe retailers who are dependent on shoes sales. . . .
>
> The American cattle grower does not even know that his livelihood depends on the sale of foreign-made shoes in the American market, for hides represent the margin between breaking even and making a profit for the livestock grower in Nebraska. Nor, conversely, does the Haitian manufacturer of the soles for these American shoes realize that he depends on hides grown in the United States. No one yet perceives the relationships. And when shoe workers' unions in the United States

or shoe manufacturers in North Carolina agitate for a ban on the importation of "cheap foreign imports," no cattle grower in the Great Plains realizes that they are actually agitating to ban the export of American hides on which his livelihood depends. When the American tanning industry—as it does—asks for a ban on sending hides abroad, American shoe retailers (let alone American consumers) do not realize that this would mean having no shoes to sell in American shops. They do not know that there are not enough American workers available to do even a fraction of the tanning needed.

Even if governments choose to continue to ignore the loss of freedom and aggression that must spring from "protectionism," they cannot ultimately ignore the facts observed by John G. Winant:

Natural resources of the world are distributed unequally among different countries and so is the population [labor] of the world. Distribution of resources is imperfectly related to the distribution of population, and trade between countries is the principal door to progress for all. It is peculiarly true of trade that the whole is greater than the sum of its parts.

By denying free trade, government not only imposes needless costs on the economy (conservatively estimated at over $60 billion for the United States in 1980), but denies us the prosperity available only through the division of labor and free movement of natural resources. Trade, by definition, is a two-way street. Countries that cannot freely sell to the United States cannot freely buy from the United States. The road to wealth is through trade. The more freedom (i.e., the less tariffs, quotas, and anti-dumping regulations), the more trade. The more trade, the more wealth. What could be more logical?

TAX CUTS

Blessed is he that expects nothing, for he shall never be disappointed.

—BENJAMIN FRANKLIN

If not now, when? [never] If not us, who? [no one]

—RONALD REAGAN

Where is the politician who has not promised to fight to the death for lower taxes—and who has not proceeded to vote for the very spending projects that make tax cuts impossible!

—BARRY GOLDWATER

I'm proud to be paying taxes in the U.S. The only thing is—I could be just as proud for half the money [currency].

—ARTHUR GODFREY

Reaganomics is not a tax cut, and (like every "tax cut" in recent history) it will not give any meaningful relief to taxpayers (although it did temporarily provide much needed relief for American corporations). When adjusted for inevitable inflation, endless increases in Social Security taxes, and increases in other existing federal taxes, this tax law will merely *temporarily* slow the federal government's pace in gaining an ever greater share of the national product.

In 1960, only 3 percent of all American taxpayers were in a marginal tax bracket of 30 percent or higher, but by 1977, 39 percent of all taxpayers were in this tax bracket, even though their real incomes had hardly increased. This is the insidious power of inflation and a progressive income tax, keeping real personal and corporate incomes stagnant, while government income and spending explode. Since 1965, federal government spending has grown 34 percent faster than GNP.

If you still believe that we have had any real tax cuts during the past thirty years, look at the following table showing the federal government's share of GNP:

Maximum Personal Tax Rates and Federal Government Spending as a Percent of Gross National Product

YEAR	MAXIMUM PERSONAL TAX RATE (Percentage)	GROSS NATIONAL PRODUCT (Billions of Dollars)	FEDERAL SPENDING (Billions of Dollars)	FEDERAL SPENDING AS A PERCENTAGE OF GROSS NATIONAL PRODUCT
1950	91	286.5	40.8	14.3
1955	91	400.0	68.1	17.0
1960	91	506.5	93.1	18.3
1965	70	691.1	123.8	17.9
1970	70	992.7	204.3	20.6
1975	70	1,549.2	356.6	23.0
1980	50	2,631.7	602.1	22.9
1984	50	3,661.3	879.9	24.0

You will notice that, in spite of all the "tax cuts" and a reduction in the maximum tax rate from 91 percent to 50 percent (which did significantly help the economy by decreasing the progressivity of the income tax, thus moving the country down the Laffer curve), the government's share of the GNP increased from 14.3 percent in 1950 to 24.0 percent in 1984.

Economist Paul Craig Roberts explained what happened to the latest "now you see it, now you don't" personal income tax cut in the January 14, 1983, issue of the *Wall Street Journal*:

According to government estimates, the 1981 tax cut measured about $960 billion (in static terms) over the 1982–87 period. It was 69 percent repealed before it was passed by scheduled Social Security tax increases and bracket creep of $660 billion, leaving a net tax cut of about $300 billion. TEFRA repealed a further $229 billion, leaving a $71 billion tax cut. The recent gasoline tax hike chipped away $16 billion leaving $55 billion. This small residual would be reduced to zero by a three-year deferral of income tax indexing or transformed into a $35-billion tax increase if scheduled payroll tax increases are moved forward to 1984. Some revolution.

Perhaps King Pyrrhus inadvertently made the best comment on Washington's idea of "tax cuts" when he said, "Another such victory and we are ruined." As you can now see, tax cuts are a dream that *rarely comes true.*

TAX REVOLT

The history of liberty is a history of resistance.

—WOODROW WILSON

If you tax too high, the revenue will yield nothing.

—RALPH WALDO EMERSON

God grants liberty only to those who love it, and are always
ready to guard and defend it.

—DANIEL WEBSTER

Anger is a prelude to courage.

—ERIC HOFFER

One of the best ways to get yourself a reputation as a dangerous
citizen these days is to go about repeating the very phrases which
our founding fathers used in the great struggle for Independence.

—CHARLES A. BEARD

We are under a Constitution, but the Constitution is what the
judges say it is.

—CHARLES EVANS HUGHS

The spirit of resistance to government is so valuable that I wish it
to be always kept alive.

—THOMAS JEFFERSON

We should not forget that our tradition is one of protest and
revolt, and it is stultifying to celebrate the rebels of the past ...
while we silence the rebels of the present.

—HENRY STEELE COMMAGER

Herbert Spencer once wrote, "Paper constitutions raise smiles
on the faces of those who have observed their results." It is obvious

that no constitution can protect a nation from the tyranny of government and its growth. Since even democratic government will always usurp as much power as it possibly can, the people must ultimately assume responsibility for forcing government to remain within the constitution. If you do not agree, take a look at the protection offered by the Russian "Constitution," or by what is left of the U.S. Constitution and the Bill of Rights after two hundred years of shredding by the Congress and "interpretation" by the courts.

What is the income tax, if not private property taken for public use without just compensation (a violation of the Fifth Amendment)? What is an income tax return, other than a signed confession in which a person is forced by law to bear witness against himself (again, a violation of the Fifth Amendment)? What is a "routine" tax audit, other than an unlawful search and investigation in which you are guilty until proved innocent (a violation of the Fourth Amendment)?

As government power, plunder, inefficiency, and waste (see WASTE) have increased year after year, some people have grown tired of waiting for Congress (Godot) to deliver meaningful tax relief (and they most assuredly never will). Rather than join the underground economy, "invest" in ridiculous or uneconomic tax shelters (such as worm farms in the Sahara, gold mines in Panama, or R&D projects in Brazil), or falsify their income tax returns, they have chosen to confront the usurption of their Constitutional rights directly by becoming tax protesters. They have grasped the unfortunate truth penned by Frederick Douglass:

> Power concedes nothing without demand. It never did, and it never will. Find out just what people will submit to, and you have found out the exact amount of injustice and wrong which will be imposed upon them; and these will continue till they have resisted with either words or blows, or with both. The limits of tyrants [governments] are prescribed by the endurance of those whom they suppress.

Many tax protesters are being severely harassed by the Internal Revenue Service, and some are being sent to jail (with massive amounts of publicity usually released just prior to every April 15), but a few are winning important jury verdicts (with no publicity). Still, the number of protestors continues to exhibit an almost geometric increase (outstripping the growth of government spending, the national debt, and campaign promises) demonstrating to the IRS, in no uncertain terms, the problems inherent in what Edmund Burke described as "shearing the wolf." (A recent IRS study also shows that even the so-called "voluntary compliance" of people still filing tax returns is dropping more rapidly than politicians' popularity ratings.) The following table, showing the latest IRS data on tax protesters, must send a chill through everyone in government while giving hope to the people who understand and love freedom:

Tax Protestors Identified by the IRS

YEAR	NUMBER OF PROTESTORS
1978	6,693
1979	9,852
1980	12,028
1981	23,007
1982	44,471

The revolt of taxpayers (like all revolutions) poses an insoluble problem for government. Once a revolt has started, any increase in the force applied by those in power merely results in added momentum for the revolution (as several Central American countries have recently discovered). But what about decreasing the amount of force and injustice? In *The True Believer* Eric Hoffer correctly perceived, "A grievance is most poignant when almost redressed." Helmut Schoeck expanded on this point in his book *Envy: A Theory of Social Behavior:*

> What Bacon has correctly noted in regard to envy's role in the early history of a revolution is this: once discontented elements have directed public suspicion, envy and resentment against unpopular government measures and institutions, little can be done to counter "the evil eye" by adulterating unpopular measures with popular ones. So long as the holder of power shows fear of envy, that state of mind will spread, and will eventually tear down the last barriers that have held back insurrection.

The U.S. government has chosen to apply more force against the tax revolt by adding staff to the IRS (five thousand new agents), placing new, more invasive rules and regulations in the tax code, plugging tax loopholes (i.e., raising taxes), and readying a new (and undoubtedly more worthless) currency that will be harder to exchange and easier to trace. These "remedies" will not work! Force cannot produce anything; it can only destroy. By these actions, Washington is becoming the greatest ally of the tax rebel leadership. The increasing number of people refusing to pay income taxes almost certainly indicates that the government and the tax revolt have passed the point of no return. As Edmund Burke observed, "People, crushed by law, have no hopes but power [mass revolt]." The government's dream of unlimited power through unlimited plunder with total impunity will come due.

TECHNOLOGY

The precedence of the moral order is clear, since useful
discoveries [i.e., technology] occur only when men secure liberty
by restraint of the political power.

—ISABEL PATERSON
THE GOD OF THE MACHINE

All genuine progress results from finding new facts. No law can
be passed to make an acre yield 300 bushels. God has already
established the laws. It is for us to discover them, and to learn
the facts by which we can obey them.

—WHEELER McMILLEN

In the mounting miracles of science, in the rapid advances of
technology, lie the foundations for almost countless new
industries and for far swifter social progress.

—EARL O. SHREVE

A political party has never accomplished anything for humanity.
Individuals and geniuses have been the pioneers of every reform
and of progress.

—LEO TOLSTOY

New discoveries in science will continue to create a thousand
new frontiers for those who still would adventure.

—HERBERT HOOVER

For myself, this matter of the disproportion between the profit
which the average man draws from science and the gratitude
which he returns—or, rather, does not return—to it; this is much
more terrifying.

—JOSÉ ORTEGA Y GASSET

What is technology? The most basic definition is the totality of the means employed to provide objects necessary for human sustenance, comfort, and advancement. Technology has been one of the central driving forces of increasing productivity, and thus of the increasing wealth of mankind. The essence of technology according to economist Murray Rothbard is power over nature. The following quote is from his book *Power and Market*. Note the difference between power over nature, and power over men (which is the only power governments have):

> Power over nature is the sort of power on which civilization must be built; the record of man's history is the record of the advance or attempted advance of that power. Power over men, on the other hand, does not raise the general standard of living or promote the satisfactions of all, as does power over nature. . . .
>
> Power of one man over another cannot contribute to the advance of mankind; it can only bring about a society in which plunder has replaced production. . . .

Since government growth is always an increase in power over men, it must represent a decline in the amount of new power over nature (technology). Without the technological advances stemming primarily from the computer, I think many political dreams would have already come due.

Technology comes from capital expenditures for education, and research and development (R&D). The source of this capital, as it is for all capital, is savings that are made available with the hope that there will be rewards for successful innovation. Since R&D spending must come from corporate profits, and real corporate profits peaked in 1966, you would expect to see a similar trend in real R&D expenditures. The chart on page 289 from the National Science Foundation shows that to be exactly the case.

As can be seen from the chart, real R&D expenditures peaked in 1968, and they have been flat to down ever since. Also note that federal "R&D" expenditures (which are largely waste) have consistently been larger than private R&D expenditures for the entire period shown, thus draining resources and new productive technology from the private sector (which still produces more than 80 percent of all patentable inventions).

With R&D spending flat to down, and American society shifting from production to "legal" plunder, the demand for professional people

R&D Funding Trends: 1953–1977.

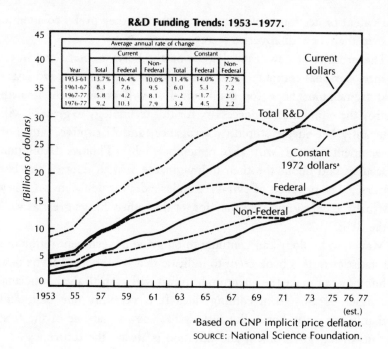

| | Average annual rate of change | | | | | |
| | Current | | | Constant | | |
Year	Total	Federal	Non-Federal	Total	Federal	Non-Federal
1953-61	13.7%	16.4%	10.0%	11.4%	14.0%	7.7%
1961-67	8.3	7.6	9.5	6.0	5.3	7.2
1967-77	5.8	4.2	8.1	-.2	-1.7	2.0
1976-77	9.2	10.3	7.9	3.4	4.5	2.2

[a]Based on GNP implicit price deflator.
SOURCE: National Science Foundation.

(and thus the ability to generate new technology) has changed accordingly. Of every ten thousand people in the United States, twenty are lawyers, forty are accountants, and seventy are engineers. In Japan, the figures are one lawyer, three accountants, and four hundred engineers. Now, perhaps, it is easier to understand our chronic balance of trade deficit with Japan and why foreigners (led by Japan) received 39 percent of the patents issued in 1981 (up from 20 percent two decades ago).

As might be expected, the government does no better job protecting intellectual property rights than it does protecting personal property rights. Congress has arbitrarily set the life of a patent at seventeen years. Intellectual property should at least have the same ownership rights as other forms of property. (How many homes would be built if the owner's rights expired in seventeen years?) Further "encouragement" for successful innovation is provided by the U.S. Patent and Trademark Office (a typical bureaucracy), which does such a poor job of researching new ideas that 50 percent of all patents challenged in court are disallowed. Many small businesses, who do not have the financial resources necessary for protracted litigation, rightly think that patent protection is of such little value that they prefer to attempt to keep their new discoveries secret.

The promise of new technology is on the horizon. Artificial intelligence, personal computers, genetic engineering, robotics, and lasers hold tremendous hope for mankind. But will government growth destroy the economic base necessary for this technology to grow? I will reluctantly bet on the stupidity, arrogance, and disruptive nature of government. But I will also remember what Thomas Babington Macaulay said about the then unimaginable British debt of the last century: "The prophets of evil were under a double delusion. . . . They saw that the debt grew; and they forgot that other things grew as well as the debt."

Maybe technology can continue to outgrow government (although the statistics in this book seem to indicate that it cannot). Maybe new technology can make the quantum leap that will keep all the politicians' ridiculous dreams from coming due. It is certainly our best, and probably our only, hope. But history has shown that one of the first victims of big government and inflation is always the future.

If we do not restore incentives and encourage capital formation by moving *significantly* down the Laffer curve (and provide more secure property rights for inventors), the United States will soon fall into a technological niche with the British, whose last great invention was the permanent recession. As Herbert Spencer said, "No man will sow when others may reap."

UNDERGROUND ECONOMY

Self-preservation is the first law of nature.

—SAMUEL BUTLER

Every actual State is corrupt. Good men must not obey the laws too well.

—RALPH WALDO EMERSON

Whenever the legislators endeavor to take away and destroy the property of the people, or to reduce them to slavery under arbitrary power, they put themselves into a state of war with the people, who are thereupon absolved from any farther obedience, and are left to the common refuge which God hath provided for all men against force and violence.

—JOHN LOCKE

Each of us has a natural right—from God—to defend his person, his liberty, and his property.

—FREDERIC BASTIAT
THE LAW

When a private citizen is robbed, a worthy man is deprived of the fruits of his industry and thrift; when the government is robbed, the worst that happens is that certain rogues and loafers have less money to play with than they had before. The notion that they have earned the money is never entertained; to most sensible men it would seem ludicrous.

—H. L. MENCKEN

The surest sign that a country is on the top side of the Laffer curve (and climbing) is the existence of a widespread, vigorous, and growing underground economy, such as America has today. As a result of confiscatory taxes and idiotic regulation, this segment of our economy is the second greatest *growth industry* in our country (government is first), with some estimates of its size running as high as 25 percent of the "official" gross national product. This would make it larger than France's "official" economy, and thus one of the ten largest economies in the world. The "hidden" economy is even more prevalent in most other countries of the world (such as Russia, Sweden, Britain, Italy, and many Latin American countries) and is always directly proportional to the size of the government (i.e., the amount of "legal" plunder). (A large underground is probably the main reason most communist economies have not completely collapsed.)

Although the existence of a large underground means that the overall economy is invariably much stronger than government figures indicate—and is perhaps one of the main reasons many political dreams have not already come due—it cannot be counted on to save us from ultimate disaster. The major limitation of this type of economic activity is its inherent inefficiency (although it is infinitely more efficient than government). The number and size of businesses that can be conducted in a relatively productive manner without government scrutiny are severely limited. AT&T, IBM, Xerox, GM, and Exxon cannot conduct their businesses underground, and they are precisely the size, in terms of human resources, capital, and technology, that our economy needs if it is to grow and prosper.

In his book *Envy: A Theory of Social Behavior* Helmut Schoeck gave a practical description of the method of operation that people are forced to employ if they wish to join the shadow economy.

Ubiquitous envy, fear of it and those who harbour it, cuts off such people from any kind of communal action directed towards the future. Every man is for himself, every man is thrown back upon his own resources. All striving, all preparation and planning for the future can be undertaken only by socially fragmented, secretive beings.

The easiest way to track the growth of the underground (and decline of the official economy) is to observe the mounting demands for currency in what was supposed to have become a cashless society. There is currently over six hundred dollars in currency for every citizen in the United States. I often wonder what additional wealth would accrue to the United States and the world if this currency were earning a return instead of being eaten away by inflation while lying hidden under mattresses or buried in backyards. (Contrary to popular belief, people in the underground still pay a significant amount of taxes through inflation and the purchases of the official economy's products and services, which have huge taxes built into their prices.) This currency could be brought back to more productive enterprise if tax rates were significantly reduced.

If you wonder why more and more people are caught in a "take the currency and run" syndrome, perhaps the following letter from the above-ground economy will give some additional insight:

Dear IRS:

You have asked why I have not sent a check for the 4th quarterly tax payment I owe you. Let me explain. The present condition of my bank account is due to laws—federal laws, state laws and city laws. The only laws that do not affect my small business are outlaws. We have never been robbed illegally; only by elected officials.

Because of these laws of many kinds I am compelled to pay taxes—a business tax, amusement tax, head tax, bank tax, gas tax, water tax, sales tax, excise tax, auto tax, phone tax, sewer tax, garbage tax, school tax, fire tax, highway tax, and three kinds of income tax—federal, state, and city.

These laws also require me to get licenses at varying fees for my small store—a business license, refrigeration license, sanitation license, inspection license, weighers' license, dairy license, carter's license, delivery truck license, interstate delivery license and a driver's license. I bought only two voluntarily: a marriage license and a dog license.

I have one employee. I must pay his Blue Cross, Blue Shield, unemployment compensation, social security, retirement pension fund, company life insurance premiums and, if anything is left over, his salary.

For the sake of my bank, my creditors and my business, I am required by law to carry life insurance, property insurance, liability insurance, fire insurance, burglar insurance, accident insurance, windstorm, flood and earthquake insurance, and freezer loss insurance. I must pay the premiums promptly or my insurance coverage like my water, gas and lights will be turned off.

I am watched, registered, counted, measured, numbered, assessed, refused, authorized, legislated, regulated, indoctrinated, checked, appraised, directed, inspected, suspected, and disrespected. I am commanded to maintain senseless flows of paperwork that violate every aspect of my privacy by bureaucrats (city, state, and federal) who cannot be removed from office, have no knowledge or concept of business, no concern for my welfare, no virtue and no compassion. If I do not comply or complain about being drilled, fleeced, exploited, monopolized, extorted, exhausted, hoaxed and robbed, I am threatened, annoyed, repressed, arrested, judged, fined, vilified, ridiculed and dishonored. Though I work sixty hour weeks, I am forced to live hand-to-mouth because I am bled white maintaining a constant flow of currency to my government and other people. There just simply does not seem to be enough to go around.

Please do not close my business or file a tax lien against my property as you threatened to do in your last correspondence, for due to a miraculous stroke of good fortune, you will get my currency. While chopping out a loin of pork this morning, I was lucky enough to miss the loin and completely sever my left thumb. It was insured and the payment should arrive next week, at which time I will endorse the check and forward it to you.

I want you to know that I am very thankful to live in a free society with a system of free enterprise and that I shall be eternally grateful for your patience.

Sincerely yours,
Ben Dover

Until mankind can find the will and the way to limit government and its senseless bureaucracy, regulation, and plunder, the rule will remain "Sauve qui peut" (Save himself who can).

UNEMPLOYMENT

I hope we never live to see the day when a thing is as bad as some of our newspapers make it.

—WILL ROGERS

The dole is utterly demoralizing; its chief effect is to turn the unemployed into the unemployable.

—DEAN INGE

Statistics are no substitute for judgment.

—HENRY CLAY

The world is full of willing people; some willing to work, the rest willing to let them.

—ROBERT FROST

The unemployment statistic is one of the poorest, most abused, misunderstood, and meaningless figures used by politicians. It is the prime excuse for the destructive interference of government in our economy.

For a start, the figure is bloated by the effect of welfare recipients' having to go through the motion of "looking for work" (this probably adds about 2 percent); extended unemployment benefits that make for long periods of "job search" (this probably adds 1 percent); the "underground economy" where people work tax-free but appear to be unemployed (this should add 1 to 2 percent); and finally, inflation and high taxes, which force into seeking work people who would otherwise choose to be homemakers or children. (If women were still seeking jobs at the same low ratio they did in 1960, unemployment would be at least 2 percent lower).

We also have the problem of inadequate capital formation showing up in unemployment statistics. When an economy is experiencing inflation and taxation of income, "investments" (i.e., speculations), and corporate profits at confiscatory rates, savings and capital formation (hence new jobs) will be much lower.

If the government were interested in reducing unemployment, it could start by reducing welfare payments (incentives to be gainfully unemployed) and abolishing price controls on human beings (minimum wage laws). But this interference in the free market will not be stopped. Consequently, the less fortunate (and taxpayers) will continue to pay the price.

In order to calculate truly accurate "unemployment" figures, the government should include every bureaucrat in the total because they add little or nothing to the gross national product and must be supported and tolerated by the productive workers in our economy. We could call this new statistic (government "employment" plus the unemployment rate) the "unproductive rate" (or "dead weight rate"). This rate has increased from 9.4 percent in 1929 to about 22.6 percent in 1980 (almost equal to the levels of the depression of the 1930s).

To dissuade government from using the unemployment statistic as an excuse for excessive spending (wasting) programs and other forms of economic interference, this statistic should be scrapped and replaced by an employment-to-population ratio. The following table reveals a picture much different from the unemployment figures:

Civilian Employment and Unemployment Statistics

YEAR	EMPLOYMENT AS PERCENTAGE OF POPULATION	UNEMPLOY- MENT RATE (Percentage)
1950	55.2	5.3
1955	55.1	4.4
1960	54.9	5.5
1965	55.5	4.5
1970	56.1	4.9
1975	55.3	8.5
1980	58.5	7.1
1984	59.5	7.5

As can be seen from the table, at the end of 1984, the employment-to-population ratio stood at 59.5 percent, down only slightly from the 1979 record of 59.9 percent, which is pretty amazing for an economy that can't create any new jobs. Using the lowest unemployment rate since 1950 (1953 at 2.9 percent), we find that the employment rate for that year was only 55.3 percent, and as previously stated, the current figures are increasingly understated because of the growing number of unreported people working in the underground economy. Only government statistics could show both employment and unemployment rising at the same time for a period of thirty-four years.

The following statement by Daniel Benjamin and Levis Kochin applies equally to America: "The army of the unemployed standing watch in Britain at the publication of the *General Theory* was largely a volunteer army." I recommend that you give the same amount of credence to the unemployment rate as you would any government promise, such as balancing the budget, or cutting wasteful spending.

UNIONS

The regular blackmail of the public, of which some American trade unions are guilty, and which cannot in any sense be ascribed to their members' real needs, is an obvious example of the way in which even economic extortion gradually comes to be seen as normal.

—HELMUT SCHOECK
ENVY: A THEORY OF SOCIAL BEHAVIOR

The trade union, which originated under the European system, destroys liberty.

—HENRY WARD BEECHER

Much of the present difficulty in industrial relations arises from the fact that too many employers as well as too many legislators take the Labor Leader more seriously than he deserves to be taken, while taking the ordinary, everyday, middle-of-the-road wage-earner less seriously than he deserves to be taken.

—WHITING WILLIAMS

I have long been profoundly convinced that in the very nature of things, employers and employees are partners, not enemies; that their interests are common, not opposed; that in the long run the success of each is dependent upon the success of the other.

—JOHN D. ROCKEFELLER, JR.

"MORE!" The battle cry of the unions is now a dream come due. There is no more to get, and jobs are leaving the United States at a staggering rate, never to return.

Unions were originally formed to prevent "abuse" of "economic power." But what is economic power, and is it inherently evil? Murray N. Rothbard gives us the following answer in *Power and Market*:

Let us analyze further the contrast between the power of violence [unions] and "economic power," between, in short, the victim of a bandit and the man who loses his job with the Ford Motor Company. Let us symbolize, in each case, the alleged power-wielder as P and the supposed victim as X. In the case of the bandit or robber, P plunders X. P lives, in short, by battening off X and all the other X's. This is the meaning of power in its original, political sense. But what of "economic power"? Here, by contrast, X, the would-be employee, is asserting a strident claim to P's property! In this case, X is plundering P instead of the other way round. Those who lament the plight of the automobile worker who cannot obtain a job with Ford do not seem to realize that before Ford and without Ford there would be no such job to be obtained at all. No one, therefore, can have any sort of "natural right" to a Ford job. . . .

Like most "systems," unions have come to oppose their own proper function and are much more oppressive than the companies that caused their formation. Prior to unions, a worker who could not obtain work with Ford might get a job with GM. But today a worker who will not join the union will not get any job in the automotive industry. In other words, the unions tell the companies whom they can hire. Workers in other industries who wish to remain independent from the union, or wish to continue working during a strike, are met with violence and vilified as "scabs." Unions try to take credit for the higher wages their workers receive, but these higher wages are just a way of "looting the future," as 250,000 auto workers recently discovered.

For years, I have watched in amazement as labor leaders have sold out their members by calling for more government regulation and higher taxes on individuals and corporations. Every one of these "new ideas" is paid for by the workers, either in higher taxes or jobs lost to more efficient foreign competition.

Wages and salaries have *always* dwarfed corporate profits (see PROFITS, CORPORATE); payments to employees at all levels now represent about 85 percent of the gross national product. This imbalance leaves insufficient profits to replace capital consumption and allow for new capital formation. Low rates of "investment," coupled with the wage differential between American labor unions (who thought they had a monopoly) and foreign workers, make it easier to understand why Japan built more cars than any country in the world for the first time in 1981.

I do not suggest that the necessary increase in corporate profits come from labor's wages, but rather, by reducing (or completely stopping) the flow of corporate profits sent to, and the flow of insane regulation coming from, earth's version of a black hole: Washington, D.C. It is time to realize that laborers cannot prosper unless employers do.

WAGES

When paper currency is depreciated, the difference has to come out somewhere; and the main cut is [always] in wages.

—ISABEL PATERSON
THE GOD OF THE MACHINE

Power over a man's subsistence is power over his will.

—ALEXANDER HAMILTON

There is not a man in the country that can't make a living for himself and family. But he can't make a living for them and his government, too, the way his government is living. What the government has got to do is live as cheap as the people.

—WILL ROGERS

Wages should be reckoned not by numbers of pounds or dollars, but in purchasing power.

—PHILIP GIBBS

I wish every blue-collar worker could see the following table showing the "real" improvement in his wages (*see next page*):

Average Weekly Earnings in Selected Private Nonagricultural Industries and Total Government Spending Adjusted to 1940 Dollars

YEAR	GROSS WAGES (CURRENCY) (Dollars)	REAL GROSS WAGES (Dollars)	TOTAL GOVERNMENT SPENDING (CURRENCY) (Billions of Dollars)	REAL TOTAL GOVERNMENT SPENDING (Billions of Dollars)
1950	53.13	30.95	61.0	35.54
1955	67.72	35.41	98.0	51.24
1960	80.67	38.20	136.4	64.59
1965	95.45	42.49	187.8	83.55
1970	119.83	43.24	313.4	113.10
1975	163.53	42.58	534.3	139.13
1980	235.10	39.97	869.0	147.73
1984	294.05	39.13	1,258.1	167.45

No surprises here: from 1950 to 1984, real wages *before taxes* were up a "whopping" 26 percent, while real government spending has managed to increase only a modest 471 percent. (In a truly free country those figures would be reversed.) Much like the Dow Jones Industrial Average, real wages in 1984 were just barely above the level achieved in 1960.

In 1983, government in America spent more than eleven thousand dollars for every civilian employee. (Could you have used an extra eleven thousand dollars in 1983?) If you think this is a government that is serving its people, the figures would indicate this concept has been reversed. The people are now serving the government.

WASTE

(A Government and Your "Money" Are Soon Parted)

We must make our choice between economy and liberty, or profusion and servitude. If we can prevent the government from wasting the labors of the people under the pretense of caring for them, they will be happy.

—THOMAS JEFFERSON

Any fool can waste, any fool can muddle, but it takes something of a man to save, and the more he saves the more of a man does it make of him.

—RUDYARD KIPLING

People try to live within their income so that they can afford to pay taxes to a government that can't live within its income.

—ROBERT HALF

Waste running into hundreds of millions [billions is much more accurate] abounds in the national government. . . . It's all around you. Some [most] of it shocking, but. . . . accepted as a necessary way of life. . . . The sad fact is that government has grown so huge that you just can't put your finger on where and how all the money [currency] is spent.

—CONGRESSMAN JACKSON E. BETTS

Economy is in itself a source of great revenue.

—SENECA

Waste is the best term to use to describe all government programs (either that, or *inefficient*). I watch Congress agonizing over what is laughingly known as the "budget process," trying to figure out where to make some minuscule cut, when, as usual, they have the question backward: The question is not where to cut, but rather where *not* to cut.

Donald Lambro has detailed some (and I mean only some) of the more wasteful spending in his excellent book *Fat City*. After reading this book, I *could* mention several "small waste" programs, such as...

1. Automatic elevator operators in the Capitol (ninety-four) and congressional office buildings, costing about $900,000 a year. (But congress has so many other numbers to worry about ... and those higher floor buttons *can* be pretty tricky to hit with a hangover. It's also said that elevators in Washington, in keeping with the spirit of government spending and taxes, only go up.)
2. Congress's Florist Service at over $40,000 a year (Say it with flowers. . . .).
3. House and Senate Gymnasium, complete with masseurs costing well over $200,000 a year. (Well, it does keep crime off the streets.)
4. Chauffeured limousines for federal officials (175), approximately $5 million a year. (In the current depressed auto market, someone has got to buy big cars.)
5. Capitol Police: about twelve hundred men at more than $23 million a year (just in case irate taxpayers storm the gymnasium).
6. Government aircraft kept on standby for members of Congress and military brass: pick a very big number. (Competition for planes unfortunately has to relegate some officials to first class on the airlines. Remember, Congressional time is "money": yours and mine.)
7. Personal chefs for Cabinet secretaries: $Unknown. (The best is just barely good enough—and it keeps drunks off the road after three-martini lunches.)

but, since I want to avoid damaging sensitive egos, I will not mention these programs.

Lambro did mention some "large waste" programs, which range from fairly irrelevant to totally absurd. I had wanted this book to be two volumes so that I could have had one for a list of the wasteful programs, but the publisher vetoed the idea. I may try for a government grant at a later date. In the meantime, I offer the following shortened list from Lambro's book:

1. U.S. Employment Service: $738 million (one of the few government agencies without an Orwellian name: they *do* employ about 38,000 people in this "service," as their name implies).
2. Revenue sharing: $6.8 billion (What revenue? Why not deficit sharing?).
3. Government film: $500 million (no plots, but an incredible number of characters).
4. Economic Development Administration: $2.4 billion (they take the economy out of "economic").
5. International Development Association: $1 billion (an association that *has* developed itself internationally, another exception to the Orwellian name syndrome).
6. Small Business Administration: $1.5 billion (designed to help small businesses which were monopolies before antitrust action).
7. U.S. Parole commission: $5.4 million (a commission to assure fair treatment of former members of Congress and other high officials).
8. HUD (Department of Housing and Urban Development): $10 billion a year. (I liked the movie better.)
9. Amtrak: $900 million a year. (If every government official were *required* to use this "service," government travel would be significantly reduced.)
10. Legal Services Corporation: $300 million ($60,000 taxpayers paying $5,000 each: protection against the ravages of attorney unemployment).

Leonard Reed, a former bureaucrat, said, "No activity in a government agency is given as high a priority as securing and enlarging its budget." The most amazing aspect of the waste in government is not that the programs are funded, but that they are so overfunded that there is a virtual panic at the end of each fiscal year to dispose of excess funds that the agency was unable to waste in the normal course of its "function." This process, which is one of the main pillars of government growth, was detailed by Charles Peters in his book *How Washington Really Works*:

> One of the most notorious results of the fear of budget cuts is the end-of-the-year spending spree. ... It was a traditional rite of spring until a few years ago, when the end of the fiscal year was changed from June 30 to September 30. Now the season — harvest time — couldn't be more perfect, and the ritual remains the same. As the midnight hour ap-

proaches each agency desperately tries to use up all its appropriated funds for that year so it won't appear to have been overbudgeted.

As if Lambro's book and Reed's insight were not enough, the Grace Commission has recently released its report (which should have been titled *In Search of Incompetence*) on stupidity, inefficiency, waste, and corruption in our beloved government. The commission's findings are staggering although no surprise to any serious student of government. If all the commission's recommendations were implemented (and there really were a Santa), they would save *taxpayers* (not the government) at least $424 billion over the next three years.

We can applaud the Grace Commission's dedication and spirit, but its fatal flaw is gullibility. It is laboring under the gross misconception that government can be made to operate efficiently. It will not and cannot! You could just as easily expect a prostitute to be celibate. Government and efficiency are as mutually exclusive as politicians and the truth. *Government is waste.* That is all it ever has been and all it ever will be. The one and only way to get greater efficiency (i.e., less waste) from any government is to cut its size. Efforts directed in any other area are, well, a waste.

WEALTH

Wealth belongs to him who creates it, and every dollar taken
from industry without an equivalent, is robbery.

—POPULIST PARTY

You cannot help the poor by destroying the rich.

—ABRAHAM LINCOLN

It requires a great deal of boldness and a great deal of caution to
make a great fortune, and when you have it, it requires ten times
as much wit to keep it.

—MEYER ROTHSCHILD

Wealth flows from energy and ideas.

—WILLIAM FEATHER

Regard your neighbor's gain as your gain, and your neighbor's
loss as your own loss.

—T'AI SHANG KAN YING

It is a very popular pastime of governments to take credit for
any new wealth that may be created (by the producers). They plan
"new economic programs," legislate new tax laws, set "fiscal" and
"monetary" policies (i.e., deficits and inflation), pass new regulations,
and set new international trade policies. It is as if a group of ticks and
roundworms had laid out a complete health program to help stimulate
the dog they are parasitizing.

The only form of wealth that can be created or can endure is private
wealth, and it is a product of free thought and free action. (The degree
of a country's freedom is the degree of its wealth.) All the wealth that
has ever been created (and that will be created in the future) was
created and preserved in spite of government. Go to any country in
the world, and any thinking person can accurately judge the size and

history of its government by the wealth, or (in most cases) poverty, of its people.

Ludwig von Mises showed that he clearly understood the nature of both government and wealth.

> By its very nature, a government decree that "it be" cannot create anything that has not been created before. Only the naive inflationists could believe that government can create anything [other than waste]; its orders cannot even evict anything from the world of reality; but they can evict from the world of the permissible. Government cannot make man richer, but it can make man poorer [and always does].

There is no better example of the way government impoverishes people than the Soviet Union's policy toward its farmers. Prior to the communists, and with much less agricultural capital and technology, Russia was the breadbasket of Europe. Currently it is unable to feed even itself. But the most shocking statistic is that more than 25 percent of the country's food is produced on private one-acre plots that equal only 1 percent of the total farm acreage. By this measure, private plots are *forty times* more productive than government farms (surprise, surprise). Imagine the exponential gains possible for the entire Soviet economy (and its people) if the private plots were increased to four acres. (This would of course "slash" the state's agricultural acreage to a mere 96 percent). There would also be large gains for the countries who are currently feeding the USSR because they would be able to redeploy the capital and resources currently in agriculture to areas of higher productivity.

The lesson here, and the one that China and India are currently learning, is that when a country is at the very top of the Laffer curve (as all statist countries are), the smallest additional freedom and incentives produce miraculous results. Even the world's current population could be well nourished if government were not involved in agriculture.

Government, in every form on earth today, is the greatest enemy of wealth and, thus, the great impoverisher of mankind. One of the most shocking thoughts to ponder is the extent to which totalitarian governments have been able to impoverish the people of the semi-free countries in the West. Citizens of these countries may argue that a foreign government cannot really affect them, but when you consider the trillions that have been taxed away and spent on weapons and armies instead of being put to productive use, you can get some idea of the scope of government depredations on humanity. Also, it is really not hard to understand that every person who has been starved, slaughtered, or oppressed by authoritarian government is one less person who can offer his productive efforts to us or purchase any of our goods or labor. Think of the incalcuable loss to the world if just one Einstein, Edison, Salk, Gandhi, Mozart, Hemingway, or Rembrandt were among the masses who have been systematically exterminated by government edict. With this thought in mind, we would do well to remember John Donne's immortal quote:

> No man is an island, entire of itself; every man is a piece of the continent, a part of the main; if a clod be washed away by the sea, Europe is the less, as well as if a promontory were, as well as if a manor of thy friends or of thine own were; any man's death diminishes me, because I am involved in mankind; and therefore never send to know for whom the bell tolls; it tolls for thee.

The eternal bell of government regulation, waste, theft, oppression, and violence tolls for all of us no matter where on earth it occurs. The dream that it could be otherwise will soon come due.

WEDGE, THAT DIRTY OLD

Taxation under every form presents but a choice of evils.

—DAVID RICARDO

We do not commonly see in a tax [or regulation] a diminution of freedom, and yet it clearly is one. The money [or currency] taken [or spent to comply] represents so much labor gone through, and the product of that labor being taken away, either leaves the individual to go without such benefit as was achieved by it or else to go through more labor.

—HERBERT SPENCER

An unlimited power to tax involves, necessarily, the power to destroy.

—DANIEL WEBSTER

The less government interferes with private pursuits, the better for general prosperity.

—MARTIN VAN BUREN

The "wedge" (a term coined by Arthur Laffer) is another word for government intervention in private economic transactions (the government, in effect, drives a wedge between the producer and consumer). Governments usually build their "wedges" from three components—taxation (income, property or sales), tariffs (import duties or "quotas") and regulation (twenty books like this one could not list all the examples). These wedges inhibit economic activity by adding excessive costs to producer's prices and depriving consumers of part of their earnings through taxes. Since most of the wealth government consumes is waste, wedges tend to impoverish everyone (except bureaucrats) to some degree.

In its simplest form, the wedge is a tax on all productive effort, and we know that taxes always lessen demand, decrease production and increase the size of the underground economy. We can see an excellent example of the wedge at work in C. Northcote Parkinson's book *The Law and the Profits* (a British surgeon has just presented a bill to his patient):

"Your fee of £4,000," he finally concluded, "represents the proportion I retain from the last £44,500 of my income. To pay you without being worse off would mean earning another £44,500 more than last year; no easy task."

"Well," replied the surgeon, "you know how it is. It is only by charging you that much that I can afford to charge others little or nothing."

"No doubt," said the patient. "But the fee still absorbs £44,500 of my theoretical income—no inconsiderable sum. Might I ask what proportion of the £4,000 you will manage to retain?"

It was the surgeon's turn to scribble calculations, as a result of which he concluded that his actual gain, after tax had been paid, would amount to £800.

"Allow me to observe," said the patient, "that I must therefore earn £44,500 in order to give you £800 of spendable income; the entire balance going to government. Does that strike you as a transaction profitable to either of us?"

"Well, frankly, no," admitted the surgeon. "Put like that, the whole thing is absurd. But what else can we do?"

"First, we can make certain that no one is listening. No one at the keyhole? No federal agent under the bed? No tape recorder in the—? Are you quite sure that we can keep this strictly to ourselves?"

"Quite sure," the surgeon replied after quickly opening the door and glancing up and down the corridor. "What do you suggest?"

"Come closer so that I can whisper. Why don't I give you a case of Scotch and so call it quits?"

"Not enough," hissed the surgeon, "but if you made it two cases ...?"

"Yes?" whispered the patient.

"And lent me your cabin cruiser for three weeks in September..."

"Yes?"

"We might call it a deal!"

"That's fine. And do you know what gave me the idea? I studied Parkinson's [Second] Law and realized that excessive taxation has made nonsense of everything!"

As has been previously stated several times, the tax wedge (*excluding* tariffs and regulatory costs) in the United States currently stands at about 42 percent of gross national product. That's at least twice what it should be.

WELFARE

(Where's the Grief?)

The democracy will cease to exist when you take away from those who are willing to work and give to those who would not.

—THOMAS JEFFERSON

There is no doubt that the real destroyer of the liberties of any people is he who spreads among them bounties, donations and largess.

—PLUTARCH

A government that robs Peter to pay Paul can always depend on the support of Paul.

—GEORGE BERNARD SHAW

Though the people support the government, the government should not support the people.

—GROVER CLEVELAND

Let us always have in mind that every attempt in the history of the world to establish a loafer's paradise has wound up in a dictator's hell-hole.

—HAROLD E. STASSEN

Those who would administer wisely must, indeed, be wise, for one of the serious obstacles to the improvement of our race is indiscriminate charity.

—ANDREW CARNEGIE

To tax the community for the advantage of a class is not protection: it is plunder.

—BENJAMIN DISRAELI

In matters of conscience, the law of the majority has no place.

—MAHATMA GANDHI

Much is written by today's liberal press about the injustice of society toward its less fortunate members. It is as if all of the poor are totally blameless for their condition. Producers have "exploited" them, and even if they haven't, they should feel guilty for working so hard and having so much wealth (that is, at least temporarily, partially out of government's reach). Herbert Spencer analyzed this fantasy in his essay "The Coming Slavery":

Sympathy with one in suffering suppresses, for the time being, remembrance of his transgressions. The feeling which vents itself in "poor fellow!" On seeing one in agony, excludes the thought of "bad fellow," which might at another time arise. Naturally, then, if the wretched are unknown or but vaguely known, all the demerits they may have are ignored; and thus it happens that when the miseries of the poor are dilated upon, they are thought of as the miseries of the deserving poor, instead of being thought of as the miseries of the underserving poor, which in large measure they should be. Those whose hardships are set forth in pamphlets and proclaimed in sermons and speeches which echo throughout society, are assumed to be all worthy souls, grievously wronged; and none of them are thought of as bearing the penalties of their misdeeds. . . . They are simply the good-for-nothings, who in one way or other live on the good-for-somethings—vagrants and sots, criminals and those on the way to crime, youths who are burdens on hard-working parents, men who appropriate the wages of their wives, fellows who share the gains of prostitutes; and then, less visible and less numerous, there is a corresponding class of women.

Is it natural that happiness should be the lot of such? Or is it natural that they should bring unhappiness on themselves and those connected with them? Is it not manifest that there must exist in our midst an immense amount of misery which is a normal result of misconduct, and ought not to be dissociated from it? There is a notion, always more or less prevalent and just now vociferously expressed, that all social suffering is removable, and that it is the duty of somebody or other to remove it. Both these beliefs are false. To separate pain from ill-doing is to fight against the constitution of things [i.e., the law of compensation], and will be followed by far more pain.

Frederic Bastiat knew that state welfare and liberty could not coexist. In *The Law* he eloquently captured the difference between welfare through government plunder (politicians' "vicarious generosity") and true charity when he wrote:

In fact, it is impossible for me to separate the word *fraternity* [charity] from the word *voluntary*. I cannot possibly understand how fraternity [charity] can be *legally* enforced without liberty being *legally* destroyed, and thus justice being *legally* trampled underfoot.

Legal plunder has two roots: One of them, as I have said before, is in human greed; the other is in false philanthropy.

Even if we ignore the immorality of redistributing plundered wealth, we are immediately faced with another disastrous problem. As welfare expenditures have exploded, so have the number of recipients (remember, what government subsidizes, *we* get more of). In spite of the government's "best efforts" to cure producers of their solvency, the percentage of U.S. population living below the "poverty level" has steadily increased since 1973. You can get some idea of the total incompetence of government and its systems as a problem solver from the following table:

Transfer Payments and the Percentage of U.S. Population Below the Poverty Level

YEAR	TRANSFER PAYMENTS (Billions of Dollars)	PERCENTAGE OF U.S. POPULATION BELOW POVERTY LEVEL
1960	28.9	22.2
1965	40.4	17.3
1970	80.1	12.6
1975	178.3	12.3
1980	297.6	13.0
1983	405.0	15.2

By studying the table, you can see that government could presumably have reduced the percentage of people living below the poverty level, by 2.9 percent down to 12.3 percent by *cutting* transfer payments back to 1975 levels of purchasing power. (In 1983, this cut would have been $226.7 billion, which, coincidentally, would have put the federal budget in surplus.)

Were Thomas Mackay still alive, he would not be even remotely surprised by the results of increasing government transfer payments. He long ago predicted this exact outcome in his book *Methods of Social Reform*:

the cause of pauperism is relief. We shall not get rid of pauperism by extending the sphere of State relief. . . . On the contrary, its adoption would increase our pauperism, for, as is often said, *we can have exactly as many paupers as the country chooses to pay for* [my emphasis].

Now Tip (I've-gotta-heart-and-my-hand-in-your-wallet) O'Neill will undoubtedly attempt to refute our inescapable conclusion and Mackay's quote, claiming that if we could just cut defense spending $100 billion or so, and transfer that amount to welfare payments, we could "solve" the nation's poverty problem once and for all (just like the various wars we fought to end all wars).

Fortunately, we don't have to rely on Tip (or more from your wallet) because we have someone who is not consumed by envy and can add, subtract, and think. Peter Grace, who chaired a panel on government waste, gave us the predictably bad news on the ineptitude of government and its programs in an article in the *Wall Street Journal*. Not surprisingly, he reaches the same conclusion about transfer payments:

> Mistargeting of benefits resulted in the poverty gap being reduced only $37.4 billion in 1982, despite expenditures of $124 billion on means-tested programs for the poor, such as Aid to Families with Dependent Children, food stamps and Medicaid. In theory, the $124 billion should have not only brought all households to 125 percent of the poverty level with $47.5 billion left over for other purposes such as reducing the federal deficit.

So where is the grief? Maybe you can find it in the following table:

Transfer Payments as a Percentage of Wages and Salaries

YEAR	TRANSFER PAYMENTS *(Billions of Dollars)*	WAGES AND SALARIES *(Billions of Dollars)*	TRANSFER PAYMENTS AS A PERCENTAGE OF WAGES AND SALARIES
1940	3.1	49.9	6.2
1945	6.2	117.5	5.3
1950	15.2	147.0	10.3
1955	17.5	211.7	8.3
1960	28.9	271.9	10.6
1965	40.4	362.0	11.2
1970	80.1	548.7	14.6
1975	178.3	806.4	22.1
1980	297.6	1,356.7	21.9
1984 (P)*	416.9	1,803.6	23.1

*(Preliminary)

As you can see, the grief, dear taxpayer, is increasingly your grief, as the producer who is being forced to support professional parasites.

A quote from William F. Buckley is worth repeating: "Idealism [i.e., dreaming] is fine, but as it approaches reality the cost becomes prohibitive [i.e., ruinous]." Government has never tired of proving this, but the dream of politicians' vicarious generosity curing poverty through ever greater plunder is beginning to come due.

Z SUMMARY

Democracy: The state of affairs in which you consent to having your pocket picked and elect the best man to do it.

—BENJAMIN LICHTENBERG

Skepticism is the highest of duties; blind faith the unpardonable sin.

—THOMAS HUXLEY

We must make war on socialism.

—M. DE MONTALEMBERT

Who can protest and does not, is an accomplice in the act.

—THE TALMUD

He who will not reason is a bigot; he who cannot is a fool; and he who dares not is a slave.

—WILLIAM DRUMMOND

Now (I hope) you know more about many things that are happening in the world and why.

The future (of what is left of freedom) depends upon the producers' changing the direction of America, while they still outnumber the parasites who live from their efforts.

In closing I would like to wish you:

HAPPINESS,

which will depend on your giving up illusions of justice in law, taxes, regulation and monetary affairs, and reality in government;

SUCCESS,

which will depend on your refusal to buy any bond or other form of debt instrument denominated in currency as opposed to money, and a personal dedication to reality at all times;

WEALTH,

which will unfortunately depend on successful speculation and exchanging your currency for precious metals (money) to protect you against empty government promises of stopping inflation; and most important;

FREEDOM,

which is waiting to be reclaimed by its rightful owner (you) if you will take personal responsibility in helping to control government (and envy) by cutting its supply of *your* currency and credit, and limiting its power to the legitimate functions for which it was originally formed.

P.S. As for present and future politicians' dreams coming due, unfortunately . . .

TO BE CONTINUED . . .